NEW TESTAMENT
EVERYDAY BIBLE STUDY SERIES

NEW TESTAMENT
EVERYDAY BIBLE STUDY SERIES

ACTS

SCOT MCKNIGHT

QUESTIONS WRITTEN BY
BECKY CASTLE MILLER

HarperChristian
Resources

New Testament Everyday Bible Study Series: Acts
© 2022 by Scot McKnight

Requests for information should be addressed to:
HarperChristian Resources, 3900 Sparks Dr. SE, Grand Rapids, Michigan
49546

ISBN 978-0-310-12939-4 (softcover)
ISBN 978-0-310-12940-0 (ebook)

HarperChristian Resources titles may be purchased in bulk for church,
business, fundraising, or ministry use. For information, please e-mail
ResourceSpecialist@ChurchSource.com.

First Printing May 2022 / Printed in the United States of America

CONTENTS

For Dave Ferguson

GENERAL INTRODUCTION

Christians make a claim for the Bible not made of any other book. Or, since the Bible is a library shelf of many authors, it's a claim we make of no other shelf of books. We claim that God worked in each of the authors as they were writing so that what was scratched on papyrus expressed what God wanted communicated to the people of God. Which makes the New Testament a book unlike any other book. Which is why Christians are reading the NT almost two thousand years later with great delight. These books have the power to instruct us and to rebuke us and to correct us and to train us to walk with God every day. We read these books because God speaks to us in them.

Developing a routine of reading the Bible with an open heart, a receptive mind, and a flexible will is the why of the *New Testament Everyday Bible Studies*. But not every day will be the same. Some days we pause and take it in and other days we stop and repent and lament and open ourselves to God's restoring graces. No one word suffices for what the Bible does to us. In fact, the Bible's view of the Bible can be found by reading Psalm 119, the longest chapter in the Bible with 176 verses! It is a meditation on eight terms for what the Bible is and what the Bible does to those who listen and read it. It's laws (*torah*) instruct us, its laws (*mishpat*) order us, its statutes direct us, its precepts inform us, its decrees guide us, its commands compel us, its words speak to us, and its promises comfort us, and it is no wonder that the author can sum all eight up as the "way" (119:3, 37). Each of those terms still speaks to what happens when we open our minds to the Word of God.

Every day with the Bible then is new because our timeless and timely God communes with us in our daily lives in our world and in our time. Just as God spoke to Jesus in Galilee and Paul in Ephesus and John on Patmos. These various contexts help us hear God in our context so the *New Testament Everyday Bible Studies* will often delve into contexts.

Most of us now have a Bible on our devices. We may well have several translations available to us everywhere we go every day. To hear those words we are summoned by God to open the Bible, to attune our hearts to God and to listen to what God says. My prayer is that these daily study guides will help each of us become daily Bible readers attentive to the mind of God.

INTRODUCTION: READING THE BOOK OF ACTS

The Book of Acts, written by the same author who wrote the Gospel of Luke, continues the narrative about Jesus into the narrative about the continued mission of Jesus and the growth of the Jesus movement, or the church, from Jerusalem to Rome. Luke informs us that such a geographical move forms the heart of his second narrative (Acts 1:8). According to Dean Fleming, a specialist on all things pertaining to God's mission in our world, what we learn is that the whole gospel is for the whole person, that God's mission shatters fleshly boundaries separating peoples and ethnic groups, and that God's mission is empowered by the Spirit of God (Fleming, *Why Mission?*). We see this mission in the speeches by the apostles, in the various communities that are formed in cities, in the various characters who sometimes make only cameo appearances, and in one story after another. In the *Bible Study* that follows the term "mission" forms the core of our observations. Everything in the Book of Acts is about God's mission about redemption in God's Son in God's Spirit through the people of God, and in Acts especially through the apostles Peter and Paul, to form churches as agents of God's redemption. Put in simpler form:

> The mission is God's mission
> About redemption in God's Son, the Lord Jesus
> In the power of God's Spirit
> Through the people of God, the church
> To form churches as agents of redemption

Our goal, however, is not just to describe what Luke wrote but also to indicate how that 1st Century mission can be like our 21st Century mission to take the gospel into new spaces. Such a transfer of two millennia requires us to become as audience-sensitive as the apostles were and to participate in what God is doing in our world.

Over and over this *Bible Study* will point us to *God's* mission through Peter and Paul, not to *Peter's or Paul's* missions. This is not the place for an extensive discussion but those with a mission frame for reading the Bible are unified in seeing that mission through Peter and Paul as God's but also as the centerpiece of what God is doing in the world today (Bosch, Christopher Wright).

As John Franke, who is an expert on missional theology, says, "The starting point for missional theology is the notion of a missional God. This means simply that God is, by God's very nature, a missionary God." Which put another way by him is that our God "has a particular desire, arising from God's eternal character, to engage the world" (1, 4). He continues, "There is mission because God loves" (8). This is the foundation of all of mission when we say God's love makes God a missionary God, namely, that God is a Trinity of love between Father, Son and Spirit, and the inevitable spillover of divine love is to love what God has created. To love in this sense is to reach out to us in missional love.

The Book of Acts speaks directly to us about our mission. We are called by God to participate in God's mission in the world to redeem it through Jesus Christ, the world's true Savior, Lord and King. Each of us participates in that mission according to the gifts given to us by God. So, when I write about the "mission" of God in the power of the Spirit through the apostles Peter and Paul in what follows, we can translate that into our lives by thinking of how we participate in God's mission in our world in the context of the community of faith, the church (Hill, 149–274).

When it comes to our mission and our missional lives, which again is participation in God's mission, Acts points us primarily at church planting but as modern practitioners of mission know, mission is more than just church planting. It is evangelism, catechism into the faith, serving those in need, active work to undo injustices and establish justice, as well as creation care (Walls, Ross). Acts focuses on the first with some hints of the second and third. None of us are 1st Century Christians and most of us are not actively planting churches so "mission" for many of us will participate in the second, third, fourth, and fifth dimensions of mission. But all of the Book of Acts motivates us to participate in all of these dimensions, but in each context the gospel will take on special nuances and connections and languages and categories and the gospel will generate new church, cultural, and social realities (Van Gelder; Guder; Franke, 97–138).

FOR FURTHER READING

David Bosch, *Transforming Mission* (Maryknoll, New York: Orbis, 1991).
Dean Fleming, *Why Mission?* (Nashville: Abingdon, 2015), 23–52.

John Franke, *Missional Theology: An Introduction* (Grand Rapids: Baker Academic, 2020).

Darell L. Guder, ed., *Missional Church: A Vision for the Sending of the Church in North America* (Grand Rapids: Wm. B. Eerdmans, 1998).

Graham Hill, *Salt, Light, and a City: Introducing Missional Ecclesiology* (Eugene, Oregon: Wipf and Stock, 2012).

Craig Van Gelder, ed., *The Missional Church in Context: Helping Congregations Develop Contextual Ministry* (Grand Rapids: Wm. B. Eerdmans, 2007).

Andrew Walls, Cathy Ross, eds., *Mission in the 21st Century: Exploring the Five Marks of Global Mission* (Maryknoll, NY: Orbis, 2008).

Christopher J.H. Wright, *The Mission of God* (Downers Grove: IVP Academic, 2006).

Commentaries cited in the Study Guide (throughout the Guide you will find the author's name and title as noted in this book listing with page numbers whenever I cite something from it):

James D.G. Dunn, *The Acts of the Apostles* (Grand Rapids: Eerdmans, 1996). [Dunn, *Acts*]

James D.G. Dunn, *Beginning from Jerusalem* (Christianity in the Making 2; Grand Rapids: Eerdmans, 2009). [Dunn, *Beginning*]

Beverly Roberts Gaventa, *Acts* (Abingdon New Testament Commentaries; Nashville: Abingdon, 2003). [Gaventa, *Acts*]

Carl R. Holladay, *Acts: A Commentary* (New Testament Library; Louisville: Westminster John Knox, 2016). [Holladay, *Acts*]

Willie James Jennings, *Acts* (Belief: A Theological Commentary on the Bible; Louisville: Westminster John Knox, 2017). [Jennings, *Acts*]

Craig Keener, *Acts* (New Cambridge Bible Commentary; Cambridge: Cambridge University Press, 2020). [Keener, *Acts*]

Dean Pinter, *Acts* (Story of God Bible Commentary; Grand Rapids: Zondervan, 2019). [Pinter, *Acts*]

William Shiell, *Acts* (Preaching the Word; Macon, Ga.: Smyth & Helwys, 2017). [Shiell, *Acts*]

N.T. Wright, *Paul: A Biography* (New York: HarperOne, 2018). [Wright, *Paul*]

THE MISSION OF JESUS

Acts 1:1–14

[1] *In my former book, Theophilus, I wrote about all that Jesus began to do and to teach* [2] *until the day he was taken up to heaven, after giving instructions through the Holy Spirit to the apostles he had chosen.* [3] *After his suffering, he presented himself to them and gave many convincing proofs that he was alive. He appeared to them over a period of forty days and spoke about the kingdom of God.* [4] *On one occasion, while he was eating with them, he gave them this command: "Do not leave Jerusalem, but wait for the gift my Father promised, which you have heard me speak about.* [5] *For John baptized with water, but in a few days you will be baptized with the Holy Spirit."*

[6] *Then they gathered around him and asked him, "Lord, are you at this time going to restore the kingdom to Israel?"*

[7] *He said to them: "It is not for you to know the times or dates the Father has set by his own authority.* [8] *But you will receive power when the Holy Spirit comes on you; and you will be my witnesses in Jerusalem, and in all Judea and Samaria, and to the ends of the earth."*

[9] *After he said this, he was taken up before their very eyes, and a cloud hid him from their sight.*

¹⁰ They were looking intently up into the sky as he was going, when suddenly two men dressed in white stood beside them. ¹¹ "Men of Galilee," they said, "why do you stand here looking into the sky? This same Jesus, who has been taken from you into heaven, will come back in the same way you have seen him go into heaven."

¹² Then the apostles returned to Jerusalem from the hill called the Mount of Olives, a Sabbath day's walk from the city. ¹³ When they arrived, they went upstairs to the room where they were staying. Those present were Peter, John, James and Andrew; Philip and Thomas, Bartholomew and Matthew; James son of Alphaeus and Simon the Zealot, and Judas son of James. ¹⁴ They all joined together constantly in prayer, along with the women and Mary the mother of Jesus, and with his brothers.

Scanning a few church websites, I noticed each had a "vision" and a "mission" statement. Prompting pastors and priests and boards at churches to reduce their ministries to vision and mission statements, the business world was leading the way. As I read them, I thought of the first few verses of the Book of Acts where we learn in bold clear language that the mission of the church is the mission of Jesus, or God's mission. What seems trite to say—"Of course it is!"—is titanic in implication. We don't have our own vision or mission statements. Jesus does. We enjoy in the eloquent opening to the Book of Acts a one-of-a-kind view. For his high-status friend "Theophilus," Luke recapitulates the story of Jesus in his Gospel ever so briefly with "about all that Jesus *began* (1) to do and (2) to teach" (1:1). Luke indicates he will now record what Jesus *continued to do through the power of the Spirit*. The mission of the church was and is nothing less than the mission of Jesus extended to new regions.

THE MISSION OF JESUS
TELLS HIS STORY

Those involved in Jesus' mission in our world will point people both to the earthly life of Jesus as well as tell what Jesus is doing in our world today. Among all that Jesus did we are to speak of his miracles, his compassion for the marginalized, the experience of God's grace at the evening table fellowship, and the formation of an alternative group (to the Pharisees) in the disciples. Among these teachings we begin with the message of the kingdom of God: "he spoke about the kingdom of God" (1:3), which is what the apostle Paul will be preaching at the end of the Book of Acts (28:31). The resurrection is the heart of the gospel in Acts: "convincing proofs that he was alive" (1:3). Unfolding out of his kingdom vision were his calls to follow him and to live according to his vision of God's will (Luke 6:17–49). That kingdom message of Jesus entailed a king, the king's redemption and rule, the king's people, the king's ethics, and physical space (the land promise; McKnight, *Kingdom Conspiracy*).

The question of his followers, "Lord, are you at this time going to restore the kingdom to Israel?" (1:6), reveals that they have not yet understood the full significance of his resurrection, which will be grasped only when they come to terms with his ascension, his rule over all, and his sending of the Spirit. They wanted to know when history was going to be wrapped up. Jesus stiff arms their concern for a bigger one, God's mission for them until the When question gets answered.

We are called along with the apostles to extend the mission of Jesus into our world: redemptive healing, table fellowship, gathering into alternative kingdom societies that practice the teachings of Jesus, and teaching and preaching God's kingdom centering on Jesus, and all this empowered by

9

the Spirit. Notice that the kingdom and the gift of the Spirit's empowering presence are virtual synonyms (1:3 and 1:4–5, 8). As Jesus was given the Spirit to open his mission (Luke 3:21–22) so too his followers (Acts 1:5, 8; 2:1–41).

This reception of the Spirit announced here does not mean the disciples had not yet been converted. Rather, they were being empowered by the Spirit for God's mission (1:8; 2:33, 38; 8:12–17). As Keener, an expert on this theme in Acts, states it, "some dimensions of the Spirit's work available in conversion might be experienced more fully subsequently" (Keener, *Acts* 104).

THE MISSION OF JESUS MAKES US WITNESSES

Those who had been with Jesus during his earthly ministry, listening intensively to his vision of the kingdom of God, were fully ready for that kingdom to be established, but Jesus' mission is a not-quite-yet-totally-done mission. First, they were to be his "witnesses" from Jerusalem "to the ends of the earth" and every place in between. A witness is someone who, on the basis of experience, verbally testifies to one's own experience and testifies by how one lives even to the point of death. Thus, "witness" translates *martus*, from which we get the word "martyr." The apostles were witnesses sent into the world as successors of Jesus (1:2).

The Book of Acts will tell that story through the lives of Peter and then Paul, ending up in Rome, the so-called Eternal City and the center of the Empire. Many have observed rightly that Acts 1:8 brings into one verse the theme of the Book of Acts.

To witness is to tell of our experience with Jesus, to tell others about Jesus and to live a life that witnesses to Jesus. Words and works. As Lesslie Newbigin, the missiologist, once said, "The words interpreted the deeds and the deeds authenticated the words" (Newbigin, *The Good Shepherd*, 62).

THE MISSION OF JESUS OPERATES FROM HEAVEN

Acts 1:9 reveals that Jesus was taken into heaven hidden by a cloud, and the text tells us where this occurred (1:12)—on the eastern hill outside the walls of Jerusalem on the Mount of Olives (where Jesus was arrested). We call this the ascension. From this moment on Jesus conducts his mission from the throne room in heaven and through the Spirit. This mission lasts until he comes back (1:11). The ascension of Jesus, which does sound a bit like the ascension of Elijah (2 Kings 2:9–12) and which is also often silently buried in the message of his resurrection, vindicates him as God's Son who has accomplished his mission of redemption while it also reveals to us that Jesus is the world's true Lord (Philippians 2:6–11) and the great intercessor (Hebrews 2:14–18; 4:14–16). Dean Pinter describes a worship service in a cathedral on Ascension Sunday when the pastor put, not ashes, but glitter on the foreheads of the chorister children. He then draws us into the implications of Jesus' resurrection and ascension: "This glory empowers us, puts wings on our feet, and gets us moving from heavenly gazing and static standing to earthly worship and energetic witness" (Pinter, *Acts*, 49).

THE MISSION OF JESUS REQUIRES PATIENT PRAYER

At Acts 1:4–5 we read that Jesus told his apostles to stay put in Jerusalem and "wait for the gift my Father promised . . . the Holy Spirit." The NIV's "gift" is not in the Greek text. Another reading is "hang around for the Father's promise that you heard from me" (Luke 24:49). In prayer they readied themselves for the Father's promise and out of that prayer they received the Spirit in Acts 2. Waiting, patient prayer for God's power remains a constant in the mission of Jesus.

The twelve apostles were present, but so too were Mary and other women and Jesus' (now converted; John 7:1–5) brothers (1:13–14). We are told they "all joined together constantly in prayer" (1:14). The word "together" in this translation could be better expressed as "emotional unity."

We might need to pause long enough to observe that this small community in Jerusalem, at the upper room where they celebrated the last supper (Luke 22:11–12), was not the entirety of the Jesus movement. There were various groups between Jerusalem and Galilee and we learn in this Book of Acts of some who were following John the Baptist way out in the diaspora (18:18–19:7). We see then Luke's intent to tell one kind of story: the one from Jerusalem to Rome, and the story that focuses on a mission that flows from Jesus' instructions in that forty-day window to the apostles (1:2–3).

QUESTIONS FOR REFLECTION AND APPLICATION

1. McKnight reminds us that the mission of the church is really the mission of Jesus. Understanding that the mission is Jesus', how does that transform your view of your place in the spread of the mission?

2. What are some examples McKnight gives of ways we can participate in the mission of Jesus?

3. What do you think of the translation of "together" expressed instead as "emotional unity"? How does that change your understanding of the text?

4. McKnight says that "to witness" means telling others about our experience with Jesus as well as living a life that speaks of him. Reflect on your experience of "witnessing." How does it compare and contrast with the vision presented here?

5. Does your church have a mission statement? How might you revise it in light of this lesson, in order to align it better with Jesus and his story?

FOR FURTHER READING

Scot McKnight, *Kingdom Conspiracy: Returning to the Radical Mission of the Local Church* (Grand Rapids: Brazos, 2014).

Lesslie Newbigin, *The Good Shepherd* (Grand Rapids: Wm. B. Eerdmans, 1977).

Cherith Fee Nordling, Becky Castle Miller, "Ascension," in *Dictionary of Paul and His Letters 2nd Edition*, (Downers Grove: IVP Academic, forthcoming).

MISSIONERS IN JESUS' MISSION

Acts 1:15–26

15 In those days Peter stood up among the believers (a group numbering about a hundred and twenty) 16 and said, "Brothers and sisters, the Scripture had to be fulfilled in which the Holy Spirit spoke long ago through David concerning Judas, who served as guide for those who arrested Jesus. 17 He was one of our number and shared in our ministry."

18 (With the payment he received for his wickedness, Judas bought a field; there he fell headlong, his body burst open and all his intestines spilled out. 19 Everyone in Jerusalem heard about this, so they called that field in their language Akeldama, that is, Field of Blood.)

20 "For," said Peter, "it is written in the Book of Psalms:

> *" 'May his place be deserted;*
> *let there be no one to dwell in it,'*

and,

> *" 'May another take his place of leadership.'*

²¹ Therefore it is necessary to choose one of the men who have been with us the whole time the Lord Jesus was living among us, ²² beginning from John's baptism to the time when Jesus was taken up from us. For one of these must become a witness with us of his resurrection."

²³ So they nominated two men: Joseph called Barsabbas (also known as Justus) and Matthias. ²⁴ Then they prayed, "Lord, you know everyone's heart. Show us which of these two you have chosen ²⁵ to take over this apostolic ministry, which Judas left to go where he belongs." ²⁶ Then they cast lots, and the lot fell to Matthias; so he was added to the eleven apostles.

Succession plans are always fraught with challenges, none more so than the replacement of Judas, who betrayed Jesus to the Roman authorities. Surely the apostles pondered over next steps and process, all the while grieving what had become of their brother. No less does this occur today when a pastor departs because of moral or leadership failure. Grief envelops the process as hope yearns for a fresh holy start. The number twelve mattered deeply to the apostles, not just because Jesus chose twelve and one had walked away, but because Israel was a twelve-tribe people. It was a symbolic number so weighty someone had to replace Judas. They needed that twelfth apostle.

Or, did they? Is it possible—and I ask this question here only to drop it—that the apostles perform two acts that belong to the old age, and both will be overturned at Pentecost? Their first act queries Jesus about when the kingdom will be restored to Israel and their second is to replace Judas with a twelfth apostle. Are both undone at Pentecost? The first act is clearly overturned by Jesus, but there is nothing about the second that appears to be overturned. Or is there? Is his replacement all those filled with the Spirit?

ACKNOWLEDGE TRUTHS

Peter stands up in the posture of a teacher before a larger audience of "about 120" (1:15)—a small group for each apostle—and addresses the story of Judas with sensitive, truth-telling candor. Three truths describe Judas: (1) that he betrayed Jesus, (2) that he was an apostle, and (3) that he died by suicide. The Gospels rehearse the betrayal, and Luke sums up the accounts with "who served as guide for those who arrested Jesus" (Acts 1:16; Luke 22:47–53). His death is summarized next (Acts 1:18–19; compare this account to Matthew 27:3–10).

Moral failures create difficulties for those who were previously close to the person, and the temptation to disown or demonize the person needs to be resisted without diminishing the failure. (Easier said than done.) I am touched by how Luke describes it: "He was one of *our* number and shared in *our* ministry" (Acts 1:17). His relationship and apostleship are not denied. The church has demonized Judas, made graphically explicit in Dante's *Divine Comedy*, which reserved the ninth ring of an icy hell for Satan who is chewing Judas headfirst. But Luke's words sound a plaintive note of grief over the loss of Judas.

Suicide occurs six times in the Old Testament: Abimelech (Judges 9:54), Samson (16:25–31), Saul and his armor bearer (1 Samuel 31:1–5), Ahithophel (2 Samuel 17:23), and Zimri (1 Kings 16:18). The ideation of suicide appears more often than many realize, as is the case with Rebekah (Genesis 27:46) and Jonah (1:12; 4:3) (Pinter, *Acts*, 56). Judas is the only instance in the New Testament, but suicide was heroic among upper status Romans. The survivors at Masada died in a mass suicide, and both the Roman and Jewish stories are shaped by an honor that refused the shame of defeat at the hands of enemies. Judas, out of remorse over his act of betraying innocent blood, hanged himself and, to put the two accounts into a harmony, his body fell apart onto a field soon called "Field of Blood" (Matthew 27:3–10; Acts 1:18–19).

Successions following tragedies and moral failures require this kind of honesty. There are some who would see these kinds of honest reports as gossip or inappropriate but the church has scriptures that tell the stories of our heroes "warts and all." Moses murdered a man; David murdered a man and was a polygamist; Solomon outdid Dad. The prophets could blow it at times and the apostle Paul got into a heated face-to-face in front of others in Galatians 2. Such stories record the truth, avoid turning Christian stories into idealistic biographies, and (frankly) put the fear of God into all of us.

BATHE IN SCRIPTURE

I grew up among people who could quote scriptures for the oddest of moments, almost none of them exegetically responsible. However, what I came to appreciate was how deep my church was in its knowledge of Scripture. Among whom were my mother and father and their close friends in our church. Their conversations at times ventured into competitions of quotations that quickly fell into humor. There was nothing irreverent about it. At other times they had the witty remark for the right situation, however connected that scripture expression or word was to its original context.

Peter pointed the small Christian community in Jerusalem to two unrelated texts in the Psalms, to Psalm 69:25 and 109:8. Psalm 69 is a complaint of David to God about his innumerable enemies "who hate me without reason" (69:4). This complaint turns into petition for deliverance and judgment on his enemies, including his desire that "their place be deserted andto Judas: the replacement there be no one to dwell in their tents" (69:25). Peter alters the plural "their" to a singular "his" and so turns the words into his own judgment of Judas for his betrayal (Acts 1:20). He then finds a scripture that legitimates replacement in Psalm 109, another psalm of complaint by David about his enemies. He prays that the days of his enemy "be few; may another take his place of leadership" (109:8). These texts, then, were not about Judas. No, Peter, bathed in scripture, articulates a succession plan with words drawn from scriptures. One could also suggest these texts about David the king and his enemies correlate with Jesus and his enemies, and with apostles representing Jesus, the apostles can be seen as standing in a place like David. That the Gospels use Psalm 69 for Jesus and his opponents in the last week confirms such a suggestion (Holladay, *Acts*, 82–83; Keener, *Acts*, 118).

FORM QUALIFICATIONS

It was as "necessary" for Judas' action (1:16; NIV has "had to be") as it was "necessary" to replace Judas (1:21). No doubt the result of conversations with others, Peter puts forward a qualification for the successor to Judas: the replacement has to "have been with us the whole time the Lord Jesus was living among us" (1:21). His name, we will see in the next section, is Matthias, and we heard not a word about the man in the Gospels. But he was an early follower of Jesus who continued with the others until the ascension and as such had witnessed the resurrection.

His giftedness and skills don't qualify him. Instead, what qualified him was following Jesus and his presence with Jesus and the others. He was a witness, and only witnesses qualify to be witnesses. Some may exaggerate this singular qualification, but more ignore it. In our searches today for ministers, we exaggerate skills and talents and job descriptions and fail to assess what matters most: character, the kind of character glowing from the person who knows Jesus and spends time with Jesus. The task, once again, of the apostle of Jesus is to be a "witness" (1:22; cf. 1:8) and most notably a witness with the others "of his resurrection."

TURN IT OVER TO GOD (BUT DON'T TOSS THE DICE)

The "search committee" discovers two who qualify, Joseph called Barsabbas (also called Justus) and Matthias. Instead of a vote, the eleven apostles turned it all over to God and tossed the dice (as it were). (You would not be alone wondering why James the brother of Jesus was not a third, or the first!) Their words were "Show us," or make it clear to us which of the two you want. The lots fell in favor of Matthias, and he was given the slot. We might look at this as a bit unspiritual but they trusted God to guide the choice, and they had scripture for that too (Proverbs 16:33; Keener, *Acts*, 120). I don't know what to make of not hearing another word about Matthias in the New Testament.

QUESTIONS FOR REFLECTION AND APPLICATION

1. When have you witnessed a moral failing of a church leader? Did others in leadership speak truth boldly, like Peter, or try to cover it up?

2. How have you seen people "disown" or "demonize" fellow Christians who fail?

3. How does Peter use Scripture to speak of Judas's death and make a succession plan?

4. What qualifications has your church formed for ministers? Which qualifications relate to their being witnesses of Jesus?

5. What in your life makes you stand out as one who would be recognized as a witness of Jesus?

THE SPIRIT OF
THE MISSION

Acts 2:1–13

¹ When the day of Pentecost came, they were all together in one place. ² Suddenly a sound like the blowing of a violent wind came from heaven and filled the whole house where they were sitting. ³ They saw what seemed to be tongues of fire that separated and came to rest on each of them. ⁴ All of them were filled with the Holy Spirit and began to speak in other tongues as the Spirit enabled them.

⁵ Now there were staying in Jerusalem God-fearing Jews from every nation under heaven. ⁶ When they heard this sound, a crowd came together in bewilderment, because each one heard their own language being spoken. ⁷ Utterly amazed, they asked: "Aren't all these who are speaking Galileans? ⁸ Then how is it that each of us hears them in our native language? ⁹ Parthians, Medes and Elamites; residents of Mesopotamia, Judea and Cappadocia, Pontus and Asia, ¹⁰ Phrygia and Pamphylia, Egypt and the parts of Libya near Cyrene; visitors from Rome ¹¹ (both Jews and converts to Judaism); Cretans and Arabs—we hear them declaring the wonders of God in our own tongues!" ¹² Amazed and perplexed, they asked one another, "What does this mean?"

[13] *Some, however, made fun of them and said, "They have had too much wine."*

The entire Old Testament reveals but one missionary, Jonah, and he was a total flop. He just didn't like the calling. The implications of Genesis 12's exhortation for Abraham's descendants to be a blessing to the nations didn't happen. History past and future proved that *a*, if not *the*, distinctive mark of the earliest Christian movement was its expansion of the people of God to include gentiles. The Pauline mission, which forms the second half of the Book of Acts, unfolded one new gentile mission church after another—across Turkey, across Greece, and all the way to Rome.

What happens in Acts 2 alters the course of history (cf. Luke 24:47–49; Acts 1:4–8). Fifty days after Passover, or in church language, Holy Week, God's Spirit creates a radically reshaped community. We call this the Day of Pentecost, while Jews named it the Feast of Weeks, named for the first-fruits of the harvest (cf. Leviticus 23:15–21). Acts 2 reveals to us the first Pentecostals.

> We are called by God to participate in God's mission in the world to redeem it through Jesus Christ, the world's true Savior, Lord and King. Each of us participates in that mission according to the gifts given to us by God.

Let us remember this Day as the Day God came among us in a new and fresh way. As Eugene Peterson once said it, "Pentecost means that God is not a spectator, in turn amused and alarmed at world history; rather, he is a participant" (*On Living Well*, 168). Yes, and this chapter in Acts reminds us that God is among us still.

PENTECOST CHRISTIANS
EXIST TOGETHER

Acts 2 tells us that Pentecost Christians (like Jesus himself in Luke 4:18–19) welcome the fresh arrival of the Spirit, they welcome the empowering of all Christians, they welcome the good news about Jesus' resurrection and ascension, and they welcome the gift of the Spirit personally. Remember that the Book of Acts is about the mission of Jesus in the world from Jerusalem to Rome. The great day of Pentecost's gift of the Spirit empowers the church to carry out that mission.

In our rush to get to the magical moment of this passage, we may miss the opening: "they were all together in one place" (2:1). It would work to say "they were together" or they were "all in one place" but Luke triples it: "all" and "together" and "in one place." One should not underestimate the potential of believers gathering in unity to wait on God. How many were the "all"? In the previous chapter we get two clues: (1) either Twelve apostles, "the women," Mary, mother of Jesus, and Jesus' brothers (1:13–14), or (2) the larger group of 120 believers (1:15). Think of these believers as a marginalized minority judged by some to be fanatics and schismatics. Regardless, they were utterly unified: all of them, together, in one place. Praying. Fellowshipping. Instructed. Encouraged. Emboldened. Inexperienced. Fearful, too. Not knowing what to do or what might happen next. Waiting. Wondering too if it might not be time to return to Galilee.

PENTECOST CHRISTIANS
EXPERIENCE THE SPIRIT

All at once, out of the blue, like a massive semi-truck's downshifting rattling windows, they *heard* a "violent wind" and it filled their house and they *observed* "tongues of fire," or flames, that split and sat on "each of them." That cloven-tongued fire *filled* them with the Holy Spirit to empower them for what God was about to do, which was that they *began to speak* "in other tongues" (2:4). Luke elsewhere informs us of the fillings of the Spirit (4:8, 31; 9:17; 13:9; Luke 1:41, 67; Ephesians 5:18). There were three, and perhaps a fourth, kinds of tongues in the early church (see Keener, *Acts*, 125–129):

(1) the spiritual gift of tongues used in an assembly
of Christians for mutual encouragement
(1 Corinthians 12:10),
(2) praying in tongues (1 Corinthians 14:14; see
14:1–18),
(3) perhaps singing in tongues (Colossians 3:16), and
(4) the Pentecost tongue of speaking God's redemption
in languages not otherwise known (Acts 2).

God anointed this small body of believers at a specific time: when the whole city was filled with foreign languages (2:5–11). Somehow their tongues-speaking is heard and understood--through a Divine Translator--by those outside the house. How that happened is unclear, but Beverly Gaventa winks at the dissolving of the walls and doors! (*Acts*, 74–75). These verses make it clear that the miracle of Pentecost was the ability to speak in an unknown foreign language (Dunn, *Beginning*, 159; Keener, *Acts*, 124) or, less likely, that the believers spoke in Aramaic but their words were *heard* by others in their own languages (2:8). Regardless, the miracle embodied the desire of God to spread the gospel (here: "the wonders of God"; 2:11) to all nations. Many have suggested Pentecost begins to unravel the curse of Babel (Genesis 11:1–9; Volf, 213–216) but it should be noticed that Acts 2 does not, like the pre-Babel days, return to one language. Rather God blesses the multiplicity of languages.

PENTECOST CHRISTIANS EXPAND THE VISION

All of this to draw our attention to the big idea: Pentecost launches the Abrahamic promise to bless all nations. Pentecost Christians don't restrict mission by ethnicity, by language, by economic class, by nation, by race, by gender, by education, by location, by geography . . . add your own . . . the gospel from the Day of Pentecost is for every human being. The more filled with the Spirit one is the wider the mission will be. As William Shiell says it, "Pentecost . . . is not a feel good, cozy, warm-and-fuzzy prayer meeting in a historic chapel . . . It is a noisy shakeup of our world that changes our lives" (Shiell, *Acts*, 21).

The truth of the gospel that Jesus is Lord of all, however, has been damaged by Christian colonialism and exploitation, by moral failures at home and abroad, and by paternalistic attitudes toward the Majority World. Missionary work continues in chastened forms. What encourages me are the efforts of local Christians who embody and express the gospel in native languages and forms. That is where the Spirit of Pentecost works.

QUESTIONS FOR REFLECTION AND APPLICATION

1. How does Acts illustrate that a distinctive mark of early Christian mission was the inclusion of gentiles?

2. What details and traits do you notice about the group gathered all together in one place?

3. What are the four types of "tongues" mentioned in Acts?

4. What examples does McKnight give of events that have damaged the truth of the gospel? Have any of these impacted your own faith?

5. How do you see the mission of God going out in your own community and world?

FOR FURTHER READING

Eugene Peterson, *On Living Well* (Colorado Springs: WaterBrook, 2021).

Miroslav Volf, *Exclusion and Embrace: A Theological Exploration of Identity, Otherness, and Reconciliation* (2d ed.; Nashville: Abingdon, 2019).

THE GOSPEL OF
THE MISSION

Acts 2:14–41

¹⁴ *Then Peter stood up with the Eleven, raised his voice and addressed the crowd: "Fellow Jews and all of you who live in Jerusalem, let me explain this to you; listen carefully to what I say.* ¹⁵ *These people are not drunk, as you suppose. It's only nine in the morning!* ¹⁶ *No, this is what was spoken by the prophet Joel:*

¹⁷ *" 'In the last days, God says,*
I will pour out my Spirit on all people.
Your sons and daughters will prophesy,
your young men will see visions,
your old men will dream dreams.
¹⁸ *Even on my servants, both men and women,*
I will pour out my Spirit in those days,
and they will prophesy.
¹⁹ *I will show wonders in the heavens above*
and signs on the earth below,
blood and fire and billows of smoke.
²⁰ *The sun will be turned to darkness*
and the moon to blood

*before the coming of the great and glorious day of the
Lord.*
*²¹ And everyone who calls
on the name of the Lord will be saved.'*

²² "*Fellow Israelites, listen to this: Jesus of Nazareth was a man
accredited by God to you by miracles, wonders and signs, which
God did among you through him, as you yourselves know.* ²³ *This
man was handed over to you by God's deliberate plan and fore-
knowledge; and you, with the help of wicked men, put him to death
by nailing him to the cross.* ²⁴ *But God raised him from the dead,
freeing him from the agony of death, because it was impossible for
death to keep its hold on him.* ²⁵ *David said about him:*

" '*I saw the Lord always before me.
Because he is at my right hand,
I will not be shaken.*
²⁶ *Therefore my heart is glad and my tongue rejoices;
my body also will rest in hope,*
²⁷ *because you will not abandon me to the realm of the
dead,
you will not let your holy one see decay.*
²⁸ *You have made known to me the paths of life;
you will fill me with joy in your presence.'*

²⁹ "*Fellow Israelites, I can tell you confidently that the patriarch
David died and was buried, and his tomb is here to this day.* ³⁰ *But
he was a prophet and knew that God had promised him on oath
that he would place one of his descendants on his throne.* ³¹ *Seeing
what was to come, he spoke of the resurrection of the Messiah,
that he was not abandoned to the realm of the dead, nor did his
body see decay.* ³² *God has raised this Jesus to life, and we are all
witnesses of it.* ³³ *Exalted to the right hand of God, he has received*

from the Father the promised Holy Spirit and has poured out what you now see and hear. [34] For David did not ascend to heaven, and yet he said,

> " 'The Lord said to my Lord:
>   "Sit at my right hand
> [35] until I make your enemies
>   a footstool for your feet." '

[36] "Therefore let all Israel be assured of this: God has made this Jesus, whom you crucified, both Lord and Messiah."

[37] When the people heard this, they were cut to the heart and said to Peter and the other apostles, "Brothers, what shall we do?"

[38] Peter replied, "Repent and be baptized, every one of you, in the name of Jesus Christ for the forgiveness of your sins. And you will receive the gift of the Holy Spirit. [39] The promise is for you and your children and for all who are far off—for all whom the Lord our God will call."

[40] With many other words he warned them; and he pleaded with them, "Save yourselves from this corrupt generation." [41] Those who accepted his message were baptized, and about three thousand were added to their number that day.

Ponder Peter a moment, the leading apostle who denied Jesus three times and who needed reinstatement. Sure, he's present in Acts 1's gathering in a home, but what we encounter in this chapter is nothing less than the transformation of a coward into a courageous preacher of the gospel.

Pause for another thought: this is the first recorded evangelistic sermon by an apostle. One great American preacher used to say he prepared his sermons by praying himself full, and by reading himself up, and then blowing it all out on

Sunday morning. Peter must have felt this way. On his own now, no more standing next to Jesus while he taught, he was put on the spot. Three years of learning and the power of the Spirit anointing him. Peter preaches the gospel plain and simple as the truth.

One more thought: Peter knew what to say, and this "cameo representation" by Luke (Dunn, *Acts*, 27) gives us a full gist of Peter's words. Opponents are calling the filling of the Spirit into question, even alleging the followers of Jesus may be intoxicated. Peter's sermon in Acts 2, the longest sermon in the Book of Acts, both explains this Holy Spirit stuff and declares the gospel. The bare bones outline of this sermon can be found in 1 Corinthians 15:1–8. Peter's gospel sermon challenges the reductions of the gospel we hear so often today. We have reduced the gospel to four simple laws (God loves you, you are a sinner, Jesus died for you, believe in Jesus and you go to heaven when you die) or to one simple truth (God loves you, or you are important). Those simplifications do tell us something true, but it is not a little surprising for many to read this first gospel sermon and realize how utterly different it is from our gospel sermons. Perhaps you are yourself surprised.

A close reading of this sermon opens a window on the earliest gospel preaching to Jews that included appealing to Old Testament *expectation, a narration* of the crucial gospel-central events in the life of Jesus, and a *declaration* of who Jesus is. The wending and winding from one Old Testament text to another can be difficult enough but when those texts are both unfamiliar (as they are to most Bible readers today) and when many of us do not understand gospel preaching, we can begin to wonder why Luke gave so much attention to this Pentecost Day sermon by Peter. We may be the ones who need some relearning.

THE MISSION'S GOSPEL EMERGES
FROM AN EXPECTATION (2:14–21)

Peter begins with what happened–the outpouring of the Spirit–and lines it up with a specific prophet's expectations of what would happen "in the last days" (2:17). That Pentecostal moment was being challenged and Peter explains that what happened was anticipated in Joel 2:28–32, a chapter that begins with the judgment of the "day of the LORD" but flows majestically into the pouring out of divine blessings, both material and spiritual. Peter knows that the spiritual blessing of that day is the Spirit-ual blessing of all spiritual blessings. The Spirit, the prophet predicted, would be poured out.

Would be just became *it happened.*

The operative expression here, much to the consternation of Peter's critics, is "all people" (Acts 2:17). God's Spirit would not be assigned only to the priests and prophets and lawgivers but to all people. So much is this the point that he quotes even more from Joel: "Your sons and daughters" and "your young men" and "your old men" and "servants, both men and women." The apostle Paul, in that famous magna carta of Christian equality, when he speaks of Jews, Greeks, free, slave, men and women, is only spelling out what Joel predicted and Peter experienced (Galatians 3:28). It was not just male leaders who "were declaring the wonders of God" (Acts 2:11). No, Peter makes clear by quoting Joel, men and women will be prophesying and both young and old will be kingdom visionaries, and all will be filled with the Spirit to speak the truths of God. The emphasis here on women must be given full weight: from Pentecost on, the Spirit no longer privileges men (Keener, *Acts*, 147–148).

The cosmic signs of Joel 2 sometimes confuse modern readers. Some think these signs–"wonders" and "signs" and "blood and fire and smoke" and a darkened sun and moon that is blood red—predict physical realities, while those more familiar with the Old Testament images see them as (apocalyptic) metaphors for political collapse caused by God's judgment on a nation (esp. Joel 2). By using these metaphors for political collapse, Peter ties the outpouring of the Spirit to God's judgment on the political powers, both Roman and Jewish, for the unjust death of Jesus. Think of it this way: the outpouring of the Spirit is the flipside of God's judgment on injustice.

THE MISSION'S GOSPEL REQUIRES A NARRATION (2:22–32)

Peter now bridges the Pentecostal moment and Joel specifically to Jesus. His report about Jesus points back to the amazing wonders God did through him (2:22), to the unjust death of Jesus (his eyes and finger pointing are aimed at his opponents here), to the providential plan of God despite the injustice, and to the mighty power of God cracking the bonds of death and raising Jesus (2:24).

Gospel preaching tells people the story of Jesus, and it is a story about his life, his teachings, his miracles, his wonders, his calling people to follow him, his embodied acts like sitting at the table with the excluded of his world, and his death and his burial and his resurrection and his ascension. Gospel preaching tells people about Jesus. Jesus is the content of the gospel message.

But for Peter's audience just after that Pentecostal moment, because they know their Bibles, he proves his point in Acts 2:25–28 by appealing to Psalm 16:8–11. That psalm was traditionally connected to David, a messianic figure, and that psalm expresses David's joy and trust in God that he will be preserved even in the face of death.

The Christian way to tell the story of Jesus is not to

reduce him to a teacher or even to a mighty prophet or a charismatic holy man. No, the Christian tradition tells us he is the Davidic Messiah, the Son of God, the one in whom life is found and who therefore cannot be contained or constrained by death itself. We are to tell the story that, like in C.S. Lewis's *The Lion, the Witch, and the Wardrobe,* the Stone Table will eventually crack and unleash the powers of life to bring Aslan back to life. This is the only gospel narration we are to tell. The man on the cross was the man who was raised.

This is the only gospel preached in the gospel sermons in Acts (chps. 2, 3, 4, 10, 11, 13, 14). It is the gospel outlined in 1 Corinthians 15 and bare-boned in 2 Timothy 2:8, and then fleshed out day by day in the four Gospels of the New Testament. To "gospel" is to tell people about Jesus. The mission lessons of the Book of Acts are instances of this gospel taking root in new locations.

One should be asking today about the various methods of actually gospeling others, and it is nothing but helpful for us to recall that the church of today can use one or more of at least eight methods. Priscilla Pope-Levison's award-winning study of these methods explains and illustrates each of the following eight methods: (1) personal evangelism, (2) small group evangelism, (3) visitation evangelism, (4) liturgical evangelism, (5) church growth principles, (6) prophetic words that evangelize, (7) revival events, and (8) the use of various media. Peter stood up and preached; we can do that and we can adjust our methods to our various audiences.

THE MISSION'S GOSPEL EXPLODES INTO A DECLARATION (2:33–41)

That narration about Jesus–his unjust death, his mighty resurrection–now turns into its implication. First, Jesus was raised to the Throne Room of God where he blows the Spirit out on all the believers in Jerusalem (2:33). (By the way, Peter said, David seemed to indicate some kind of ascension, but it was not about himself so it was about Jesus! Acts 2:34–35.)

Second, the Spirit-sending Jesus–crucified and raised–is "both Lord and Messiah" (2:36). Death seemingly defeated him, but God cracked open the powers of death, and life was unleashed on Jesus and he was raised to the Throne Room with God (the Father). This makes him Lord over all, and "Lord" probably indicates over the Roman empire and "Messiah" indicates king over Israel. But it was Pentecost that unleashed the power to announce this gospel. The gospel *not only tells us the story of Jesus, but it identifies with titles Who He Is!* Gospel preaching is not done until someone is asked to identify what they think of Jesus, to express what term best captures who he is and what he has accomplished. The proper terms are Lord and Messiah, along with others not used here like Lamb of God and Son of God and King of Kings (Wright; McKnight; Bates).

Third, what's the proper response to the story about Jesus and who he is? The ones at whom Peter was looking this whole time ask the million dollar question: What shall we do? (2:37). The answer is simple: Repent and be baptized. Which means to admit your sin, to reverse one's thinking about who Jesus is, and to turn from our previous sinful ways to following him with the other believers (see Acts 3:19; 5:31; 8:22; 11:18). The act of baptism, which plunges a person into the death and resurrection of Jesus, embodies one's identification with Jesus and sets up a pattern for how best to follow Jesus: by dying to self and living in the life Christ gives us through the Spirit. The response made to the gospel is not the achievement of indubitable certainty, as Lesslie Newbigin wrote in his important study *Proper Confidence*, in coming to faith "There is no possibility of the kind of indubitable certainty that Descartes claimed. . . . There is no insurance against risk. We are invited to make a personal commitment to a personal Lord and to entrust our lives to his service" (Newbigin, 66). In that relationship we grow in a proper confidence in the truth of the gospel that such a relationship empowers us to have.

Fourth, and only now does this theme appear, those who learn the story about Jesus and who he is and who repent and are baptized *experience the benefits of the gospel*. That benefit is (1) "the forgiveness of sins" and (2) the gift of the Spirit (2:38; see Pinter, *Acts*, 76–80). Those sins took shape in Acts 2 in rejection of Jesus but should not be limited to that. And, as Lord at the right hand of God, Jesus sends the Spirit *upon all who repent and are baptized* (2:38). This much-anticipated promise from Joel 2, already indicated at Acts 1:4–5, is for "you and your children and for all who are far off" (2:39). That is, for all who, as Joel said (Acts 2:21), are called by God (2:39).

It's exciting, isn't it, to see that the small church of 120 grew by 3000? (Acts 2:41)

QUESTIONS FOR REFLECTION AND APPLICATION

1. How does the gospel preaching in Peter's sermon differ from "gospel" sermons you have heard before in churches or crusades?

2. What does it mean for the Spirit to be poured out on all people?

3. How do the cosmic signs from Joel 2 function as metaphors?

4. McKnight says, "To 'gospel' is to tell people about Jesus." What are some of the "gospeling" methods mentioned here, and which are you most familiar with? Which are new to you that you would like to try?

5. What is the proper response to the story of Jesus? How have you experienced responses to and benefits of the gospel?

FOR FURTHER READING

Matthew Bates, *Gospel Allegiance* (Grand Rapids: Brazos, 2019).

Scot McKnight, *King Jesus Gospel* (rev. ed.; Grand Rapids: Zondervan, 2016).

Lesslie Newbigin, *Proper Confidence* (Grand Rapids: Wm. B. Eerdmans, 1995).

Priscilla Pope-Levison, *Models of Evangelism* (Grand Rapids: Baker Academic, 2020).

N.T. Wright, *What Saint Paul Really Said* (Grand Rapids: Wm. B. Eerdmans, 1997), 39–62.

THE RESPONSE TO THE MISSION

Acts 2:42–47

42 They devoted themselves to the apostles' teaching and to fellowship, to the breaking of bread and to prayer. 43 Everyone was filled with awe at the many wonders and signs performed by the apostles. 44 All the believers were together and had everything in common. 45 They sold property and possessions to give to anyone who had need. 46 Every day they continued to meet together in the temple courts. They broke bread in their homes and ate together with glad and sincere hearts, 47 praising God and enjoying the favor of all the people. And the Lord added to their number daily those who were being saved.

The baptized of the previous passage were all-in, that is, they committed themselves to what today we call "formation," with one major caveat. We use "formation" more individualistically than what we see in this passage. For the earliest churches after the great Day of Pentecost, spiritual formation was both very personal but also meant learning how to live in a new Christian fellowship with others. To be a mature Christian was to be one who both loved God *and* loved others. Luke describes this all-in way of life in no fewer than seven categories.

His opening words–*they devoted [or were devoting] themselves*–describe their *commitment* vividly as his words stir us to watch their daily commitments. Theirs was a resolute, persistent, active commitment to four practices (Dunn, *Beginning*, 172–206):

(1) to listening to and learning the apostolic instructions, which would have been the basics about Jesus' life and teachings and mission, now all empowered by the resurrection;

(2) to "fellowship," a term that speaks of a common way of life;

(3) to the "breaking of bread," which either means the Lord's supper (Pinter, *Acts*, 83–84) or eating meals with one another as is stated in 2:46 (Dunn, *Beginnings*, 199–200), or perhaps one leading to the other (Keener, *Acts*, 171–172); and

(4) to prayer, which for 1st Century Jews would mean evening, morning, and mid-afternoon prayers.

Accompanying their commitment was an explosion of Spirit-empowered *charismatic* "wonders and signs" (2:43), terms indicating miracles that revealed the redemptive work of God in Christ.

What distinguished the early churches was a spontaneous *commonality* that included resources and possessions (2:44–45), a kind of accountability and liability for one another that exhibited their "fellowship" (2:42). Many are struck with a sense of anxiety by these descriptions about sharing. "What is far more dangerous than any plan of shared wealth or fair distribution of goods and services is a God who dares impose on us divine love" (Jennings, *Acts*, 40). Unity in this common way of life comes out in his next description, which I have labeled *concord*. That is, "every day they continued to meet together in the temple courts" (2:46). The warm glow of fresh faith formed at a summer youth camp or, in our case at Northern Seminary, of new cohorts gathering all day Monday through Friday, evokes what Luke describes in verse forty-six. Not willing to part from one another, again like our cohorts, they then proceeded to one another's homes for evening meals and deepening discussion of this new way of life, which can be called *commensality* (2:46) or "sacred sociality" (Jennings, *Acts*, 39). There is a lack of discrimination at work: all the believers were living a common way of life and all are gathering together. Status has been erased. The impact of this common way of life, including its worship in song, among these Jewish believers are both *commendation* from "all the people" in Jerusalem, which means they had a wonderful public reputation, and an increased number of *commitments* to the gospel about Jesus (2:47).

One of the modes of Bible reading for some is to go back to the early church and retrieve all one can for our day, adjusting for what can be done and what can't be done (we're not gathering at a no-longer-existing temple!). Such an approach leads at times to unfortunately rigid attempts to imitate rather than to recognizing (1) that this experience is an early example of only some of what was happening, (2) that these practices were not always do-able in other contexts and for all Christians, and (3) that at times we need to adapt to new social conditions in other parts of the world. The Book of Acts, when read alongside the letters of the apostles and the history of the church, reveals that we can learn from these various commitments while not slavishly copying them. Yet, in a day when Christians have dropped out of eating at one another's homes, where they pray together only on Sundays (if then), and when that sense of family liability for one another has been handed over to the government, perhaps what we need all over again is a renewed persistent commitment to a common way of life (Mamula).

Questions for Reflection and Application

1. Describe the difference between the individual way we approach spiritual formation with the communal form Luke writes about.

2. What are the "c" words McKnight uses here to describe the community that formed in the early church?

3. Have you seen any group of Christians try to live out a literal attempt to imitate the early church? How did that appear to you?

4. When you consider the radical sharing that took place among early Christians, what emotion does it provoke in you? Anxiety, joy, concern, comfort, wonder, or others?

5. What are some practices you could take on that might increase your sense of "family liability" for other believers?

FOR FURTHER READING

Greg Mamula, *Table Life: An Invitation to Everyday Discipleship* (Valley Forge, Penn.: Judson Press, 2020).

AUDIENCE-SENSITIVE MISSION

Acts 3:1–26

¹ One day Peter and John were going up to the temple at the time of prayer—at three in the afternoon. ² Now a man who was lame from birth was being carried to the temple gate called Beautiful, where he was put every day to beg from those going into the temple courts. ³ When he saw Peter and John about to enter, he asked them for money. ⁴ Peter looked straight at him, as did John. Then Peter said, "Look at us!" ⁵ So the man gave them his attention, expecting to get something from them.

⁶ Then Peter said, "Silver or gold I do not have, but what I do have I give you. In the name of Jesus Christ of Nazareth, walk." ⁷ Taking him by the right hand, he helped him up, and instantly the man's feet and ankles became strong. ⁸ He jumped to his feet and began to walk. Then he went with them into the temple courts, walking and jumping, and praising God. ⁹ When all the people saw him walking and praising God, ¹⁰ they recognized him as the same man who used to sit begging at the temple gate called Beautiful, and they were filled with wonder and amazement at what had happened to him.

¹¹ While the man held on to Peter and John, all the people were astonished and came running to them in the place called Solomon's Colonnade. ¹² When Peter saw this, he said to them:

"Fellow Israelites, why does this surprise you? Why do you stare at us as if by our own power or godliness we had made this man walk? [13] The God of Abraham, Isaac and Jacob, the God of our fathers, has glorified his servant Jesus. You handed him over to be killed, and you disowned him before Pilate, though he had decided to let him go. [14] You disowned the Holy and Righteous One and asked that a murderer be released to you. [15] You killed the author of life, but God raised him from the dead. We are witnesses of this. [16] By faith in the name of Jesus, this man whom you see and know was made strong. It is Jesus' name and the faith that comes through him that has completely healed him, as you can all see.

[17] "Now, fellow Israelites, I know that you acted in ignorance, as did your leaders. [18] But this is how God fulfilled what he had foretold through all the prophets, saying that his Messiah would suffer. [19] Repent, then, and turn to God, so that your sins may be wiped out, that times of refreshing may come from the Lord, [20] and that he may send the Messiah, who has been appointed for you— even Jesus. [21] Heaven must receive him until the time comes for God to restore everything, as he promised long ago through his holy prophets. [22] For Moses said, 'The Lord your God will raise up for you a prophet like me from among your own people; you must listen to everything he tells you. [23] Anyone who does not listen to him will be completely cut off from their people.'

[24] "Indeed, beginning with Samuel, all the prophets who have spoken have foretold these days. [25] And you are heirs of the prophets and of the covenant God made with your fathers. He said to Abraham, 'Through your offspring all peoples on earth will be blessed.' [26] When God raised up his servant, he sent him first to you to bless you by turning each of you from your wicked ways."

The early church's spiritual practice of prayer, tied to the Jewish prayer traditions, prompts two of the apostles to attend the afternoon prayers in the temple courts of Jerusalem.

At the gate called "Beautiful" they encounter a daily-begging, physically challenged man. (Scholars are unsure about the location of this gate, but most likely it was to the east of the holy of holies and perhaps was the gate between the court of women and men.) The power of Jesus works through Peter to heal, setting off a series of events beginning with the second evangelistic sermon in the Book of Acts (4:1–31).

CONTEXT

The outpouring of the Spirit and speaking in tongues prompted the first public act of gospeling. The second was a healing. During the earthly life of Jesus and (at least) the early days of the apostles, miracles were abundant, both as demonstrations of the presence of God among us, the reality of the kingdom of God, and the unleashing of the Spirit (Matthew 12:28; Acts 2:43; 3:6). No other explanation other than "God at work" can explain the power and presence of these miracles (Keener, *Miracles; Miracles Today*). Some contend that gospeling and miracles still go hand in hand (Twelftree).

The lame man's request for money meets Peter's much better solution. He doesn't have money, but he's got the power of Jesus and the lame man begins to walk. The sudden and complete healing finds no better words than "instantly" and "he jumped to his feet" (3:7–8). As a healed man he can enter into the court of men, and this in a world where disabilities disqualified humans from close proximity to the Holy of Holies (cf. Leviticus 21:19; 22:19–25). He was recognized as a routine beggar and as one giving glory to God for the healing, he declares the Source of the miracle: God.

Healing stories spread; healers and explanations demanded. All of which creates the opportunity for Peter, with John seemingly standing silently taking it all in, to explain what has happened in a way that gospels a new group.

AUDIENCE-SENSITIVE GOSPELING

For many, the Four Spiritual Laws (4SL) approach has diminished in value as a gospel presentation. Its assumptions, culture, and phrasing worked for mostly church-going or church-raised Americans. It was audience-sensitive; it is no longer so. *Every gospeling event requires audience-sensitivities* so we should remember that the 4SL was profoundly audience-sensitive in its day.

Peter's message appeals to those curious about a healing they both accepted as an event and for which they wanted an explanation. So Peter responds to an "unexpected opportunity" (Dunn, *Acts*, 42). In so doing he becomes a model for gospeling today by illustrating nothing less than *pastoral sensitivity* to the people to whom he speaks at Solomon's portico (eastern side of temple complex from which one looked down into the Kidron Valley and at Gethsemane and Mt. Olivet). What follows is not eight steps of audience-sensitivity but instead illustration of one sensitive gospeler (Peter).

First, he denies that he and John ("us" "our" "we") did this. It was an act of God in the name of Jesus (3:6). Which means we have to *get over ourselves and get into the centrality of Jesus* (cf. 3:16; 4:7, 10, 12, 17–18, 30). Amen?

Second, to explain what happened *Peter tells the story of Jesus* that occurred not that many days earlier. He doesn't draw attention to himself or the healed man but throws the whole story onto Jesus. The source of the miracle was that Jesus had been "glorified," which means crucified, raised, ascended to the right hand of God (3:13).

Third, Peter is not afraid to *call attention to their sins* so he points a long finger at those complicit in the unjust crucifixion of Jesus (3:15), aiming his words at the crowd frenzy before Pilate: "you handed him over" and "you disowned him" and "you disowned the Holy and Righteous One" and you "asked that a murderer be released to you" and "you killed the author of life." He's blaming only those complicit in the death deed done to Jesus.

Fourth, in the process of accusing them, *Peter keeps the subject matter focused on the identity of who Jesus is:* he is "glorified," he is God's "servant," he was innocent, he is the "Holy and Righteous One" and he is the "author of life." The contrasts between what they did and who Jesus is jar the listener. Even more jarring perhaps for them was that God "raised him from the dead" and Peter and John once again are not the source of all this because they are but "witnesses" (3:15). An unjust capital sentence is bad, the death of one unjustly accused is worse, but overturning both by resurrection is beyond good. That's the gospel: the one they killed came back to life. The God who raised Jesus is "still rollin' stones," Lauren Daigle sings, and this is the first post resurrection rolling stone. The lame man is now jumping like a Pentecostal singer and it's all because of "faith in the name of Jesus" (3:16).

That's Peter's explanation, but he's a Pentecostal gospeler sensitive to his audience so, fifth, *he softens the accusations* he's just made when he says "you acted in ignorance" (3:17). He pushes behind their own injustices to remind them that their God is sovereign and used even that unjust death to accomplish redemption, drawing out the Messiah's suffering indicated in the prophets (3:18). There are numerous connections in this "sermon" to the Old Testament, each illustrating how audience-sensitive Peter was to his Jewish world.

Peter now has a back and forth between softening and warning. Sixth, with a soft hand on their shoulder he tells them *they need conversion* so their unjust acts and complicity in unjust acts can be forgiven (3:19). He then declares the benefits for those who turn to Jesus. They will discover God's refreshing redemption (3:19–21). Seventh, he points at them again *as he warns them* about rejecting the gospel about Jesus' resurrection. Moses himself, considered by many to be the ultimate prophet, predicted a prophet to come. Not listening to that prophet would lead to be being cast out of God's people (3:22–23). In fact, not just Moses but "all the prophets" predicted the Messiah's redemption (3:24). A warning given is not the final word for Peter. He turns again, eighth, to the positive, shifting to *an appeal based on their privileged status* in God's redemption. He calls his audience "heirs of the prophets and of the covenant" (3:25). Then he reminds them of another privilege, namely the expansive reach of their mission from God to bless the nations, and then yet another one when he says God "sent" that prophet Jesus "first to you." Why? To bless you by turning each of you from your wicked ways" (3:26).

You can ask where Peter became so proficient at this back-and-forth pastorally and audience-sensitive gospeling and there is but one answer to that, and it's the only answer the New Testament presents: he learned this from Jesus. The gospel is capable of adjusting to every audience.

QUESTIONS FOR REFLECTION AND APPLICATION

1. In what ways does a miraculous healing set the scene for the second gospeling sermon in Acts?

2. How does Peter give us a model for audience-sensitive gospeling?

3. How does Peter incorporate the identity and story of Jesus into his sermon?

4. Sin can be an uncomfortable topic for many people. What are some lessons you can learn from Peter's example here for pastorally talking about sin?

5. How do you need to adjust the gospel for your audience today?

FOR FURTHER READING

Craig Keener, *Miracles: The Credibility of the New Testament Accounts* (Grand Rapids: BakerAcademic, 2011).

Craig Keener, *Miracles Today: The Supernatural Work of God in the Modern World* (Grand Rapids: BakerAcademic, 2021).

Graham Twelftree, *The Gospel according to Paul: A Reappraisal* (Eugene, Oregon: Cascade, 2019).

COURAGE IN
THE MISSION

Acts 4:1–22

¹ *The priests and the captain of the temple guard and the Sadducees came up to Peter and John while they were speaking to the people.* ² *They were greatly disturbed because the apostles were teaching the people, proclaiming in Jesus the resurrection of the dead.* ³ *They seized Peter and John and, because it was evening, they put them in jail until the next day.* ⁴ *But many who heard the message believed; so the number of men who believed grew to about five thousand.*

⁵ *The next day the rulers, the elders and the teachers of the law met in Jerusalem.* ⁶ *Annas the high priest was there, and so were Caiaphas, John, Alexander and others of the high priest's family.* ⁷ *They had Peter and John brought before them and began to question them: "By what power or what name did you do this?"*

⁸ *Then Peter, filled with the Holy Spirit, said to them: "Rulers and elders of the people!* ⁹ *If we are being called to account today for an act of kindness shown to a man who was lame and are being asked how he was healed,* ¹⁰ *then know this, you and all the people of Israel: It is by the name of Jesus Christ of Nazareth, whom you crucified but whom God raised from the dead, that this man stands before you healed.* ¹¹ *Jesus is*

" 'the stone you builders rejected,
which has become the cornerstone.'

[12] *Salvation is found in no one else, for there is no other name under heaven given to mankind by which we must be saved."*
[13] *When they saw the courage of Peter and John and realized that they were unschooled, ordinary men, they were astonished and they took note that these men had been with Jesus.* [14] *But since they could see the man who had been healed standing there with them, there was nothing they could say.* [15] *So they ordered them to withdraw from the Sanhedrin and then conferred together.* [16] *"What are we going to do with these men?" they asked. "Everyone living in Jerusalem knows they have performed a notable sign, and we cannot deny it.* [17] *But to stop this thing from spreading any further among the people, we must warn them to speak no longer to anyone in this name."*
[18] *Then they called them in again and commanded them not to speak or teach at all in the name of Jesus.* [19] *But Peter and John replied, "Which is right in God's eyes: to listen to you, or to him? You be the judges!* [20] *As for us, we cannot help speaking about what we have seen and heard."*
[21] *After further threats they let them go. They could not decide how to punish them, because all the people were praising God for what had happened.* [22] *For the man who was miraculously healed was over forty years old.*

Peter healed a begging lame man in the temple courts. Some were utterly dumbfounded that Peter worked a wonder. Peter explained the power as God's power at work by faith in the name of Jesus and called his audience to repent and recognized God's promises were now at work. A few religious and political authorities monitoring that audience were disturbed by the crowd's positive response to Peter so they locked both apostles up for the night. A more official group of Jerusalem's authorities hailed Peter before themselves the next day and Peter explains to them the power of God at work in the name of Jesus. Since the response to this movement was bursting at the seams (now at 5000 according to Acts 4:4) the authorities demanded the apostles to cease from their preaching. The apostles refuse to be silent and the authorities release them anyway.

The earliest missioners of the gospel about Jesus were filled not only with the Spirit but also with courage. Gospelers need the sort of courage especially drawn upon when the pressure is on.

WE SOMETIMES ENCOUNTER PRESSURE

Take a good look at the labels for leaders applying pressure on Peter and John. In 4:1 we read about *priests* who ran the temple, *a captain of the temple guard* (police), and the Rome-friendly, politically influential *Sadducees* who were mostly the elite priestly families of Jerusalem. That is, Jerusalem's WASPs (if I may). Then in 4:5–6 we discover *rulers*, which is a general term for authorities, *elders* who are the preeminent synagogue sages of Jerusalem, and *teachers of the law* who are the canon lawyers or official legal interpreters of the law of Moses (cf. Luke 9:22). In that meeting are the top brass, including *Annas the high priest*, and *Caiaphas, John, Alexander* and *others of the high priest's family*. He calls the gathering the *Sanhedrin* (4:15).

Galilee had its own versions of local authorities, but there is only one authority above this group, and it's Rome. Rome had the back of this group because this group scratched the back of Rome. You think this is scary, just try Miss Dameyer at Lincoln School when you are called into her (the principal's) office for mischief in third grade. I had gotten used to the drill by the time I had Mr. Petersen in fifth grade and Mr. Bratcher in sixth. But I can still break out into a sweat thinking about Miss Dameyer, the ol' battle-axe.

The authorities were *agitated* (4:2) enough that they resorted to physical confinement. The higher-ups stood the apostles in their presence to *interrogate* them (4:7). They gave Peter an opportunity to explain himself. He was so good rhetorically they were "astonished" (4:13), they were silenced by the reality of the lame man's healing, they *demanded* they leave their presence so they could deliberate, and they decided the best course of action was to *command* the apostles to stop their gospeling. The two apostles informed them that was not about to happen so they *threatened* them and released them, fearing that any physical punishment would create even more chaos with the crowds.

Power shapes these scenes, and the authorities had the power to do some nasty stuff to the apostles. Surely the apostles knew that. They are not that many days beyond the torturous crucifixion of their Lord. The apostles did not, probably because they could not, appeal to rights or due process. They had none. All they had was the courage to gospel anyone close enough to hear.

WE ARE CHALLENGED TO MEET PRESSURE WITH COURAGE

We should begin with 4:3 and repeat what Willie James Jennings says. These apostles are now officially "criminal-disciples" because their message and boldness disturb the peace of Jerusalem (Jennings, *Acts*, 45–46). They are dissidents.

Some translations use the term "courage" in Acts 4:13. Saying the apostles were also "unschooled" in the verse adds for the authorities some recklessness to their courage. But courage can also be translated "boldness" (NRSV) or "confidence" (CEB; Dunn calls it "super confidence" in *Acts*, 51). Behind these translations is the Greek word *parrēsia*, a term routinely used for those around a political leader who spoke "frankly" to the leader to steer him away from pride and toward wise, humble decisions. One Greek writer in the ancient world (Plutarch) wrote a whole book on the need for kings to have frank counselors. So this term in this context suggests not only courage but also steely frankness.

Such courageous frankness comes to expression in Luke's reduction of Peter's explanation. First, he is courageous because he was "filled with the Holy Spirit" (4:8). I love what Peter does next. He wonders before the moral authorities, *What could be wrong with his act of goodness* (translated "kindness" in the NIV)? Peter's term evokes a term for public acts of mercy for the common good, that is public "benefactions" (Keener *Acts*, 194–195). With "benefactions" he's got them now in his hand, so he returns some pressure.

He says it's all because of the "name of Jesus," the one *you* crucified but the one *God* raised. Resurrection provoked the temple authorities in 4:2 and it was the center of the gospeling of the apostles. The power of the authorities is turned upside down by the power of the Resurrected One. The gospel again is the story about Jesus. He anchors his gospel in their scriptures (Psalm 118:22), a text that speaks of God reversing the judgments of humans. Next come words that are bold, frank, and central to all gospel preaching:

> Salvation is found in no one else, for there is no other name under heaven given to mankind by which we must be saved (Acts 4:12).

The Reformation's slogan of "Christ alone" grounds itself in a text like this. *Solus Christus*, or "Christ alone," Mike Bird observes, points us to the "absolute and final go-between for God the Father and humanity" (*Evangelical Theology*, 418).

That courageous frankness, that confidence to speak such bold words to the top leaders in Jerusalem, had another resource. Yes, the authorities knew Peter and John did not have their power and social status, that they had not been trained rhetorically, calling them "unschooled, ordinary men" (4:13), with "ordinary" suggesting something like our "layman." But they also perceived "that these men had been with Jesus." Which connects them both to Jesus' healing powers and his own boldness before leaders in Jerusalem.

The authorities, making use of their powers, decided to silence them but courage appears yet one more time when the two apostles, like the three Hebrew children in Daniel 3 (Pinter, *Acts*, 115), speak frankly when they state their options. Are they to follow them or God? They give the authorities the power to decide for themselves, and they decide against God (Jennings, *Acts*, 48), but Peter and John have made their choice when they state, "we cannot help speaking about what we have seen and heard" (4:20). That is, they are yet again witnesses (1:8, 22; 2:32; 3:15).

Off they go for their next adventure in the gospel mission, their courage now burnished and their mission learning curve steeper than a high-rise stairway, though a whole lot more adventurous.

QUESTIONS FOR REFLECTION AND APPLICATION

1. Who are the leaders putting pressure on Peter and John? What do these leaders have in common with each other?

2. How do the leaders try to use power to silence the proclaimers of the gospel?

3. Where did the apostles get their courage from?

4. The term used for courage can also be translated "frankness." To whom in your life do you need to be speaking with "steely frankness"?

5. Have you ever been silenced by those in power? What kind of courage do you need God to give you to face that situation?

FOR FURTHER READING

Michael Bird, *Evangelical Theology* (2d ed.; Grand Rapids: Zondervan, 2020).

PRAYERS IN
THE MISSION

Acts 4:23–31

²³ *On their release, Peter and John went back to their own people and reported all that the chief priests and the elders had said to them.* ²⁴ *When they heard this, they raised their voices together in prayer to God. "Sovereign Lord," they said, "you made the heavens and the earth and the sea, and everything in them.* ²⁵ *You spoke by the Holy Spirit through the mouth of your servant, our father David:*

> *" 'Why do the nations rage*
> *and the peoples plot in vain?*
> ²⁶ *The kings of the earth rise up*
> *and the rulers band together*
> *against the Lord*
> *and against his anointed one.'*

²⁷ *Indeed Herod and Pontius Pilate met together with the Gentiles and the people of Israel in this city to conspire against your holy servant Jesus, whom you anointed.* ²⁸ *They did what your power and will had decided beforehand should happen.* ²⁹ *Now, Lord, consider their threats and enable your servants to*

speak your word with great boldness. [30] *Stretch out your hand to heal and perform signs and wonders through the name of your holy servant Jesus."*

[31] *After they prayed, the place where they were meeting was shaken. And they were all filled with the Holy Spirit and spoke the word of God boldly.*

Not all prayers in the Bible have the dramatic results of this prayer, which is nothing less than a shaking of the place as a sign of God's presence (Gaventa, *Acts*, 98) and "all" being "filled with the Holy Spirit" (Acts 4:31), but many prayers in the Bible fit the *pattern* of this prayer. This is the second prayer of the earliest church (1:24–25 is the first).

LEARNING A PRAYER PATTERN FOR THE MISSION

The pattern of petitionary prayer we find here opens with an address to God that gives God a name (Sovereign Lord) and is followed by a description of truths about God that deserve to be recounted before God (4:24–28), and then follows the petition itself (4:29–30). In the history of how the church has learned to pray, especially in Sunday worship, these three elements of petitionary prayers are called Invocation, Acknowledgement, and Petition. Most of our prayers then finish such petitions with an expression of the goal of God's answering the prayer (e.g., "that we may perfectly love") and some expression of the grace foundation for all petitions ("through Christ our Lord" or "in Jesus' name"). Such a form for praying, made eloquently succinct over the years in church "collects" (McKnight, *To You All Hearts Are Open*), arises especially from Old Testament prayers like Deuteronomy 3:23–25, 9:26–29, and 1 Kings 8 (Solomon's long petition).

Jesus prayed like this, too (Matthew 6:9–13; 11:25–26; John 11:41–42; 12:27–28; 17:1–25) as did the early church (Acts 1:24–25). The prayer in Acts 4 "collects" together a response of resistance to those opposing the witness to Jesus' resurrection while it also reflects a together-ness. In fact, the word translated "together" could be translated as "shared passion" (Walton). Their response to opposition is to petition God for power to become courageous witnesses.

To *address God* as "Sovereign Lord" (see Luke 2:29) is an affirmation that God is creator, that God is above all and over all and through all and in all, that what God has designed for all creation and God's people will come about, and that history is moving through Rome toward the New Jerusalem in the new heavens and new earth. In this prayer the pray-ers have the courage to petition God to do something stunning because they know God is sovereign.

The depth of theology at work in this prayer points its finger at us for how hastily we move from addressing God ("Our Father") to petitioning God ("Gimme, gimme, gimme"). The Bible's and church's prayer pattern has always been to ponder what truths about God anchor the viability of our petitions. James said we don't have because we ask amiss (4:3), and one of our "amisses" is that we barge in without reverencing the God we are asking. Acts 4's petition brings into expression these truths about God: (1) creator, (2) communicator through the Spirit in a scripture (Psalm 2:1–2) that stands in their own context against those opposing the Messiah's movement, (3) anointer of Jesus as Messiah, and (4) controller of all that happens (4:24–28).

PRAYING FOR THE MISSION

The truth about God, that God is the "Sovereign Lord," prompts the church to form three very clear petitions:

1. Consider their threats. (James D.G. Dunn)
2. Enable your servants to witness with courageous frankness (4:29).
3. Stretch out your hand to heal and perform signs and wonders (4:30).

These three petitions are *anchored or grounded* "through the name of your holy servant Jesus" (4:30).

The Book of Acts is about mission and reveals to us how the early churches learned mission. One of its lessons was prayer, and what is revealed is a theological approach to prayer valuable today in mission work. The providence of God over all anchors mission prayers in the work of God in this world, often called the *missio Dei*. They asked God to do what God alone can do: empower their witness. James D.G. Dunn observes this is the third time for Peter to be filled (2:4; 4:8, Dunn, *Acts*)!

LEARNING TO PRAY
LIKE THE CHURCH

Here's my experience of learning to pray like this. First, I need to get hold of what I want to ask so I start with what I want to ask God. Second, I ponder what name for God is most appropriate for that specific request. If I want God to shake the world, "Sovereign Lord" or "God over all" are best, but if I want God to heal my student I might choose "Father, the Great Physician." Then, third, I ponder by wandering into reflections about God that show why the answer to my request fits the God I am addressing. Try to ask your petitions by:

1. Formulating your petition.
2. Assigning the right title for God.
3. Pondering the God who answers such a petition.

And ask.

Praying like this may slow you down but I assure you that pondering our God leads as much to worship as it does petition, and worshipful petitions are what we all need more of.

QUESTIONS FOR REFLECTION AND APPLICATION

1. Are you familiar with prayers in the style of "collects"? What do you think of this pattern for prayer McKnight lays out here?

2. How do you usually address God in prayer? What truths about God does this communicate?

3. What are the three steps McKnight suggests for formulating a petition?

4. How could you incorporate more "pondering" time into your approach to prayer?

5. Write your own prayer using the pattern in this lesson. Reflect on the experience. How can you include such prayers in your ongoing prayer life?

FOR FURTHER READING

Scot McKnight, *To You All Hearts Are Known: Revitalizing the Church's Pattern of Asking God* (Brewster, Mass.: Paraclete, 2021).
Steve Walton, "*Homothumadon* in Acts: Co-location, Common Action or 'Of One Heart and Mind'?" in *The New Testament in Its First Century Setting* (ed. P.J. Williams, et al.; Grand Rapids: Wm. B. Eerdmans, 2004), 89–105.

GENEROSITY MARKS
THE MISSION

Acts 4:32–5:11

[32] *All the believers were one in heart and mind. No one claimed that any of their possessions was their own, but they shared everything they had.* [33] *With great power the apostles continued to testify to the resurrection of the Lord Jesus. And God's grace was so powerfully at work in them all* [34] *that there were no needy persons among them. For from time to time those who owned land or houses sold them, brought the money from the sales* [35] *and put it at the apostles' feet, and it was distributed to anyone who had need.*

[36] *Joseph, a Levite from Cyprus, whom the apostles called Barnabas (which means "son of encouragement"),* [37] *sold a field he owned and brought the money and put it at the apostles' feet.*

[5:1] *Now a man named Ananias, together with his wife Sapphira, also sold a piece of property.* [2] *With his wife's full knowledge he kept back part of the money for himself, but brought the rest and put it at the apostles' feet.*

[3] *Then Peter said, "Ananias, how is it that Satan has so filled your heart that you have lied to the Holy Spirit and have kept for yourself some of the money you received for the land?* [4] *Didn't it belong to you before it was sold? And after it was sold, wasn't the*

money at your disposal? What made you think of doing such a thing? You have not lied just to human beings but to God."

⁵ When Ananias heard this, he fell down and died. And great fear seized all who heard what had happened. ⁶ Then some young men came forward, wrapped up his body, and carried him out and buried him.

⁷ About three hours later his wife came in, not knowing what had happened. ⁸ Peter asked her, "Tell me, is this the price you and Ananias got for the land?"

"Yes," she said, "that is the price."

⁹ Peter said to her, "How could you conspire to test the Spirit of the Lord? Listen! The feet of the men who buried your husband are at the door, and they will carry you out also."

¹⁰ At that moment she fell down at his feet and died. Then the young men came in and, finding her dead, carried her out and buried her beside her husband. ¹¹ Great fear seized the whole church and all who heard about these events.

Calls to provide and care for the poor, not least widows and orphans, are found in many passages in the Old Testament law and prophets. Such acts of compassion were the way of life for Israel. Those calls to care for the poor are not so much regulations or rules as they are the inevitable implications of how to live before God in a covenant life. Generosity, like the laws on gleaning, stood in bold contrast with much of the ancient world, and by the time of the New Testament, the Greco-Roman world's rather harsh treatment of the poor made Christian generosity all the more visible (Longenecker). Skimming Isaiah 58 reveals compassion for the poor as the measure of true spirituality, and it becomes so with force in the 1st Century Jewish Christian community.

GRACE PROMPTS GIVING

Luke mentions the unity of the believers in a number of ways (1:14; 2:1, 44, 46) but "one in heart and mind" could suggest for some today little more than kumbayah or "we are one in the Spirit, we are one in the Lord" youth group singfests. But we need to recall that this unity is Pentecostal and thus sprouts from the soil of God's gracious redemption and Spirit-power (4:33). The growth of believers in Jerusalem included an increase of the poor among them. Unity then was material liability for one another and that meant a loosening of the grip of one's resources (including real estate). Luke makes his point with vivid hyperbole when he says "*no one* claimed that *any* of their possessions was their own" and instead they parted ways with "*everything* they had" (4:32).

The consequence of such generosity was that no one was needy (4:34), which reminds of the manna story of Exodus 16 or Jubilee in Leviticus 25. Management of so much generosity becomes systemic enough that Luke describes monies being laid "at the apostles' feet" (4:35), who themselves passed it on to those in need (4:35). Luke occasionally drops a line or two, moves on, only to return to that topic later. Here he drops a first note about one of Paul's mission companions, Joseph named Barnabas.[1] He was a "Levite" (a temple assistant), he was from Cyprus, was renamed by the apostles for his encouraging disposition, and of course he is mentioned here because he was very generous (4:36). This positive example forms a contrast with the negative example to follow.

The systemic nature of this doesn't require us to think of it as anything more than a spontaneous outburst of

---

1. Using "son of encouragement" as a translation of "Barnabas" requires a little fudging because the Aramaic name means "son of a prophet." But if a "prophet" encourages or exhorts, then the name Barnabas can be extended to the son of encouragement (Keener, *Acts* 203), which he is (9:27; 11:19–26).

compassion that required organization. Generosity marks the early Christian ideal. Peter's early experiences with generosity become part of his routine instructions for the churches under his care. In 1 Peter he speaks several times of "good works," which describe public acts of generosity (2:15, 20; 3:6, 17), his companion at this time (John, I presume) speaks of the same (3 John 11). The apostle Paul knows the same teaching of mutual obligation (2 Corinthians 8:13–14; McKnight, *Pastor Paul*, 79–101).

BUT NOT FOR PERSONAL GLORY

Public acts of generous donations by the wealthy brought honor and praise to the donors and obligation on the part of those who received the donations. A yearning for honor, then, at times motivated the wealthy. Which best explains the sad story of a married couple, Ananias and Sapphira (5:1–11). Their problem was a Satan-inspired (5:3), selfish, sovereign desire for a recognition greater than their honesty. His wife fully knowing what was up, Ananias pretended to surrender the total sale while keeping back some for himself.

One of Peter's Spirit-gifts prompts his discernment of the deceit and theft (Gaventa, *Acts*, 102), a recognition of the man's freedom and responsibility, and a clarification of the depth of that sin. He not only is lying just to "human beings but to God" (5:4). His wife later becomes knowingly and intentionally complicit in the same deceitful purloining. Both collapse on the spot (5:5, 10). The almost casualness of describing the bodies being taken away arrests our attention but not so much as the deaths, which fit Old Testament narratives about God's acts of judgment at crucial moments (e.g., Leviticus 10:1–5; 2 Samuel 6:6–7).

The words "great fear" in 5:5 and 5:11 combine solemnity, dread, and utter reverence for the omniscience and penetrating judgment of God. Dunn describes the scene as "holy and aweful" (Dunn, *Acts*, 61). The scene reminds us that our world and their world are at odds, and their world had an "almost tangible presence of raw, uncontainable energy" (Dunn, *Acts*, 62). What may strike us as over-the-top extravagance was God's attempt to get the church's attention (Pinter, *Acts*, 136–137). Which it still does.

Stories like this can be abused as easily as they can be ignored. Luke designs this act of judgment as a solemn warning to the church (used here for the first time in Acts) about pretense, about the sacredness of holy practices, about the need for honesty, about the necessary connection of discipleship and our resources, and about the fundamental holiness of generosity.

QUESTIONS FOR REFLECTION AND APPLICATION

1. Why is care for the poor so essential to the Christian life?

2. What stands out to you about Barnabas and his story here?

3. How is Barnabas's story contrasted with that of Ananias and Sapphira?

4. Have you ever been tempted to seek "recognition greater than your honesty"? What happened?

5. What might radical-yet-honest generosity to other believers look like in your life? How would you like to grow in giving that pairs grace with integrity?

FOR FURTHER READING

Bruce Longenecker, *Remember the Poor: Paul, Poverty, and the Greco-Roman World* (Grand Rapids: Wm. B. Eerdmans, 2010).

Scot McKnight, *Pastor Paul* (Grand Rapids: Brazos, 2019).

UPS AND DOWNS
OF MISSION

Acts 5:12–42

12 The apostles performed many signs and wonders among the people. And all the believers used to meet together in Solomon's Colonnade. 13 No one else dared join them, even though they were highly regarded by the people. 14 Nevertheless, more and more men and women believed in the Lord and were added to their number. 15 As a result, people brought the sick into the streets and laid them on beds and mats so that at least Peter's shadow might fall on some of them as he passed by. 16 Crowds gathered also from the towns around Jerusalem, bringing their sick and those tormented by impure spirits, and all of them were healed.

17 Then the high priest and all his associates, who were members of the party of the Sadducees, were filled with jealousy. 18 They arrested the apostles and put them in the public jail. 19 But during the night an angel of the Lord opened the doors of the jail and brought them out. 20 "Go, stand in the temple courts," he said, "and tell the people all about this new life."

21 At daybreak they entered the temple courts, as they had been told, and began to teach the people.

When the high priest and his associates arrived, they called together the Sanhedrin—the full assembly of the elders of Israel—and sent to the jail for the apostles. *22* But on arriving at the jail, the officers did not find them there. So they went back and reported, *23* "We found the jail securely locked, with the guards standing at the doors; but when we opened them, we found no one inside." *24* On hearing this report, the captain of the temple guard and the chief priests were at a loss, wondering what this might lead to.

25 Then someone came and said, "Look! The men you put in jail are standing in the temple courts teaching the people." *26* At that, the captain went with his officers and brought the apostles. They did not use force, because they feared that the people would stone them.

27 The apostles were brought in and made to appear before the Sanhedrin to be questioned by the high priest. *28* "We gave you strict orders not to teach in this name," he said. "Yet you have filled Jerusalem with your teaching and are determined to make us guilty of this man's blood."

29 Peter and the other apostles replied: "We must obey God rather than human beings! *30* The God of our ancestors raised Jesus from the dead—whom you killed by hanging him on a cross. *31* God exalted him to his own right hand as Prince and Savior that he might bring Israel to repentance and forgive their sins. *32* We are witnesses of these things, and so is the Holy Spirit, whom God has given to those who obey him."

33 When they heard this, they were furious and wanted to put them to death. *34* But a Pharisee named Gamaliel, a teacher of the law, who was honored by all the people, stood up in the Sanhedrin and ordered that the men be put outside for a little while. *35* Then he addressed the Sanhedrin: "Men of Israel, consider carefully what you intend to do to these men. *36* Some time ago Theudas appeared, claiming to be somebody, and about four hundred men rallied to him. He was killed, all his followers were dispersed, and it all came to nothing. *37* After him, Judas the Galilean appeared in the days of the census and led a band of people in revolt. He too was killed, and all his followers were scattered. *38* Therefore, in the present case I *advise you: Leave these men alone! Let them go! For if their purpose or activity is of human origin, it will fail. 39 But if it is from God, you will not be able to stop these men; you will only find yourselves fighting against God."*

40 His speech persuaded them. They called the apostles in and had them flogged. Then they ordered them not to speak in the name of Jesus, and let them go.

41 The apostles left the Sanhedrin, rejoicing because they had been counted worthy of suffering disgrace for the Name. 42 Day after day, in the temple courts and from house to house, they never stopped teaching and proclaiming the good news that Jesus is the Messiah.

I routinely have coffee or lunch with persons engaged in the gospel mission. If I ask, "How's it going in the mission work?," I more often than not know the answer: "Some great things, some awful things." Full-hearted engagement in the mission of God in this world has always been like that. There's Judas and there's Mary, there's the generous and honest Barnabas flanked by the deceiving Ananias and Sapphira. In our passage, we rush from that awful episode of the deceitful couple into the glories of charismatic displays of the Spirit's power right into episodes of opposition at the hands of the authorities. How to deal with all these ups and downs?

The Book of Acts's answer is "Daily."

MISSION WORK HAS THE OCCASIONAL MOUNTAINTOP UPS

We perhaps need a reminder that Acts 4–5 is a bit like a second Pentecost. Recall that Peter and John were released from confinement and returned to a home where they prayed for power and courage and miracles in the name of "your holy servant Jesus." The place shook and they were filled with the Spirit (4:23–21). That led, as the Spirit-filling Pentecost did, to a new kind of community life (4:32–35). Such a community life was challenged by the deceitful couple, but the judgment of God on them renewed the reverence of the church (5:1–11). Which leads to "signs and wonders" (5:12–16).

These miracles provoked some social distancing from the apostles and believers, who were again together in unity (cf. 5:12 with 1:14; 2:46; 4:24). One wonders too if their location, the porch on the eastern side of the temple platform overlooking the Kidron valley, created status concerns for those who might participate, as they could be easily spotted. This was the location of Peter's sermon in chapter three (3:11). There is tension in Luke's descriptions. In v. 13 he says "no one else dared join them" while in v. 14 we read "more and more men and women believed in the Lord," and v. 16 speaks of large numbers gathering from local towns. The signs and wonders stand out both in their number (5:12) and in their impact of promoting more believers (5:13–14). God's power moved even through Peter's shadow to heal (5:15), and Luke says "all of them were healed" (5:16). God was at work among these people in a way that provoked fear and reverence and social caution.

The text evokes a kingdom enthusiasm that reminds me of my high school days when a number of us had gotten "right with the Lord." We were holding a 7am Bible study at our church for about a dozen Christians, and one friend after another was turning her or his life over to Christ. That's a more common sort of enthusiasm than the signs, wonders, and shadow healing we see in this text. I stand with James D.G. Dunn who is unafraid of facing the realities of these wonders when he says, "The fervour . . . which attend[s] . . . movements of spiritual renewal, particularly in their initial enthusiasm, can arouse such excitement and expectation" (Dunn, *Acts*, 66).

Some think faithfulness requires the same for our day. Dean Pinter offers wisdom: "we may either dismiss them or try to duplicate them" but the Book of Acts does not offer us a "prescriptive account of how God is supposed to answer our prayers or meet our needs" (*Acts*, 141). This Book, Pinter continues, shows us that God does not do the same thing in every context or for every person. God opens the prison gates for Peter but James is put to death, Paul recovers from being stoned but Stephen was killed by stones. We are called to pray, to petition, and to wait upon God. Only God knows what might happen.

MISSION WORK HAS ITS DOWNS AND UPS

Ministry combines the glories of touching and feeling and smelling redemption and the degradations of betrayals, deceits, frauds, and hypocrisies. Daily, not just every now and then. Emotions run high and flounder in the pits of despair. Tears flow from joy and from pain. God designed the mission for the big-hearted, hearts that can handle the racket of ups and downs. What parents experience in rearing children, especially teens and young adults, finds its way into the daily schedule of those doing gospel mission. Gospel mission work is a daily emotional rollercoaster. Willie James Jennings rightly invades our comfort when he says we like the unity of the earliest believers until we realize their unity involved incarcerations and whippings (Jennings, *Acts*, 61).

Down: The stupendous miracles come to a shrieking halt when the priestly establishment arrests and incarcerates the apostles (5:17–18). There is a sharp tension in this passage between the high priest (5:17, 21, 27) and the apostles and those following the apostles. That is, between the occasionally violent priests and their prisons and the sometimes suffering populists who rely on the powers of resurrection. That tension carries over then to the temple as institution and the redemptive work of God in the name of Jesus that challenges that temple institution.

Up: The downer of their first arrest is outmatched by God-sent angels opening the doors at night without anyone noticing (cf. 5:19–20 with 12:6–11), which gives the apostles the opportunity to return to the temple courts and proclaim "this new life" (5:20; the word "new" is added by the NIV). This beautiful expression—"this new life"—summarizes the gospel of the earliest church as the gospel of the resurrection of Jesus.

Down: Their miraculous release only led the authorities to fetch them back to the Sanhedrin and the full assembly (5:21–27) who ordered them once again to cease their public teaching "in this name [of Jesus]" (5:28). Gaventa points out the irony of this event when she says, "Instead of the apostles being afraid of the powerful, the powerful are afraid of the apostles" (Gaventa, *Acts*, 107).

Up: The downer of being grabbed again meets nothing less than a gospeling of Jerusalem's establishment. Their "strict orders not to teach" meets the apostles' higher orders, which says "We must obey God rather than human beings!" (5:29), and this launches Peter into a tailored gospel presentation that simultaneously accuses the leaders. His message can be summarized in these points:

1. *You* killed Jesus on a cross.
2. *Our God* raised him.
3. *Our God* exalted him as "Prince [or Founder, Hero] and Savior"
4. So that *he* could offer "repentance" and forgiveness.

5. *We* are witnesses (cf. 1:8, 22; 2:32; 3:15; 4:33) and
6. So is *the Holy Spirit* whom God gives to the repentant.

The heart of the gospel is #2 following #1 because the really good in the good news is that death had no final grip on God's Son, whom Peter here calls "Prince and Savior."

Down: Peter's direct gospel message accuses the authorities of murdering Jesus. They become enraged enough to pursue the death of the apostles, a response that hardly surprised anyone after Peter's accusing words (5:33).

Up: Every now and then someone gets rational, reasonable, logical (as we learned from Supertramp's *The Logical Song*). Gamaliel, a Pharisee (notice 15:5; 26:5), a Bible lawyer, a man of public status, a teacher of the apostle Paul (Acts 22:3), and eminently reasonable and asks that the apostles be "put outside" as he calms down what has become hysterical. He appeals to the Sanhedrin for tolerance the basis of experience, in particular the episodes with the revolutionaries Theudas, which seems to have occurred after this speech in 44 AD, and Judas the Galilean whose movements died out because they were not from God (5:36–37). Time will tell, he urges upon them, if the apostles are from God or not. His words confirm the resurrection of the gospel when he says, "If it [this movement] is from God, you will not be able to stop these men" (5:39). Gamaliel divides the temple establishment into pro (Pharisees) and con (priests, Sadducees), but the question still lingers: Does he, as Jennings suggests (Jennings, *Acts*, 62–63), avoid taking sides by posturing from the sidelines?

The shift from hysteria to persuasion, which happens almost never among politically agitated leaders, leads only to "flogging" and the common-by-now command for them to cease preaching "in the name of Jesus." (Which ain't gonna happen.)

This Up leads to another Up. They adored that they were "counted worthy of suffering disgrace for the Name" (5:41) and they daily gospeled at the temple and in homes, "proclaiming the good news that Jesus is the Messiah" (5:42). Their message was about figuring out who Jesus was. I have studied the process of Jews converting to Jesus and the entire process can be reduced to a studied examination of one question: Is this Jesus of the Christians the Messiah announced in (our) Bible? The entire gospel for Jews is about the identity of Jesus, and it should be ours too. The gospel is an announcement of Who Jesus is and conversion is the affirmation that Jesus is who the Bible says he is (McKnight and Ondrey).

QUESTIONS FOR REFLECTION AND APPLICATION

1. What are some Ups that the early church experienced?

2. What Downs did they go through in this section of Scripture?

3. How does Peter turn a Down into an Up with his gospeling sermon? What does Peter say?

4. When have you experienced times of the church growing in numbers in your community as seen in this passage and like McKnight describes in his life? What did it feel like to be part of an exciting movement?

5. When you have been on mission for God, what have been your biggest Ups and Downs?

FOR FURTHER READING

Scot McKnight, Hauna Ondrey, *Finding Faith, Losing Faith* (Waco, Texas: Baylor University Press, 2008) 65–121.

ETHNIC-SENSITIVITY IN THE MISSION

Acts 6:1–7

¹ In those days when the number of disciples was increasing, the Hellenistic Jews among them complained against the Hebraic Jews because their widows were being overlooked in the daily distribution of food. ² So the Twelve gathered all the disciples together and said, "It would not be right for us to neglect the ministry of the word of God in order to wait on tables. ³ Brothers and sisters, choose seven men from among you who are known to be full of the Spirit and wisdom. We will turn this responsibility over to them ⁴ and will give our attention to prayer and the ministry of the word."

⁵ This proposal pleased the whole group. They chose Stephen, a man full of faith and of the Holy Spirit; also Philip, Procorus, Nicanor, Timon, Parmenas, and Nicolas from Antioch, a convert to Judaism. ⁶ They presented these men to the apostles, who prayed and laid their hands on them.

⁷ So the word of God spread. The number of disciples in Jerusalem increased rapidly, and a large number of priests became obedient to the faith.

Many read this passage as the need for a division of labor because of the rapid growth of the church. That theme does stand out, but we need to look with a wider lens. Behind the decision to divide labor is an ethnic tension that threatened the note of unity Luke has emphasized and that is resolved in a way that reveals the heart of the gospel. To clarify terms, "ethnicity" is about a common culture, history, and heritage while "race" bases hierarchy in a location upon physical characteristics.

The dispute that arose in our passage emerges from ethnic tension, but in the USA, most ethnic tensions are rooted even more in race. This passage pierces through the protective walls of our society and churches. So, the text speaks far more into ethnic tensions than into the simple division of labor.

RECOGNIZING ETHNIC TENSIONS

One of my favorite writers about ethnic and racial tensions in the church today, Korie Edwards, teaches us about race and whiteness as a construct of power and hierarchy. She observes that white Americans do not perceive the color of the ethnic waters in which they swim and bathe and have their being, and neither do they know they've made everyone else swim their way in their waters. What is normal to whites is cross-cultural or suppressive or even oppressive to Native, African, Latin, and Asian Americans. Another of my favorite writers on this topic is Isabel Wilkerson. In her new book, *Caste*, she proposes that we learn to think of our society in terms of caste, which presses again on the problem of power, hierarchy, and an inability for whites to perceive the negative impacts of their social dominance. Put in terms of church life today, the structures, policies, and virtues of churches are ethnically constructed to favor those in power, who are white.

Some will balk at these bald claims so I give a different example. Ask introverts if Sunday services are designed for extroverts or introverts. The "passing of the peace" moment so common in many churches is a time for some introverts to head to the bathroom until that moment is over. Do extroverts think Sunday services are comfortable? Yes. Do they know the color of the water they are swimming in? Mostly not (McHugh). The same applies to ethnic and racial constructs. At least one major reason our churches are segregated on Sunday morning is because minority cultures immediately sense the dominant culture at work in typical white churches and choose to worship somewhere else where the power differential is not present.

This explanation of our ethnic and racial connection produces an opportunity to see our passage from a different perspective. So here's the context: Hebraic (or Hebrew-speaking[1]) Jewish believers had the power and were distributing dole to their widows more favorably than to the Hellenistic (or Greek-speaking) Jewish believers, who are immigrant minorities. We cannot dismiss the power the different languages had to cordon off a group to form its own culture and identity.

The term "overlooked" suggests the Greek widows were unnoticed and invisible to those distributing the food. The Hebrew speakers didn't notice, but the (minority culture) Greek speakers did. Prejudice was running the system invisible to one group and doubly visible to another. Widows were especially vulnerable, and to neglect them counters the Torah's common instructions to care for widows and orphans (Exodus 22:24; Deuteronomy 24:17–21; Isaiah 10:1–2; also James 1:27).

What to do? What they chose to do should astound us more than it does.

---

1. Actually they spoke a dialect of Hebrew called Aramaic. The word "Jewish" has been added by the NIV to clarify what is implicit.

Resolving Ethnic Tensions

The apostles realize they don't have enough hours in a day to do both their "ministry of the word of God" and prayer as well as "to wait on tables" (6:2, 4), the latter an expression for the service to the widows. For some even today this stinks of an air of superiority, but if we nod a little trust toward the apostles, we can understand this more as a division of labor (Gaventa, *Acts*, 114). Such would include a commitment to serve the widows with justice without degrading service ministries. So, yes, there is a division of labor here, but there's more.

What's their resolution? The apostles recommend that the believers of Jerusalem "choose seven men" with the character traits of being "full of the Spirit and wisdom" (6:3) and "faith" (6:5). They are chosen not by talents but by character.

But their choice had a radical edge, a choice that forms into a monument of Christlikeness shaped by ethnic-sensitivity. Many miss it. The names chosen are not Jewish but Greek names. Not an Akiva or a Ya'akov or a Benyamin among them. The unidentified choosers decided to turn the power over to the Greek-speaking believers (Dunn, *Acts*, 83), no doubt because the Hebrew-speaking believers were blind to the injustices they inflicted upon the overlooked widows. Ethnic sensitivity is about sharing and even surrendering power. Think about this, and let's ask ourselves this question: How many of us, when realizing we have failed a group in our church, hand the power over to that group going forward? Do we do this with women, with African Americans, with Asian Americans, with Latin Americans, with Native Americans? To surrender power is to be like Christ (Mark 10:35–45; Philippians 2:6–11).

What happened in the earliest churches might just happen if we too become ethnically sensitive. "So the word of

God spread. The number of disciples in Jerusalem increased rapidly" and some priests, who had participated in silencing Peter and John, were converted (6:7).

QUESTIONS FOR REFLECTION AND APPLICATION

1. Are you an introvert or an extrovert? How does this analogy help you understand the difficulty of the dominant culture to understand their dominance?

2. After reading this study, how would you explain the conflict over the distribution of resources?

3. What do the names of the chosen seven tell us about the decision behind the scenes here?

4. Consider McKnight's question: "How many of us, when realizing we have failed a group in our church, hand the power over to that group going forward?" What groups do you think your community has failed?

5. What might happen if your church followed this model of ethnic sensitivity?

FOR FURTHER READING

Korie L. Edwards, *The Elusive Dream: The Power of Race in Interracial Churches* (New York: Oxford, 2008).

Adam S. McHugh, *Introverts in the Church* (2d ed.; Downers Grove: IVP Books, 2017).

Isabel Wilkerson, *Caste: The Origins of our Discontents* (New York: Random House, 2020).

MARTYR FOR
THE MISSION

Acts 6:8–15; 7:1–8:3

⁸ Now Stephen, a man full of God's grace and power, performed great wonders and signs among the people. ⁹ Opposition arose, however, from members of the Synagogue of the Freedmen (as it was called)—Jews of Cyrene and Alexandria as well as the provinces of Cilicia and Asia—who began to argue with Stephen. ¹⁰ But they could not stand up against the wisdom the Spirit gave him as he spoke. ¹¹ Then they secretly persuaded some men to say, "We have heard Stephen speak blasphemous words against Moses and against God." ¹² So they stirred up the people and the elders and the teachers of the law. They seized Stephen and brought him before the Sanhedrin. ¹³ They produced false witnesses, who testified, "This fellow never stops speaking against this holy place and against the law. ¹⁴ For we have heard him say that this Jesus of Nazareth will destroy this place and change the customs Moses handed down to us." ¹⁵ All who were sitting in the Sanhedrin looked intently at Stephen, and they saw that his face was like the face of an angel.

⁷:¹ Then the high priest asked Stephen, "Are these charges true?"

² To this he replied: "Brothers and fathers, listen to me! The God of glory appeared to our father Abraham while he was still in

Mesopotamia, before he lived in Harran. ³ 'Leave your country and your people,' God said, 'and go to the land I will show you.'

⁴ "So he left the land of the Chaldeans and settled in Harran. After the death of his father, God sent him to this land where you are now living. ⁵ He gave him no inheritance here, not even enough ground to set his foot on. But God promised him that he and his descendants after him would possess the land, even though at that time Abraham had no child. ⁶ God spoke to him in this way: 'For four hundred years your descendants will be strangers in a country not their own, and they will be enslaved and mistreated. ⁷ But I will punish the nation they serve as slaves,' God said, 'and afterward they will come out of that country and worship me in this place.' ⁸ Then he gave Abraham the covenant of circumcision. And Abraham became the father of Isaac and circumcised him eight days after his birth. Later Isaac became the father of Jacob, and Jacob became the father of the twelve patriarchs.

⁹ "Because the patriarchs were jealous of Joseph, they sold him as a slave into Egypt. But God was with him ¹⁰ and rescued him from all his troubles. He gave Joseph wisdom and enabled him to gain the goodwill of Pharaoh king of Egypt. So Pharaoh made him ruler over Egypt and all his palace.

¹¹ "Then a famine struck all Egypt and Canaan, bringing great suffering, and our ancestors could not find food. ¹² When Jacob heard that there was grain in Egypt, he sent our forefathers on their first visit. ¹³ On their second visit, Joseph told his brothers who he was, and Pharaoh learned about Joseph's family. ¹⁴ After this, Joseph sent for his father Jacob and his whole family, seventy-five in all. ¹⁵ Then Jacob went down to Egypt, where he and our ancestors died. ¹⁶ Their bodies were brought back to Shechem and placed in the tomb that Abraham had bought from the sons of Hamor at Shechem for a certain sum of money.

¹⁷ "As the time drew near for God to fulfill his promise to Abraham, the number of our people in Egypt had greatly increased. ¹⁸ Then 'a new king, to whom Joseph meant nothing, came to power

in Egypt.' [19] He dealt treacherously with our people and oppressed our ancestors by forcing them to throw out their newborn babies so that they would die.

[20] "At that time Moses was born, and he was no ordinary child. For three months he was cared for by his family. [21] When he was placed outside, Pharaoh's daughter took him and brought him up as her own son. [22] Moses was educated in all the wisdom of the Egyptians and was powerful in speech and action.

[23] "When Moses was forty years old, he decided to visit his own people, the Israelites. [24] He saw one of them being mistreated by an Egyptian, so he went to his defense and avenged him by killing the Egyptian. [25] Moses thought that his own people would realize that God was using him to rescue them, but they did not. [26] The next day Moses came upon two Israelites who were fighting. He tried to reconcile them by saying, 'Men, you are brothers; why do you want to hurt each other?'

[27] "But the man who was mistreating the other pushed Moses aside and said, 'Who made you ruler and judge over us? [28] Are you thinking of killing me as you killed the Egyptian yesterday?' [29] When Moses heard this, he fled to Midian, where he settled as a foreigner and had two sons.

[30] "After forty years had passed, an angel appeared to Moses in the flames of a burning bush in the desert near Mount Sinai. [31] When he saw this, he was amazed at the sight. As he went over to get a closer look, he heard the Lord say: [32] 'I am the God of your fathers, the God of Abraham, Isaac and Jacob.' Moses trembled with fear and did not dare to look.

[33] "Then the Lord said to him, 'Take off your sandals, for the place where you are standing is holy ground. [34] I have indeed seen the oppression of my people in Egypt. I have heard their groaning and have come down to set them free. Now come, I will send you back to Egypt.'

[35] "This is the same Moses they had rejected with the words, 'Who made you ruler and judge?' He was sent to be their ruler

and deliverer by God himself, through the angel who appeared to him in the bush. ³⁶ He led them out of Egypt and performed wonders and signs in Egypt, at the Red Sea and for forty years in the wilderness.

³⁷ "This is the Moses who told the Israelites, 'God will raise up for you a prophet like me from your own people.' ³⁸ He was in the assembly in the wilderness, with the angel who spoke to him on Mount Sinai, and with our ancestors; and he received living words to pass on to us.

³⁹ "But our ancestors refused to obey him. Instead, they rejected him and in their hearts turned back to Egypt. ⁴⁰ They told Aaron, 'Make us gods who will go before us. As for this fellow Moses who led us out of Egypt—we don't know what has happened to him!' ⁴¹ That was the time they made an idol in the form of a calf. They brought sacrifices to it and reveled in what their own hands had made. ⁴² But God turned away from them and gave them over to the worship of the sun, moon and stars. This agrees with what is written in the book of the prophets:

" 'Did you bring me sacrifices and offerings
    forty years in the wilderness, people of Israel?
⁴³ You have taken up the tabernacle of Molek
    and the star of your god Rephan,
    the idols you made to worship.
Therefore I will send you into exile' beyond Babylon.

⁴⁴ "Our ancestors had the tabernacle of the covenant law with them in the wilderness. It had been made as God directed Moses, according to the pattern he had seen. ⁴⁵ After receiving the tabernacle, our ancestors under Joshua brought it with them when they took the land from the nations God drove out before them. It remained in the land until the time of David, ⁴⁶ who enjoyed God's favor and asked that he might provide a dwelling place for the God of Jacob. ⁴⁷ But it was Solomon who built a house for him.

⁴⁸ *"However, the Most High does not live in houses made by human hands. As the prophet says:*

> ⁴⁹ *" 'Heaven is my throne,*
>   *and the earth is my footstool.*
> *What kind of house will you build for me?*
>   *says the Lord.*
> *Or where will my resting place be?*
> ⁵⁰ *Has not my hand made all these things?'*

⁵¹ *"You stiff-necked people! Your hearts and ears are still uncircumcised. You are just like your ancestors: You always resist the Holy Spirit!* ⁵² *Was there ever a prophet your ancestors did not persecute? They even killed those who predicted the coming of the Righteous One. And now you have betrayed and murdered him—*⁵³ *you who have received the law that was given through angels but have not obeyed it."*

⁵⁴ *When the members of the Sanhedrin heard this, they were furious and gnashed their teeth at him.* ⁵⁵ *But Stephen, full of the Holy Spirit, looked up to heaven and saw the glory of God, and Jesus standing at the right hand of God.* ⁵⁶ *"Look," he said, "I see heaven open and the Son of Man standing at the right hand of God."*

⁵⁷ *At this they covered their ears and, yelling at the top of their voices, they all rushed at him,* ⁵⁸ *dragged him out of the city and began to stone him. Meanwhile, the witnesses laid their coats at the feet of a young man named Saul.*

⁵⁹ *While they were stoning him, Stephen prayed, "Lord Jesus, receive my spirit."* ⁶⁰ *Then he fell on his knees and cried out, "Lord, do not hold this sin against them." When he had said this, he fell asleep.*

^{8:1} *And Saul approved of their killing him. On that day a great persecution broke out against the church in Jerusalem, and all except the apostles were scattered throughout Judea and Samaria.* ² *Godly men buried Stephen and mourned deeply for him.* ³ *But Saul began to destroy the church. Going from house to house, he dragged off both men and women and put them in prison.*

At times a follower of Jesus becomes a double witness. Again, the term "witness" translates the Greek term *martus*, from which we get our word "martyr." In the 1st Century, "witness" points to a person who witnesses or testifies to something she has seen or heard or experienced and, at times, it costs her her life. There are a number of women double witnesses in the early church, including Thecla, Perpetua, and Felicitas (Cohick, Brown). Our passage is about the church's first double witness, Stephen, who both preached an angular gospel to a hostile audience and paid for it with his life (6:8–8:3; cf. 22:20).

Luke was a skilled narrator. In the choosing of the seven Greek-speaking believers to lead the dole for the widows, Luke sketches the term "Hellenists" into his narrative, naming Stephen first (6:5), and that sketch anticipates the story of the Hellenist Stephen in our lengthy passage, one of Luke's finest vignettes of an otherwise unknown early follower of Jesus. Stephen in turn sets the stage both for the apostle Paul and the gentile mission. The narrative about Stephen can be broken into four parts: (1) Stephen's initial witness (6:8, 10), (2) Opposition to Stephen's Witness (6:9, 11–15), (3) Stephen's long witness (7:1–53), and (4) Stephen's final witness (7:54–8:3).

STEPHEN'S INITIAL WITNESS

Stephen is the New Testament's most charismatic man, for Luke simply can't mention him without attributing Spirit powers and wisdom to him (6:5, 8, 10; 7:55). Thus, he is a "man full of God's grace and power" and as such "performed great wonders and signs" (6:8), an expression connecting Stephen to Jesus (2:22), the apostles (2:43; 5:12), and to Moses (7:36). No doubt about it, Stephen may have become a figure as significant as Paul had he lived. His opponents did not have the strength to stand against the Spirit at work through him. In fact, he had an angelic appearance (6:15). Though we cannot draw out all the examples, there are numerous instances in this passage where Luke describes Stephen as he had described Christ (Keener, *Acts*, 228–229), indicating at another level that "witness" to Christ occurs best in Christlikeness.

One's witness is tied to one's story, one's integrity, and to the trust one's circle puts in the person. Stephen's power was at work in his own neighborhood. Not all liked it, however.

OPPOSITION TO
STEPHEN'S WITNESS

The previous episode (6:1–7) revealed a fissure in the earliest churches between Greek-speaking and Aramaic-speaking Jewish believers. We now discover in 6:9 a fissure cracking between Greek-speaking believers and non-believers. Jerusalem then was like Jerusalem or Rome today, with a synagogue or church or holy site on every corner. One of the synagogues was sponsored by diaspora of Greek-speaking "Freedmen," or former slaves who had been manumitted. Since most slaves were not liberated until they were no longer able to put in a yeoman's effort, it is not overly speculative to think of this synagogue as populated by the older generation (Dunn, *Acts*, 86).

They seem to have no problem with Stephen's witness to Jesus but instead their deep worry is about the implications the witness draws about the temple and the Torah. The Freedmen persuaded (or suborned) some "men" to accuse Stephen of blasphemy (6:11). Jerusalem frequently lived on the edge of tumult so the accusers, like modern day social media experts who can make things go viral, got the attention of the religious authorities who arrested Stephen and hailed him, as they had done to Peter and Stephen, before the Sanhedrin. Their accusation was that Stephen believed Jesus would destroy their cherished temple (cf. Mark 14:57–58) and, upon his return, would alter Moses' cherished "rules and regs." It's like drumming up a charge that some public figure denies inerrancy or the Republican Party or the millennium. The secret is to find something that threatens a cherished identity marker. Stephen's speech to follow gives them all they need.

The hottest issue of the gospel mission in the earliest churches, the gossip over every skin of wine and the graffiti on every wall, was the relationship of gentile converts to Torah observance. This will pop up now and then in Acts, it's all over Paul's letters, and Stephen is the first hint in the earliest churches of such a tension. Stephen's theology, which we will discover in his long speech, calls into question the centrality of the temple and at least creates tension over Torah observance and its interpretation. Jewish identity revolves around the covenant election of Israel, the observance of the Torah, and the centrality of temple and Jerusalem. Stephen's death at the feet of Saul is irony for it is Saul who becomes Paul who carries Stephen's mantle all the way to Rome because he dared to defy the very authorities who put down Stephen.

Dunn again provides fresh words when he reminds us that there "are not passions like religious passions, no charges so exaggerated and intemperate as made by those whose deepest religious sensibilities have been wounded" (Dunn, *Acts*, 87). Witnesses to Jesus cannot expect their critics to represent their viewpoint dispassionately or even fairly.

STEPHEN'S LONG WITNESS

Luke represents Stephen as a skilled orator, and the orator of that day earned honor in law court speeches. The most famous orator was (and still is) Cicero. What to say about his oration before the Sanhedrin? What is his answer to the high priest's question, "Are these charges true?" (7:1)

First, instead of direct rebuttal or defense, Stephen *re-tells the story of Israel,* favoring the Book of Genesis and Exodus. This allows him to locate the present moment in the plan of God. Willie James Jennings captures the power of storytelling when he says "Give me storytellers, and I will rule the world. Indeed all worldly power begins in storytelling and reaches its greatest leverage in story believing" (Jennings, *Acts,* 68). Second, *Stephen includes major figures* in his story of Israel (Abraham, the patriarchs, Joseph, Moses, David, Solomon). To tell Israel's story well you must fit the major players in their proper roles. Third, *he ties into his story the most important identity markers of the people* (land/Jerusalem/ temple, inheritance, exile, liberation, return, circumcision, Egypt). Fourth, *he connects himself,* not all that subtly, *to Moses* when Stephen says, "This is the same Moses they had rejected with the words, 'Who made you ruler and judge?'" (7:35) Moses comes off in Stephen's narrative as the central figure in Israel's story, and Stephen emphasizes Israel's rejection of Moses. Fifth, he reminds the Sanhedrin that *God told Moses that a prophet like him was to come in the future* (7:37), which now turns the audience into wondering if Stephen will say the prophet to come is Jesus. Sixth, *the sound of rejection,* which began in 7:35, *grows louder* in 7:39 ("our ancestors refused to obey" Moses) and, seventh, he *turns to Amos for proof* in Acts 7:41–43 of their failure to worship God properly.

A decisive phase occurs in this (now becoming very polemical) speech and it reveals the hand of Stephen. He intends for his speech to persuade, convince, or convict the Sanhedrin of complicity in the death of the Messiah. His first step in the new phase is to make the radical, but still Jewish, claim that *God cannot be contained by the temple or in one location* (Jerusalem; 7:48–50). He does this *by shifting focus from important figures (Abraham, Joseph, Moses) to the temple edifice itself* (Gaventa, *Acts*, 128). As God was not contained by a temple prior to Solomon, so God is not contained by it now. Which is a bit like telling country musicians that Nashville doesn't matter.

Like a bolt out of little more than a hint of gray clouds, going eyeball to eyeball, he calls them "You stiff-necked people!" Having already mentioned the well-known covenant rite, he says "Your hearts and ears are still uncircumcised" and, like their "ancestors," they "always resist the Holy Spirit!" (7:51). Weightier words can't be uttered. And he's not done because he claims they're like the persecutors of the prophets. How so? He says "your ancestors . . . even killed" the prophets "who predicted the coming of the Righteous One" (7:52), who is Jesus, and rejected the Torah itself (7:53).

This oration shifts from accusations against Stephen into his blaming them for the crucifixion of Jesus. The strength of Stephen's language, unpalatable as it is to many today, sounds like 1st Century Jewish prophetic denunciations (Dunn, *Acts*, 98). Dean Pinter in fact says "Stephen's words are inflammatory and condemnatory—and biblical" (Pinter, *Acts*, 185).

A double witness comes to expression both in words and works, in what one says and how one lives (and dies).

STEPHEN'S FINAL WITNESS

In our terms, his opponents go ballistic as the Sanhedrin becomes a mob. Stephen's witness could not be bolder, for he now reveals that he can see Jesus whom he calls "the Son of Man standing at the right hand of God." Informing the Sanhedrin of Jesus' location is a way of announcing, proclaiming, and witnessing that Jesus is the world's true ruler. Which means they are not. In their rage, they drag him from the city and stone him to death. As they are throwin' stones at Stephen, God is rollin' a stone called Saul, and that stone will roll to the end of the Book of Acts. Stephen becomes the first double witness of the church. He witnesses about Jesus, and his death witnesses to faith in the indestructible body of Jesus and those who believe in him. His final words are like the Lord's: he asks the Lord to receive him and for the forgiveness of his murderers (7:59–60).

One of those accusing Stephen was a zealous budding rabbi, Saul who becomes Paul the apostle. Saul approved of the stoning and was part of a systemic persecution against the church, which led to the Greek-speaking believers to scatter from Jerusalem. As they buried Stephen, Saul was seeking to destroy the churches.

One's witness often does not make an immediate impact. Time has a way of revealing the power of that witness.

QUESTIONS FOR REFLECTION AND APPLICATION

1. What are the four parts of Luke's narrative about Stephen?

2. What markers did Jewish identity revolve around at the time of this story?

3. How does Stephen use storytelling in his oration?

4. Stephen was accused of blasphemy, which was a way of attacking a "cherished identity marker." What identity markers does your community hold, and what happens to people who transgress them?

5. If time reveals the power of a witness, what might time eventually reveal about your witness, based on the witnessing of Jesus you are doing now?

FOR FURTHER READING

Lynn Cohick, Amy Brown Hughes, *Christian Women in the Patristic World: Their Influence, Authority, and Legacy* (Grand Rapids: Baker Academic, 2017).

THE UNEXPECTED
IN THE MISSION

Acts 8:4–40

⁴ Those who had been scattered preached the word wherever they went. ⁵ Philip went down to a city in Samaria and proclaimed the Messiah there. ⁶ When the crowds heard Philip and saw the signs he performed, they all paid close attention to what he said. ⁷ For with shrieks, impure spirits came out of many, and many who were paralyzed or lame were healed. ⁸ So there was great joy in that city.

⁹ Now for some time a man named Simon had practiced sorcery in the city and amazed all the people of Samaria. He boasted that he was someone great, ¹⁰ and all the people, both high and low, gave him their attention and exclaimed, "This man is rightly called the Great Power of God." ¹¹ They followed him because he had amazed them for a long time with his sorcery. ¹² But when they believed Philip as he proclaimed the good news of the kingdom of God and the name of Jesus Christ, they were baptized, both men and women. ¹³ Simon himself believed and was baptized. And he followed Philip everywhere, astonished by the great signs and miracles he saw.

¹⁴ When the apostles in Jerusalem heard that Samaria had accepted the word of God, they sent Peter and John to Samaria. ¹⁵ When they arrived, they prayed for the new believers there that they might receive the Holy Spirit, [16] because the Holy Spirit had not yet come on any of them; they had simply been baptized in the name of the Lord Jesus. [17] Then Peter and John placed their hands on them, and they received the Holy Spirit.

[18] When Simon saw that the Spirit was given at the laying on of the apostles' hands, he offered them money [19] and said, "Give me also this ability so that everyone on whom I lay my hands may receive the Holy Spirit."

[20] Peter answered: "May your money perish with you, because you thought you could buy the gift of God with money! [21] You have no part or share in this ministry, because your heart is not right before God. [22] Repent of this wickedness and pray to the Lord in the hope that he may forgive you for having such a thought in your heart. [23] For I see that you are full of bitterness and captive to sin."

[24] Then Simon answered, "Pray to the Lord for me so that nothing you have said may happen to me."

[25] After they had further proclaimed the word of the Lord and testified about Jesus, Peter and John returned to Jerusalem, preaching the gospel in many Samaritan villages.

[26] Now an angel of the Lord said to Philip, "Go south to the road—the desert road—that goes down from Jerusalem to Gaza." [27] So he started out, and on his way he met an Ethiopian eunuch, an important official in charge of all the treasury of the Kandake (which means "queen of the Ethiopians"). This man had gone to Jerusalem to worship, [28] and on his way home was sitting in his chariot reading the Book of Isaiah the prophet. [29] The Spirit told Philip, "Go to that chariot and stay near it."

[30] Then Philip ran up to the chariot and heard the man reading Isaiah the prophet. "Do you understand what you are reading?" Philip asked.

[31] "How can I," he said, "unless someone explains it to me?" So he invited Philip to come up and sit with him.

[32] This is the passage of Scripture the eunuch was reading:

"He was led like a sheep to the slaughter,
and as a lamb before its shearer is silent,
so he did not open his mouth.
33 In his humiliation he was deprived of justice.
Who can speak of his descendants?
For his life was taken from the earth."

34 The eunuch asked Philip, "Tell me, please, who is the prophet talking about, himself or someone else?" 35 Then Philip began with that very passage of Scripture and told him the good news about Jesus.

36 As they traveled along the road, they came to some water and the eunuch said, "Look, here is water. What can stand in the way of my being baptized?" 38 And he gave orders to stop the chariot. Then both Philip and the eunuch went down into the water and Philip baptized him. 39 When they came up out of the water, the Spirit of the Lord suddenly took Philip away, and the eunuch did not see him again, but went on his way rejoicing. 40 Philip, however, appeared at Azotus and traveled about, preaching the gospel in all the towns until he reached Caesarea.

Cookie cutter theories about mission, evangelism, and church planting fail more often than they succeed. What worked in 1st Century Asia Minor does not always work in 21st Century Mediterranean cities. What works in Peoria does not work in Pretoria, what works in Sacramento does not work in Sarajevo, and what works in Berlin does not work in Boston. You can determine in advance what you will do, but you can never determine the results. The moment different people are gathered you will discover humans are agents with different ideas and different histories with different agendas and priorities and purposes. Ministry is all about adjusting to the unexpected.

The missioner participating in God's mission will experience regular unexpected challenges and will then discern what's most needed in that context and at that moment. In Acts 8 two unexpected events occur, one with Simon the sorcerer and the other with an Ethiopian eunuch. Each required a contextually-shaped response in gospeling, and those who do mission like this will experience the "adventurous nature of faith" (Shiell, *Acts*, 67).

Unexpected Dispersion

Power-based opposition to the gospel mission at the hands of Saul scattered Jerusalem-based believers. Their response is singular: they "preached the word wherever they went" (Acts 8:4). We should not imagine evangelistic sermons or dropping tracts at convenient locations or door-to-door evangelism. Rather, as they journeyed home—say to Alexandria or Antioch or Caesarea—wherever they overnighted or ate or drank or found themselves cooling under the shade of a tree, they told people about Jesus. Gospelers talk about Jesus from Jerusalem and Judea into Samaria (1:8). You may need to refresh your memory about Samaria. I suggest 2 Kings 17:24–41, Ezra 4, Nehemiah 4, and the entry in your favorite Bible dictionary. You will learn from these passages that Samaria (1) was perceived by many in Israel/Judea as populated by a different ethnic group, (2) by those unfaithful to the laws of Moses, and (3) Samaria was considered to be a dangerous area for Jewish travelers.

Traveling to a different location often unmasks our assumptions that God is at work in all places with all people. Kris and I have worshiped with state-sponsored charismatics in Denmark, with Presbyterians in the Republic of Ireland, with Anglicans and Methodists in England, with church plants in Austria, with Catholics on a small island off

Venice, Italy, with the Reformed and non-denominationalists in South Africa, and with an evangelical church in Seoul Korea. Not to mention believers all over the United States and Canada. We've tasted the goodness of God at work all over the world.

THE (EXPECTED) POWER OF THE GOSPEL

What was not unexpected was the gospel's power. Philip, one of the seven (6:5), was an evangelist (21:8), was from Caesarea (21:8), and had four daughters who prophesied (21:9). He scattered at the persecution and traveled up to Samaria. He was the first to preach the gospel to a gentile (the Ethiopian). Samaria, despised by some Jews (Luke 9:52–54; John 8:48), was a region comprised of a different ethnicity with an "unorthodox" form of the faith of Israel (John 4). In Samaria, Philip "proclaimed the Messiah" (Acts 8:5), which is shorthand for "announced that Jesus of Nazareth was the long-awaited Messiah." That message unleashed what Jesus unleashed: the power of the kingdom of God (Matthew 12:28). In this boundary-breaking location, Philip performed signs of God's unleashed kingdom that resulted in exorcising evil powers from persons and healing the "paralyzed or lame" (Acts 8:6–7). Beverly Gaventa's words perfectly express what happens in this episode: "Luke shows not only the foolishness of the persecution in Jerusalem, but also the powerlessness of magic, as well as its author Satan, in the face of Jesus Christ" (Gaventa, *Acts*, 135).

AN UNEXPECTED OFFER

Supernatural powers impress everyone, and words surrounding miracles point that out: verses six and seven speak of signs and shrieks. So impressive are they a sorcerer named Simon (Magus) both lost his audience to Philip and got himself baptized with others. He was himself "astonished" (8:13). The amazed people exalted him by referring to him as The Power of God called Great (8:10). His Greatness takes a hit when Philip's powers exceed his so much his audience moves *en masse* to Philip. Comparisons between the two in this passage are rich. (Note "great power" in 8:10 and 8:13.)

News of the gospel's expansion into Samaria, which again illustrates the programmatic plan of Luke (1:8), grabbed the attention of the apostles so they commissioned Peter and (his shadow companion) John to review this unexpected expansion, where they prayed for the new believers that they might be flooded with the Holy Spirit (8:14–17). Which happened and which brought something totally unexpected.

Simon offered Peter and John money for the power for him to make Pentecost happen (8:18–19). Money and divine powers are often in cosmic battle. What seemed permissible to him was not with the apostles. Peter's rebuke of Simon (8:20–24) is sterner even than Jesus' rebuke of Peter (Mark 8:33). Peter engages Simon more pastorally than most who tell this story. In fact, I find Peter's grace here unexpected. Peter urges him to repent and pray "in the hope" of the Lord's forgiveness. Peter and John return to Jerusalem and they too preach the gospel all the way back (8:25).

Those who have a habit of seeing only Simon the sorcerer's sins often fail to read how he responded to Peter's stern rebuke. Simon asks him to pray that God's judgment will not rest on him (8:24). Perhaps we need not only to lament our uncharitable treatment of this man but also ask ourselves who we might be deeming unforgiveable. Upon genuine repentance, which often requires a period of probation and evidence of repentance, as well as spiritual discernment, what God forgives we are to forgive as well. However, we need to remind ourselves of what we can call "justifiable forgiveness" because in human experience (death of a parent guilty of sexual abuse, pastoral abuse, etc.), forgiveness cannot always and need not always lead to reconciliation or even to restoration to ministry (McKnight, *Jesus Creed*). Of course, we don't know with certainty what happened to Simon after this and many have supported the negative portrayal of the man (Gaventa, *Acts*, 138–139). Luke leaves it open, perhaps so you and I can ponder and discern what we would have done–or what Simon did (Dunn, *Beginnings*, 286–287).

An Unexpected Conversion

The unexpected continues. First, an angel gives Philip specific directions to a new location for gospel mission (8:26). This attentiveness to the Lord's guidance indicates the intimacy Philip had with the Lord. Second unexpected event: on the way he meets up with an African, the "Ethiopian eunuch." Now catch this: the Ethiopian was a castrated official for the queen of Ethiopia who was at least attracted to Judaism and was on his way back home after worshiping the God of Israel in Jerusalem. As castrated he could not enter into the temple beyond the court of the gentiles (8:27; cf. Deuteronomy 23:1 with Isaiah 56:3–5).

Third unexpected moment: the man's reading Isaiah, and not just any part of Isaiah, but a passage the earliest believers knew was a prophecy about Jesus–that is, Isaiah 53:7–8! It's about like finding a seeker reading Billy Graham and yearning for someone to explain the stuff. The man was not entirely welcome at the temple but he was welcomed by Jesus, and that should be enough for fellowship for any of us (Pinter, *Acts*, 213).

More unexpected stuff: the Spirit (angels and Spirit are often interchangeable in Jewish texts) commands Philip to get near to the eunuch's chariot, a bit like someone standing near someone else on a phone so they can snoop on the conversation. (Don't say you haven't done that.) All these unexpected events lead to an amazing conversation as the chariot moved onward: Philip asks if the man can understand the text. Of course he can't, which is the response Philip needed. Philip then "told him the good news about Jesus" (8:35). Notice how the man is "gospeled": Philip tells the man about Jesus, about his life and his death and his burial and his resurrection and ascension.

Another unexpected occurrence: water, enough for an immersion (which you don't have to mention if you're Anglican). So the man gets baptized. He's now a believer in Jesus and no sooner are they done with the baptism and, you guessed it, one more unexpected experience: the Spirit whisks Philip away so swiftly the eunuch is left standing. The Spirit lands Philip at Azotus and the whole thing begins all over again. Back to gospeling as he travels to Caesarea (where Paul will spend time in prison later in this book).

Just ask anyone who has served the Lord for a few decades about unexpected encounters with God at work and may discover you a thrill in some stories (and be late to your next scheduled event).

QUESTIONS FOR REFLECTION AND APPLICATION

1. Have you ever worshipped with a different people group? What did that experience teach you about God's expansive work?

2. Are there groups that "your people" view with suspicion, as the Israelites viewed the Samaritans? How might God's power be at work among them as well as among you?

3. Do you think Simon the sorcerer repented and changed over time? Are there people you consider unforgiveable? What might forgiving what God forgives look like for you? (Keeping in mind appropriate boundaries with destructive people.)

4. Of all the unexpected occurrences in this section, which is the most surprising to you?

5. Think about an unexpected experience you've had while on mission with God. How was the Spirit at work in what happened?

FOR FURTHER READING

Scot McKnight, *The Jesus Creed: Loving God, Loving Others* (Brewster, Mass.: Paraclete, 2019), 218–226.

CONVERSION IN THE MISSION

Acts 9:1–19

[1] *Meanwhile, Saul was still breathing out murderous threats against the Lord's disciples. He went to the high priest* [2] *and asked him for letters to the synagogues in Damascus, so that if he found any there who belonged to the Way, whether men or women, he might take them as prisoners to Jerusalem.* [3] *As he neared Damascus on his journey, suddenly a light from heaven flashed around him.* [4] *He fell to the ground and heard a voice say to him, "Saul, Saul, why do you persecute me?"*

[5] *"Who are you, Lord?" Saul asked. "I am Jesus, whom you are persecuting," he replied.* [6] *"Now get up and go into the city, and you will be told what you must do."*

[7] *The men traveling with Saul stood there speechless; they heard the sound but did not see anyone.* [8] *Saul got up from the ground, but when he opened his eyes he could see nothing. So they led him by the hand into Damascus.* [9] *For three days he was blind, and did not eat or drink anything.*

[10] *In Damascus there was a disciple named Ananias. The Lord called to him in a vision,*

"Ananias!" "Yes, Lord," he answered.

[11] *The Lord told him, "Go to the house of Judas on Straight*

Street and ask for a man from Tarsus named Saul, for he is pray-ing. [12] *In a vision he has seen a man named Ananias come and place his hands on him to restore his sight."*

[13] *"Lord," Ananias answered, "I have heard many reports about this man and all the harm he has done to your holy people in Jerusalem.* [14] *And he has come here with authority from the chief priests to arrest all who call on your name."*

[15] *But the Lord said to Ananias, "Go! This man is my chosen instrument to proclaim my name to the Gentiles and their kings and to the people of Israel.* [16] *I will show him how much he must suffer for my name."*

[17] *Then Ananias went to the house and entered it. Placing his hands on Saul, he said, "Brother Saul, the Lord—Jesus, who appeared to you on the road as you were coming here—has sent me so that you may see again and be filled with the Holy Spirit."* [18] *Immediately, something like scales fell from Saul's eyes, and he could see again. He got up and was baptized,* [19] *and after taking some food, he regained his strength. Saul spent several days with the disciples in Damascus.*

Saul, who won't be named "Paul" until later (13:9), has a conversion story that appears three times in Acts (9:1–19; 22:3–26; 26:9–18), and Paul himself tells much of that story in Galatians 1 and Philippians 3. One of my favorite writers, the English Catholic G.K. Chesterton, once wrote an essay called "My Six Conversions," which has given his readers a glimpse into phases of his journey of personal faith. His final sentence says it well: "We have come out of the shallows and the dry places to the one deep well; and the Truth is at the bottom of it." We get a few glimpses, too, of Paul's journey into faith in Jesus as Messiah, the One whom Paul saw as Truth incarnate.

It understates the matter to say "on his way to Damascus

he met the Lord." But he did, and understatement still tells the truth: meeting the Lord radically altered not only his life, it shifted the course of the Jesus story from a Jerusalem, Galilee-based movement to a world-wide story. This chapter, to quote from *Hamilton*, is the "room where it happens."

What happens most pushes us ahead to one simple line of Paul's: "If anyone is in Christ, the new creation has come: The old has gone, the new is here!" (2 Corinthians 5:17). That radically new life sprouts in Acts 9, and by the time we get to end of this book (or of Paul's life), everything has become new for the man. Conversion tells the story of an old life transformed into new life. Paul's life, it needs to be said, does not tell us of a conversion story from Judaism to Christianity but from what we can clumsily call "non-messianic Judaism" to "messianic Judaism." The tell-tale sign of conversion is a rewritten autobiography (McKnight, *Pastor Paul*, 127–146).

OLD LIFE

Luke has the wonderful habit of dropping us off somewhere, heading off somewhere else, and then circling back to pick us up and take us onward again. Chapter nine opens by circling back to Saul's participation in the murder of Stephen (7:58–8:1). We can fill in some lines. Saul may have been born in Galilee, but he was reared in the university town Tarsus (modern day's southeastern Turkey) and then was taught Torah in Jerusalem by Gamaliel (Acts 22:3; 26:4) where he became famously zealous for his devotion (Philippians 3:4–6). Dunn says Paul in Tarsus may have been like "an Orthodox Jew living outside the land of Israel" (Dunn, *Beginnings*, 329). In Tarsus, Saul became adept at Hellenistic culture and the Greek language. In short, he was tailor-made for a gentile mission, something he does not yet know in this chapter of Acts.

Acts describes Saul's ferocity when it says he "was still breathing out murderous threats" and got "letters" to nab Jesus' followers 150 miles north of Jerusalem in Damascus (9:1–2; cf. Galatians 1:13–14, 23). In Saul's view, these Jesus people were verging from accommodation and assimilation into dangerous apostasy, so his zeal kicked in. Zeal, by the way, never let up for Saul even if he may have preferred other terms for his post-zeal-for-Torah life.

THE ENCOUNTER WITH JESUS

Very few believers have the kind of body-shaking conversion Saul had, and most churches probably don't want a church full of Sauls, but his conversion has become a paradigm for many for mapping a story of conversion. Here are some of the highlights:

Jesus knows Saul's name (9:4);

Jesus informs him that opposing the followers of Jesus is opposing Jesus (9:4; cf. Luke 10:16);

Saul and Jesus converse with one another (Acts 9:5);

Jesus orders Saul to Damascus where he will get directions (9:6);

Saul was "blinded by the light" (9:9);

Jesus coordinates those orders with orders to Ananias in Damascus, which Ananias tries to shake off by telling Jesus Saul is one dangerous man (9:10–16);

Ananias obeys, places his hands on Saul, Saul is filled with the Spirit and is restored to health (9:17–19).

Conversions to Jesus derive from personal encounters with Jesus. Dean Pinter's reminder remains for us today when he says "No follower of Christ is anonymous" (Pinter, *Acts*, 229). He knows my name, he knows yours. Invisibility is not possible with God.

There are at least three features in Saul's conversion story in chapter nine that deserve our attention. First, Saul's conversion rolls out his mission too. He not only enters into new creation or new birth or a new life, but Jesus tells Ananias that Saul will preach the gospel to gentiles and will suffer for it (9:15–16). Notice the flipping of the script as Saul moves from persecutor to persecuted (note Galatians 1:23). A mission to the gentiles was not common for Judaism of the day, no matter how rooted it is in the promise to Abraham at the beginning of Genesis 12. But there was a hope emerging like dolphins alongside a sea vessel indicating that someday, maybe soon, all nations would stream to Zion to worship Israel's God. That day was here, and Saul is that day's first major agent. Gaventa entitles the whole chapter "From Persecutor to Proclaimer" (Gaventa, *Acts*, 146). The reality is that from this point on, Saul has a new story about himself, and that revised autobiography indicates conversion.

Second, conversion is the work of God through the Spirit of God to draw people from the lordless lords of life to the lordly Lord Jesus. If you read from Acts 1 through Acts 9 and highlight in your Bible every reference to the Spirit, you will no doubt conclude that the Spirit that came down at Pentecost converted Saul the persecutor to the missioner for Jesus, which is nothing less than a radical disruption of one man's life.

Third, we need to notice how important and common advocates, that is those who speak to us on behalf of Jesus, are to conversions. To be sure, Saul's major advocate is the Lord Jesus who dazzles the man with blinding light, but Ananias becomes another advocate of God's work of redemption. Conversion is the work of God's Spirit, but God has chosen to use people to lead people to the face of Jesus. Here's my ranking of the order of influence by advocates: mom, dad, siblings, friends, youth pastors, evangelistic youth rallies, teaching and senior pastors, and various forms of media (books, videos, social media).

NEW LIFE

Saul receives the Spirit (9:17) just as those at Pentecost did, as those in the prayer meeting did, as the deacons did, as those in Samaria did (2:1–4, 38; 4:31; 6:3, 5; 7:55; 8:15–17). His filling meant the end of blindness, his baptism, and his restoration to full health.

Conversions affect people in such different ways. Some like Paul see the Lord; others pray a quiet prayer and wonder if anything happened. Barbara Brown Taylor described her own story of conversion as nothing less than surprising and totally unsuspected when some friends visited her dorm room:

The whole thing took less than twenty minutes. It was quick, simple, direct. They did not have any questions about who Jesus was. You are here, God is there, Jesus is the bridge. Say these words and you are a Christian. Abracadabra. Amen. It is still hard for me to describe my frame of mind at the time. I was half-serious, half-amused. I cooperated as much out of curiosity as anything, and because I thought that going along with them would get them out of my room faster than arguing with them. . . . Most of it was just embarrassing, the kind of simplistic faith I liked the least, but something happened to me that afternoon. After they left I went out for a walk and the world looked funny to me, different. People's faces looked different to me; I had never noticed so many details before. I stared at them like portraits in a gallery, and my own face burned for over an hour. Meanwhile, it was hard to walk. The ground was spongy under my feet. I felt weightless, and it was all I could do to keep myself from floating up and getting stuck in the trees.

We would do well to respect the variety of conversions. Some are little more than gentle nods of the soul, and the change is a bit like watching the evening shadows move across the lawn. Others are dramatic like Saul's. We are not all Sauls. (Thank you, Jesus.)

QUESTIONS FOR REFLECTION AND APPLICATION

1. McKnight says, "Conversions to Jesus derive from personal encounters with Jesus." What was your personal interaction with Jesus that led you to follow him?

2. What are the three features of Saul's conversion story that deserve our attention?

3. How was Saul's old life different from his new life?

4. One of the key signs that someone has converted is that they change the way they tell their life story. How has your conversion experience with Jesus led you to rewrite your autobiography, to view your history in a different way?

5. Who were the advocates for Jesus on your journey to knowing him? How can you serve as a better advocate for Jesus to others?

FOR FURTHER READING

G.K. Chesterton, "My Six Conversions," in *The Collected Works of G.K. Chesterton* (San Francisco: Ignatius, 1990), 3:357–391, quoting from p. 391.

Barbara Brown Taylor, *The Preaching Life* (Cambridge, Mass.: Cowley, 1992), 110–111.

For a good new life of Paul, N.T. Wright, *Paul: A Biography* (San Francisco: HarperOne, 2018), 27–59.

QUESTIONS ABOUT CONVERTS IN THE MISSION

Acts 9:19b-31

¹⁹ Saul spent several days with the disciples in Damascus.

²⁰ At once he began to preach in the synagogues that Jesus is the Son of God. ²¹ All those who heard him were astonished and asked, "Isn't he the man who raised havoc in Jerusalem among those who call on this name? And hasn't he come here to take them as prisoners to the chief priests?" ²² Yet Saul grew more and more powerful and baffled the Jews living in Damascus by proving that Jesus is the Messiah.

²³ After many days had gone by, there was a conspiracy among the Jews to kill him, ²⁴ but Saul learned of their plan. Day and night they kept close watch on the city gates in order to kill him. ²⁵ But his followers took him by night and lowered him in a basket through an opening in the wall.

²⁶ When he came to Jerusalem, he tried to join the disciples, but they were all afraid of him, not believing that he really was a disciple. ²⁷ But Barnabas took him and brought him to the apostles. He told them how Saul on his journey had seen the Lord and that the Lord had spoken to him, and how in Damascus he had preached fearlessly in the name of Jesus. ²⁸ So Saul stayed with

them and moved about freely in Jerusalem, speaking boldly in the name of the Lord. [29] He talked and debated with the Hellenistic Jews, but they tried to kill him. [30] When the believers learned of this, they took him down to Caesarea and sent him off to Tarsus.

[31] Then the church throughout Judea, Galilee and Samaria enjoyed a time of peace and was strengthened. Living in the fear of the Lord and encouraged by the Holy Spirit, it increased in numbers.

Frauds find platforms. It doesn't matter what kind of platform. They desire being noticed because being seen for them measures their success. Deeper yet, publicity means identity. Some frauds are deceivers from the get-go while others morph from somewhat genuine to fakes. Some churches like "to platform" celebrities in order to draw a bigger crowd, and the resulting decisions for Christ legitimate the platforming. Not a few of the platformed celebrities reveal themselves as frauds over time with not a word from the church that gave them Christian endorsements. Consequently, cynicism's cold tentacles grip us when we hear of the next celebrity who has become a believer. It doesn't matter if these are Hollywood stars or NBA heroes or financial entrepreneurs. "A pox on all of them," cynicism chatters in our minds.

Such cynicism was already at work in the early churches, and the two most important gospel centers, Damascus and Jerusalem, did not want to believe the stories about Saul's conversion. His past was too clear and, as the adage goes, past behavior is the best predictor of future behavior.

Perhaps instead of cynicism we should say questions are good when we hear of some celebrity, or some notorious sinner, being platformed. Willie James Jennings opens a window on this entire passage by stating Saul's "life is now a question" (Jennings, *Acts*, 96). Indeed, he is the question that makes others ask questions!

GOOD QUESTIONS

The believers in Damascus had two questions.

> **First**: "Isn't he the man who raised havoc in Jerusalem
> among those who call on this name?"
> **Second**: "And hasn't he come here to take them as
> prisoners to the chief priests?" (9:21)

The second question indicates Saul chased the scattered believers from Jerusalem all the way to Damascus. The believers raised doubts about the credibility of Saul's confession and preaching just as they wonder about their own safety. They just don't trust him. How does one move from questions and even cynicism to trust about a person's claims to being a follower of Jesus? This passage provides two common pathways to bridging from a person's past to a persons' profession of faith.

PREACHING AND SUFFERING

Immediately after Paul gained his strength "he announced Jesus–that he is God's Son" (Acts 9:20; my translation). Jesus–his life, his teachings, his actions, his death, his burial, his resurrection, his ascension–is the gospel. Saul was telling everyone about Jesus, and his angle was that he was the world's true king. "Son of God," like Messiah, is early Christian lingo for a king in the line of David (cf. 2 Timothy 2:8). As a seminary professor who believes in preparation before going public, I pinch my nose when it says "at once" (9:20). But let's recall Saul's past: nurtured in the home in the world-class city of Tarsus, theologically educated at the feet of Gamaliel in Jerusalem, and the Torah so well known it was in the pouch of his tunic. The moment he realized

Jesus was the Messiah of Israel's expectation, the whole Bible came to life for him as if for the first time. Plus, it's not at all unreasonable to think Luke uses a bit of hyperbole. No doubt Saul was mentored a bit in Damascus.

Saul preached the identical gospel to the apostles that these believers had embraced in Jerusalem. In fact, he had a Spirit-empowered gift of persuasion, so much so that he was mixing it up with the Jews of Damascus, or perhaps confounding them. We hear echoes of Jesus in the temple at twelve as this brand-new believer takes on the Torah-informed in the local assembly halls. He was winning converts (9:22).

One step toward credibility.

A second step can be missed. The believers in Damascus had freshly experienced a scattering prompted by this very man, so when the tables tip over and land in his lap, the believers know he's on their side (9:23), so much so they protect him from the plot to kill him and plan an escape from Damascus (9:24–25; cf. 2 Corinthians 11:32–33). Luke tells us this occurred "after many days," which is flexible enough for us to appeal to Paul telling us he spent time in Arabia and only after three years did he return to Jerusalem (Galatians 1:16–20). So the suggestion is sometimes made that Saul's zealous young faith explains the problems in Damascus and Jerusalem needs a refresher. Perhaps Damascus but not Jerusalem. Not if he had three years to grow in his faith before he got to Jerusalem. Was it his zeal that caused the problems? Probably so. Paul was all-in.

AN ADVOCATE MATTERS

The questions start all over again the moment Saul walked through the walls of Jerusalem. Luke tells us "they were all afraid of him, not believing that he really was a disciple" (9:26). It's just like Luke as a storyteller to pull out a character in his story, Barnabas, who had already appeared earlier (4:36–37). He will figure so prominently in the rest of the Book of Acts. Barnabas believed the story about Saul's conversion and commission and used his "platform" to empower Saul the way many today open up their platforms to empower the next generation. So Barnabas led Saul before the apostles in Jerusalem, explained his conversion story and his confounding preaching in Damascus. Luke surprisingly omits the apostles' response, and many of us assume they were persuaded, but we should not be so certain. Tension remained for Saul/Paul with at least some Jerusalem church leaders.

What we do know is that Saul went in and out of Jerusalem speaking frankly (boldly, directly, clearly, on point) "in the name of the Lord" (9:28). What we also know is that, as was the case later in his life (23:12–30), the disturbances the man's preaching caused in Jerusalem with the "Hellenistic Jews" landed him in front of Roman authorities on the coast at Caesarea. The edge of Paul's preaching never lost its sharpness for the Jewish believers in Jerusalem, and they somehow knew this man was made for a different location–so they sent him back home to Tarsus (9:30). Later Paul will tell us he was visited by the Lord and told to leave (22:18).

Saul's conversion story, his giftedness in persuading others that Jesus was the Messiah, and the affirmation of a leader like Barnabas never led to total affirmation in Jerusalem. A fissure in the unity of the church, so important for Luke in the early chapters of Acts, forms over this man Saul. Some may be a bit saddened by this tension over Saul, or at least my explanation of it, but Paul himself, about fifteen or so years later, will write that he was called to the gentile world while Peter was more fit for a Jewish context (Galatians 2:1–10). Their fellowship was firm but at a social distance.

It is not surprising then that Luke now turns back to

where he had left us off with Peter. Two apostles, two different ministry foci. Perhaps only after Saul's departure is it appropriate to say the "church throughout Judea, Galilee and Samaria" now found itself in a "time of peace" as it flourished in the power of the Spirit (Acts 9:31–32).

QUESTIONS FOR REFLECTION AND APPLICATION

1. What suspicions did the Damascus believers have about Saul and the legitimacy of his conversion?

2. How did Saul's previous training work toward making him a skilled witness for Jesus as soon as he was converted?

3. What steps proved Saul's credibility over time to the believers in Damascus and Jerusalem? How did Barnabas make a difference in the story?

4. What is your perspective on notorious sinners or celebrities who convert to Christianity and are given a public platform? Has your cynicism even been proven right, and/or have you ever been surprised by a true change in someone?

5. God sent Paul out on a mission to the Gentiles, and the discomfort of the leaders in Jerusalem that led to their sending him away played a part in getting him onto that mission. Have you, like Paul, ever been led into God's particular mission for you by way of certain people's rejection?

MINISTERING LIKE JESUS IN THE MISSION

Acts 9:32–43

32 As Peter traveled about the country, he went to visit the Lord's people who lived in Lydda. 33 There he found a man named Aeneas, who was paralyzed and had been bedridden for eight years. 34 "Aeneas," Peter said to him, "Jesus Christ heals you. Get up and roll up your mat." Immediately Aeneas got up. 35 All those who lived in Lydda and Sharon saw him and turned to the Lord.

36 In Joppa there was a disciple named Tabitha (in Greek her name is Dorcas); she was always doing good and helping the poor. 37 About that time she became sick and died, and her body was washed and placed in an upstairs room. 38 Lydda was near Joppa; so when the disciples heard that Peter was in Lydda, they sent two men to him and urged him, "Please come at once!"

39 Peter went with them, and when he arrived he was taken upstairs to the room. All the widows stood around him, crying and showing him the robes and other clothing that Dorcas had made while she was still with them.

40 Peter sent them all out of the room; then he got down on his knees and prayed. Turning toward the dead woman, he said,

"Tabitha, get up." She opened her eyes, and seeing Peter she sat up. [41] He took her by the hand and helped her to her feet. Then he called for the believers, especially the widows, and presented her to them alive. [42] This became known all over Joppa, and many people believed in the Lord. [43] Peter stayed in Joppa for some time with a tanner named Simon.

You may be like me and wonder if what happens in these accounts with Peter–healing a paralyzed man, raising a dead woman–happens in our world. I know of healings, but resurrections, not so much. I wonder if we don't stumble before we start because we move too quickly. Neither act by Peter was common in the Jewish world. That is, until Jesus. If we read Matthew 4:23–25 we discover that Jesus' ministry involved three actions: teaching, preaching, and healing. Five chapters later Matthew says it all over again: Jesus was teaching, preaching, and healing. Then he sends out the twelve apostles and tells them to extend and expand what he was doing: preaching and healing (they don't get told to teach until the last paragraph of Matthew's Gospel). The ministry of an apostle is nothing other than the ministry of Jesus.

Which is exactly what we see here in two brief episodes about Peter. What he does replicates and extends the ministry of Jesus. Or, as Jennings puts it, "Peter repeats Jesus" (Jennings, *Acts*, 99). So much so that Peter tells Aeneas, the paralyzed man. "*Jesus Christ* heals you" (Acts 9:34). Seeing these actions by Peter as extensions of Jesus' ministry shifts the focus from "Can we still do miracles?" to "How can I be like Jesus for the marginalized and suffering?" In our compassion for the suffering, perhaps the Lord will work a redemptive healing.

> We are called by God to participate in God's mission in the world to redeem it through Jesus Christ, the world's true Savior, Lord, and King. Each of us participates in that mission according to the gifts given to us by God.

Be Like Jesus with Persons with Disabilities

Peter disappears into the shadows after baptizing and rebuking Simon in Samaria and then returning to Jerusalem (8:14, 20, 25). After Philip and then Saul's conversion story we find Peter again. He has left Jerusalem to traverse the Mediterranean to Lydda (Old Testament "Lod") and then to the Mediterranean coastal city, Joppa. Both were mostly Jewish communities. In Lydda he visits the "Lord's people," which is commonly translated "saints," and these saints were perhaps converts of the ministry of Philip (8:40). In Lydda Peter meets Aeneas, a man who was unable to walk and so spent his life on a mat. Like Jesus, who responded to such persons with compassionate empowering (Luke 5:18–26), Peter declares Jesus as his healer (Acts 9:34). Luke seems to turn to hyperbole for impact: everyone in Lydda and Sharon "turned to the Lord" (9:35).

How would Jesus respond in our day to persons with various disabilities? How do we? Instead of doing nothing because we may not see miraculous healings, perhaps we can ask what we do have the power to do. And do it.

Be Like Jesus with the Dying and Dead

As my father lay dying for more than a week in complete silence and unresponsiveness, he was attended by family and friends and nurses and hospice staff with utmost respect. He was bathed, shaved, his sheets and blankets changed, and he was spoken to by name. It was a sacred compassion and a solemn mercy. Pastors, I have learned, become the epitome of pastoring in the presence of the dying and dead and their families. Our hope in resurrection does not diminish care for the dying or respect for those who have died. Peter learned solemn mercy from Jesus, who had raised a girl from the dead (Luke 8:40–42, 49–56), so when he saw Tabitha, also named Dorcas, he became like Jesus.

Noticeably Tabitha, who lived in Joppa (modern day Jaffa) about ten miles from Lydda, is called a "disciple" (9:36).[1] Like Jesus (and Peter), her life-basket was filled with "good works" (NIV has "doing good") and donations for the poor, including making clothing for widows (9:39). We don't know her age, but the image of Mother Theresa comes to mind for me. (How about for you?) She acquires a sickness and dies (the average length of life in the 1st Century was in the 30s and 40s), and her body is treated with sacred compassion (9:37).

The locals entreat Peter, who is now known for the powers of healing, to come to Joppa. He does and, no doubt incurring corpse impurity (again like Jesus), enters the upper room where Tabitha lay. He has witnessed Jesus raising the dead, so he kneels, intercedes, and petitions for God's power to be unleashed. He orders the dead woman to stand up, and God answers the prayer, so Peter presents her alive to those in the home. Extending the compassionate ministries of Jesus makes the gospel credible so "many people believed in the Lord" (9:42). When a healer touches the corpse and is defiled by corpse impurity, raising that person from the dead completely cleanses the healer! (I would think.)

---

1. The term used, *mathētria*, a woman disciple of Jesus, occurs only here in the entire New Testament.

By the way, ministry to persons with disabilities, the dying, and the dead awakens our own neediness and makes us more receptive to those in need. Which is what Peter is about to learn on an even larger scale.

QUESTIONS FOR REFLECTION AND APPLICATION

1. What is your perspective on miracles in the Bible and miracles today? Do you expect that Christians today should see miraculous healings? Why or why not?

2. How does Peter use situations of healing to point people to Jesus?

3. How does compassion to sick, disabled, and dying people help to make the gospel credible?

4. How have other Christians cared for you when a loved one died or was very ill? What touched you the most?

5. How are you continuing as an extension of Jesus' ministry in your teaching, healing, and compassion for suffering people?

FOR FURTHER READING

On miracles today, see Craig Keener, *Miracles: The Credibility of the New Testament Accounts* (2 vols.; Grand Rapids: Baker Academic, 2011); on raisings from the dead, see volume 1, 536–579.

GOD'S TIMING IN
THE MISSION

Acts 10:1–23a

¹ At Caesarea there was a man named Cornelius, a centurion in what was known as the Italian Regiment. ² He and all his family were devout and God-fearing; he gave generously to those in need and prayed to God regularly. ³ One day at about three in the afternoon he had a vision. He distinctly saw an angel of God, who came to him and said, "Cornelius!"

⁴ Cornelius stared at him in fear. "What is it, Lord?" he asked.

The angel answered, "Your prayers and gifts to the poor have come up as a memorial offering before God.

⁵ Now send men to Joppa to bring back a man named Simon who is called Peter. ⁶ He is staying with Simon the tanner, whose house is by the sea."

⁷ When the angel who spoke to him had gone, Cornelius called two of his servants and a devout soldier who was one of his attendants. ⁸ He told them everything that had happened and sent them to Joppa.

⁹ About noon the following day as they were on their journey and approaching the city, Peter went up on the roof to pray. ¹⁰ He became hungry and wanted something to eat, and while the meal was being prepared, he fell into a trance. ¹¹ He saw heaven opened and something like a large sheet being let down to earth by its four corners. [12] It contained all kinds of four-footed animals, as well as reptiles and birds. [13] Then a voice told him, "Get up, Peter. Kill and eat."

[14] "Surely not, Lord!" Peter replied. "I have never eaten anything impure or unclean."

[15] The voice spoke to him a second time, "Do not call anything impure that God has made clean."

[16] This happened three times, and immediately the sheet was taken back to heaven.

[17] While Peter was wondering about the meaning of the vision, the men sent by Cornelius found out where Simon's house was and stopped at the gate. [18] They called out, asking if Simon who was known as Peter was staying there.

[19] While Peter was still thinking about the vision, the Spirit said to him, "Simon, three men are looking for you. [20] So get up and go downstairs. Do not hesitate to go with them, for I have sent them."

[21] Peter went down and said to the men, "I'm the one you're looking for. Why have you come?"

[22] The men replied, "We have come from Cornelius the centurion. He is a righteous and God-fearing man, who is respected by all the Jewish people. A holy angel told him to ask you to come to his house so that he could hear what you have to say." [23] Then Peter invited the men into the house to be his guests.

What some call luck or coincidence or serendipity, Christians call providence or the Lord's timing. Susie Larson, a radio host for KTS in Minnesota, has suffered with Lyme disease for decades. One of her greatest reliefs is riding her bicycle at top speed in 90 degree weather. Who knew! Once on a ride, in prayer and pushing the pedals, she began to catch up to a man but, when she was about to pass him, he spied her and said "Not on your life!" and took off. Later she actually caught up to him at a stoplight. He leaned over and said, "Embrace each day. It's a gift." He took off and she's never seen him again. But it blessed her in suffering with Lyme disease. Those living with suffering both affirm living one day at a time and need constant reminders. She got hers, and it made her day. Coincidence? When she said that, I whispered to myself, "That was an angel." The woman in front of me in the audience muttered aloud, "God sent her an angel." Providence. Maybe even an angel.

When the church needed servants who would be Greek-speaking widow-sensitive people, God "found" some for them (Acts 6:1–6). When the Samaritans were ready for the gospel, God sent Philip; when a eunuch needed someone to explain Isaiah's words, God sent Philip (Acts 8:4–40). When the gentile world needed a Jewish-trained, Greek-speaking, energy-abundant, organization-skilled apostle, God prepared the apostle Paul and sent him (Acts 9:1–31). When Aeneas needed healing and when Tabitha needed resurrection, God sent Peter (9:32–43). Providence, not luck or coincidence. I don't believe God micro-manages everything that happens on planet earth, which is called meticulous sovereignty (Olson), but I do believe we perceive the hand of God's plan at times in the coordination of events. Grateful (to God) reception of such timing is the appropriate response.

We discover such providential coordination in the two visions in our passage, one to Cornelius and one to Peter. The Spirit is at work over and over.

THE BIG PICTURE

The point of all of Acts ten and eleven is that the gospel expands to the gentiles. Soon we will read that "the gift of the Holy Spirit had been poured out even on Gentiles" (10:45).

The two coordinated visions of Acts 10 prepare a gentile for the gospel and a Jewish apostle to preach to a gentile and for the audience to experience the palpable receipt of salvation by gentiles. Think again of Luke's basic plot in Acts 1:8: Jerusalem, Judea and Samaria, and to the ends of the earth. Here Peter becomes the coordinated agent of spreading the gospel to a gentile.

A Gentile's Vision

Not just any gentile either. He was in the Roman empire's ever-increasing army, he was in the major port city of Caesarea rebuilt by Herod the Great, and he was a ruler of up to 100 soldiers. But he straddled the emperor's world and the Jewish world. Luke describes as a man who had a civilized piety or a publicly respectable (cf. 10:22) form of religious practice (NIV: "devout"; Hoklotubbe), he was "God-fearing," which most likely means he was a convert to Judaism without circumcision. (Which is a bit like being an unbaptized Baptist.) Plus, Cornelius participated in two of Judaism's top acts of piety, namely, charity for the poor and the public hours of prayer. An angel appears to him at the time of the afternoon prayer (3pm; 10:3).

God honors the gentile's prayer and generosity, so the angel gives him a simple task: send servants, one of whom was a "devout soldier" (10:7), to Joppa to fetch Peter to meet with Cornelius.

I don't know about you, but I cheat at this point because I know what's going to happen. But imagine your way back to the life of Cornelius and choose to know only what Cornelius knows. All the empire-man knows is "get Peter." He doesn't have any idea why or what will happen when Peter returns. Perhaps he spent the next day or two wondering.

A JEW'S VISION

Peter's vision pierces into the heart of the Book of Acts. This vision empowers Peter to take steps that will only be finished off by Paul's trip to Rome, both stepping into the expansion of the gospel to gentiles.

Peter's vision, like Cornelius's, occurs while praying. Peter's hunger at the time sets the stage for an ecstatic reverie that, metaphorically speaking, pushes Peter over a fifty-foot high and thirty-foot thick wall, a wall called kosher food laws. The food prohibited in Leviticus 11 was observed and spelled out by the time of the 1st Century. A voice tells Peter, who is surrounded at Simon the tanner's house by unclean skins (Shiell, *Acts*, 84–85), to kill the animals on this most unwelcome menu and eat them. Peter argues with the voice: "I have never eaten anything impure or unclean" (10:14). Evidently Peter learns that God can "break" the laws he has given to Israel because the voice tells him to use more caution with his labels. What he's calling "impure" God has "made clean" (10:15). In an offhanded manner Luke informs us that this happened three times. Peter was not exactly gung-ho about eating shrimp or pork. (Little did he know what he would discover in taste.) This becomes "a moment in time" when a threshold is crossed and the new movement is born (Dunn, *Acts*, 138).

It's all over without explanation. As Peter ponders the meaning of eating non kosher food, Cornelius's party arrives and the "Spirit" informs Peter their arrival is kosher! They inform Peter of their vision, and he welcomes them into Simon the tanner's home. So why the vision? What Peter *acts out* in the vision could be called a "prophetic symbolic action." That is, the act of eating non-kosher food symbolizes the mission Peter is to experience in gospeling the gentiles.

Peter's hesitations are obvious, not only in his own words but in the need for God to command him to eat three times. That hesitation needs our respect. Nothing prepared Jews of even ordinary piety to become mission agents to gentiles. Even more, of becoming agents to bring them into the people of God. And one more, of becoming agents that do not require circumcision. What, many may have been asking, about following the law of Moses?

God coordinates two visions to two agents so that one of them can become a paradigm of gospeling and the other the paradigm of gentile conversion. That question about the law of Moses would fester into a major boil within a few years. The gentile mission provoked the question.

QUESTIONS FOR REFLECTION AND APPLICATION

1. What does McKnight call "the point" of Acts 10 and 11?

2. How do the two visions in this passage function to further God's mission to the gentiles?

3. What were the two main acts of piety for Jews, which Cornelius practiced? What did these acts of piety accomplish?

4. What is your view on God's involvement in the details of our life situations? How do you understand divine providence?

5. Imagine yourself in Peter's shoes, called by God to challenge some long-held religious beliefs in order to gospel people outside the norm for you and to welcome them into the people of God. What do you think he experienced? How can his obedience encourage you when you face similar barriers to bringing the gospel?

FOR FURTHER READING

Christopher Hoklotubbe, *Civilized Piety: The Rhetoric of Pietas in the Pastoral Epistles and the Roman Empire* (Waco, Texas: Baylor University Press, 2017).
Roger Olson, *Arminian Theology: Myths and Realities* (Downers Grove: IVP, 2006), 115–136.

GENTILES IN THE MISSION

Acts 10:23b–11:18

²³ The next day Peter started out with them, and some of the believers from Joppa went along.

²⁴ The following day he arrived in Caesarea. Cornelius was expecting them and had called together his relatives and close friends. ²⁵ As Peter entered the house, Cornelius met him and fell at his feet in reverence. ²⁶ But Peter made him get up. "Stand up," he said, "I am only a man myself."

²⁷ While talking with him, Peter went inside and found a large gathering of people. ²⁸ He said to them: "You are well aware that it is against our law for a Jew to associate with or visit a Gentile. But God has shown me that I should not call anyone impure or unclean. ²⁹ So when I was sent for, I came without raising any objection. May I ask why you sent for me?"

³⁰ Cornelius answered: "Three days ago I was in my house praying at this hour, at three in the afternoon. Suddenly a man in shining clothes stood before me ³¹ and said, 'Cornelius, God has heard your prayer and remembered your gifts to the poor. ³² Send to Joppa for Simon who is called Peter. He is a guest in the home of Simon the tanner, who lives by the sea.' ³³ So I sent for you immediately, and it was good of you to come. Now we are all here in the

presence of God to listen to everything the Lord has commanded you to tell us."

³⁴ Then Peter began to speak: "I now realize how true it is that God does not show favoritism ³⁵ but accepts from every nation the one who fears him and does what is right. ³⁶ You know the message God sent to the people of Israel, announcing the good news of peace through Jesus Christ, who is Lord of all. ³⁷ You know what has happened throughout the province of Judea, beginning in Galilee after the baptism that John preached—³⁸ how God anointed Jesus of Nazareth with the Holy Spirit and power, and how he went around doing good and healing all who were under the power of the devil, because God was with him.

³⁹ "We are witnesses of everything he did in the country of the Jews and in Jerusalem. They killed him by hanging him on a cross, ⁴⁰ but God raised him from the dead on the third day and caused him to be seen. ⁴¹ He was not seen by all the people, but by witnesses whom God had already chosen—by us who ate and drank with him after he rose from the dead. ⁴² He commanded us to preach to the people and to testify that he is the one whom God appointed as judge of the living and the dead. ⁴³ All the prophets testify about him that everyone who believes in him receives forgiveness of sins through his name."

⁴⁴ While Peter was still speaking these words, the Holy Spirit came on all who heard the message. ⁴⁵ The circumcised believers who had come with Peter were astonished that the gift of the Holy Spirit had been poured out even on Gentiles. ⁴⁶ For they heard them speaking in tongues and praising God. Then Peter said,

⁴⁷ "Surely no one can stand in the way of their being baptized with water. They have received the Holy Spirit just as we have." ⁴⁸ So he ordered that they be baptized in the name of Jesus Christ. Then they asked Peter to stay with them for a few days.

¹¹:¹ The apostles and the believers throughout Judea heard that the Gentiles also had received the word of God. ² So when Peter went up to Jerusalem, the circumcised believers criticized him [3] and said, "You went into the house of uncircumcised men and ate with them."

[4] Starting from the beginning, Peter told them the whole story: [5] "I was in the city of Joppa praying, and in a trance I saw a vision. I saw something like a large sheet being let down from heaven by its four corners, and it came down to where I was. [6] I looked into it and saw four-footed animals of the earth, wild beasts, reptiles and birds. [7] Then I heard a voice telling me, 'Get up, Peter. Kill and eat.'

[8] "I replied, 'Surely not, Lord! Nothing impure or unclean has ever entered my mouth.'

[9] "The voice spoke from heaven a second time, 'Do not call anything impure that God has made clean.' [10] This happened three times, and then it was all pulled up to heaven again.

[11] "Right then three men who had been sent to me from Caesarea stopped at the house where I was staying. [12] The Spirit told me to have no hesitation about going with them. These six brothers also went with me, and we entered the man's house. [13] He told us how he had seen an angel appear in his house and say, 'Send to Joppa for Simon who is called Peter. [14] He will bring you a message through which you and all your household will be saved.'

[15] "As I began to speak, the Holy Spirit came on them as he had come on us at the beginning. [16] Then I remembered what the Lord had said: 'John baptized with water, but you will be baptized with the Holy Spirit.' [17] So if God gave them the same gift he gave us who believed in the Lord Jesus Christ, who was I to think that I could stand in God's way?"

[18] When they heard this, they had no further objections and praised God, saying, "So then, even to Gentiles God has granted repentance that leads to life."

The moment Peter, with other (probably Jewish) believers from Joppa, crossed the threshold at Simon the tanner's home, he broke into a new world. Cornelius had issued invitations to his "relatives and close friends" (10:24), so even though the conversation and sermon in this chapter seemed to be between these two men, we need to keep in mind that it is "a large gathering" (10:27).

COORDINATED EXPLANATION

It is "biblical" for an author to describe an event and then repeat it all over again in redescribing it later. This happens in Acts 10 with the initial events (10:1–23), then in a brief summary conversation between Peter and Cornelius (10:27–33), and then before Jerusalem's leaders (11:1–18).

In Peter's explanation (10:27–29), we get his official interpretation of the vision of various foodstuffs. He knew God was telling him to spread the gospel to the gentiles because no one was unclean. Peter's words ironically describe his situation: "it is against our law [or, better, "unconventional"] for a Jew [like me] to associate with or visit a Gentile [which I'm doing in your home]" (10:28). No, God told him he was not to pin the "unclean" label on any human. Passing over his own initial hesitations, he came without objection (10:29). Only then does he ask why Cornelius asked him to come. Cornelius' explanation adds nothing significant to the vision. The military man finishes it off with a receptive mood: "Now we are all here in the presence of God to listen to everything the Lord has commanded you to tell us" (10:33).

The visions of each are now summarized in a coordinated fashion, all to set up Peter to preach the gospel to a gentile audience. God is the One doing all of this redemptive work.

GOSPEL PROCLAMATION

I love this sermon by Peter. It's marked by an honest admission. He only now realizes God is non-prejudiced, non-favoritistic, and welcomes any who are reverent and do what is right (10:34–35). I grew up with religious prejudice and pride, so I read Peter's words through that lens. We were fundamentalist Baptists, and the people of influence for me essentially taught me all other Christian denominations were not true Christians. Peter knows his Bible, which has informed him of God's special election of Israel and of Israel's destiny in the plans of God for the redemption of all creation. Gentiles sometimes made breakthroughs into the people of Israel, but by and large most were pagan idolaters headed straight for judgment. That vision of the foodstuffs converted Peter. So here he stands in front of gentiles with an opportunity for gospel proclamation to a people who had been excluded from the covenant.

He tells them about Jesus. I summarize Luke's summary of what would take less than a minute to say. Each of these points was elaborated with instances in the ministry of Jesus. (1) Jesus' message was about peace (not so much of soul but between peoples) through the Jesus who is "Lord of all," that is, of Jews and gentiles (10:36). (2) From John's baptism on, God "was with him," that is, God anointed Jesus "with the Holy Spirit and power" so that he could traverse the Galilee "doing good and healing" (10:37–38). (3) Like God the Father, Jesus showed no favoritism. He showed redemptive compassion on "all who were under the power of the devil" (10:38). Peter turns momentarily from plainspoken descriptions of Jesus to a personal claim: he was there, he saw it, he heard it all. That is, Peter is a witness (10:39).

He continues telling the story of Jesus, and again this is what apostolic gospel preaching was: (4) "They [the Roman-sponsored authorities] killed him by hanging him on a cross," which describes for many the victory of the powers over the way of Jesus (10:39). But (5) "God raised him from the dead" (10:40), and (6) we saw him and ate again with him (10:41).

Stay right there. Don't run ahead. Pause to hear this: *that* is the gospel. His death was overcome by resurrection. The gospel is about the *victory of God over death through the power of the resurrection*. The gospel story about Jesus continues only because of Easter. (7) Jesus ordered us–the witnesses–to announce (NIV: "preach") and to "testify" that the Raised One will return as the Judge (10:42). Only now does the benefit of the gospel get mentioned in Peter's gospel. (8) The entire sweep of the Bible witnesses about Jesus and the gift of forgiving sins "through his name" (10:43).

One of my favorite verses in the Bible, in part because I love to teach about Jesus, comes next, sometimes called the "Gentile Pentecost." Jennings captures it beautifully when he says "While Peter speaks, God moves" (Jennings, *Acts*, 112) or, as Luke records it, "While Peter was still speaking . . . the Holy Spirit came on all who heard the message" (10:44). A gospel truth is that *whenever we are talking Jesus with others the Spirit is at work*. The Spirit's falling on the gentiles tossed the Jewish believers (from Joppa) into consternation. They were "astonished" (cf. 10:45–46) that God's Spirit would come even on gentiles! That's what you call prejudice, the kind that Peter was learning to unlive and the kind they were about to see blown apart.

Peter is one step ahead of the Joppa believers. If these gentiles have the Holy Spirit, then they need to be baptized. This is an argument from experienced reality. Peter heard them speaking in tongues and praising God, and that's all he needed. "They've got what we've got" was his witness, and this witness would be needed if he was to get approval in Jerusalem. The order of redemptive moments in a person's life is inconsistent in the Book of Acts. Which is to say, these elements are not in the same order each time they appear: faith, repentance, forgiveness, baptism, and the coming of the Spirit (Dunn, *Acts*, 152).

TWO OBSERVATIONS

Two features in this passage are usually missed by Bible readers. One thing Jewish believers, whether from Joppa or Jerusalem, would not have missed: no circumcision. Which will come to mean for some Jerusalem believers that Peter (and then especially Paul) was no longer observant of Moses. What also many readers skip by is that this decision by Cornelius would have created a demanding decision. Would Cornelius, the leader of his battalion, ever be able to offer the required sacrifice to the gods and declare emperor the ruler of all? The answer is No. The man makes a decision that would have led to dismissal if not his death (Kalantzis, 66–68).

JERUSALEM ACCLAMATION

Though we have assumed all along that the eunuch of Acts 8 was a gentile and the first to hear the gospel, the apostles and believers in Judea only seem to recognize gentile conversions with the story of Cornelius (11:1). In fact, not all Jerusalem believers were affirming these gentile conversions. The "circumcised believers," which is lingo for believers who were also Torah observant (11:2), pointed at Peter's flagrant violation of custom in that he "went into the house of uncircumcised men and ate with them" (11:3).

So Peter rehearses the whole story: his vision, Cornelius' vision, the coordination of those visions leading to his gospeling of Cornelius in his home, and the outpouring of the Spirit on them as he had experienced at Pentecost, and his baptizing of them. "Who was I," Peter asks aloud, "to think I could stand in God's way?" (11:4–17).

Criticisms wither under the heat of this magnificent story. "They had no further objections," Luke tells us (but this book will show not all were convinced). Like Peter, like the Joppa believers, so the Jerusalem authorities admit, still with a tone of condescension, "So then, even to Gentiles God has granted repentance that leads to life" (11:18). Peter's mission is embraced as was the conversion of a gentile.

QUESTIONS FOR REFLECTION AND APPLICATION

1. What is Peter's own thought process and experience of coming to terms with God accepting gentiles, rather than excluding them?

2. Which points of Peter's sermon do you think are the most important? Why?

3. How will Cornelius's conversion likely change his military life?

4. Look up the following verses and observe how they are echoed in Peter's speech about Jesus without quoting them (Deuteronomy 10:17–18; Psalms 15:1–2; 107:20; Isaiah 52:7; 61:1). What do you see in such echoes?

5. Have you ever had to overcome prejudice to accept certain people as part of God's family? What changed your heart?

FOR FURTHER READING

George Kalantzis, *Caesar and the Lamb: Early Christian Attitudes on War and Military Service* (Eugene, OR: Cascade, 2012).

FELLOWSHIP IN THE MISSION

Acts 11:19–30

19 Now those who had been scattered by the persecution that broke out when Stephen was killed traveled as far as Phoenicia, Cyprus and Antioch, spreading the word only among Jews. 20 Some of them, however, men from Cyprus and Cyrene, went to Antioch and began to speak to Greeks also, telling them the good news about the Lord Jesus. 21 The Lord's hand was with them, and a great number of people believed and turned to the Lord.

22 News of this reached the church in Jerusalem, and they sent Barnabas to Antioch. 23 When he arrived and saw what the grace of God had done, he was glad and encouraged them all to remain true to the Lord with all their hearts. 24 He was a good man, full of the Holy Spirit and faith, and a great number of people were brought to the Lord.

25 Then Barnabas went to Tarsus to look for Saul, 26 and when he found him, he brought him to Antioch. So for a whole year Barnabas and Saul met with the church and taught great numbers of people. The disciples were called Christians first at Antioch.

27 During this time some prophets came down from Jerusalem to Antioch. 28 One of them, named Agabus, stood up and through the Spirit predicted that a severe famine would spread over the entire Roman world. (This happened during the reign of Claudius.) [29] *The disciples, as each one was able, decided to provide help for the brothers and sisters living in Judea.* [30] *This they did, sending their gift to the elders by Barnabas and Saul.*

No one had a blueprint for how to develop a gospel mission to the whole world. The Book of Acts opens doors for us to peer inside the attempts, the failures, and the successes of the apostles and early believers. Luke is not providing a map or even a template. He's telling stories of what happens when the Spirit of God leads missioners to do mission. We are tempted to imitate, but instead of imitating them, we are best off learning to discern, as they did, the Spirit's guidance of us in our world as they did in their world. Mission is not only evangelizing and operating church services. Mission involves, as we indicated in the Introduction to his book, catechizing new believers, caring for the needs of others, working for justice, and caring for creation—all wrapped up in participating in God's love for all. That love motivates us in relationships, which are on display in this passage.

Luke opens four doors in this passage that reveal various dimensions of the mission: (1) about growth, (2) about official approval, (3) about instruction, and (4) about fellowship.

GOSPEL GROWTH

Luke wants us to read these chapters as a connected report of the growth of the gospel mission. These are verses that keep us moving forward in that progress toward Rome: 8:4, 25, 40; 9:22, 31; and 11:19. On this path, Luke pauses to recount vignettes of people and churches, and in our passage he turns our attention to the Jewish church in Antioch where we take notice that evangelistic believers from Cyprus and Cyrene travel to Antioch to share the gospel with Greeks (gentiles) (11:20). Their gospel, notice once again, is "about the Lord Jesus" (11:20). This is a new breakthrough and once again not a word about the need for circumcision.

Mission expansion throbs from the very beginning of the church and beats in every healthy church. I grew up in a missionary-soaked church. Every year we had a missionary conference where we heard stories about the gospel in foreign countries. Perhaps you can pause to consider your own church's participation in God's mission outside your own community.

JERUSALEM APPROVAL

Jerusalem's approval of the mission work punctuates an event in Samaria (8:14–17), Paul's conversion (9:26–30), the conversion of Cornelius through Peter (11:1–18), as well as the growth of the church in Antioch (11:19–30). We will learn in this Book of Acts that there will be plenty of tension between Jerusalem's leaders and the Pauline mission, but that story will be told later in this book.

Upon hearing of the expansion of the gospel to the Hellenists in Antioch, the Jerusalem leaders send the peace-making and encouraging Barnabas to evaluate (9:27). Barnabas' pastoral giftedness shines in this text as we hear these words from him: "he saw what the grace of God had done" and "he was glad and encouraged them" and "he was a good man, full of the Holy Spirit and faith" (11:23–24). Barnabas learned the important lesson in mission work to "go with the flow of God" (Jennings, *Acts*, 123), that is, to enter into God's mission. What we see in Barnabas is not control but discernment of the Spirit's work.

APOSTOLIC TEACHING

Barnabas was a networker and, perceiving a need, he knew the resolution so he traveled (200 miles or more!) to Tarsus to persuade Saul, who dropped out of our story after leaving Jerusalem (9:30). He solicits Saul to join him as a teacher in Antioch (11:25–26), so Saul spent a year in Antioch instructing the disciples. This is early in Paul's career, so we can assume the foundations that later became Galatians and Romans were first laid in Antioch. Yet, any study of Paul's own writings show that he adjusted to each context in such a way that he was both faithful to the gospel and context-sensitive.

I have avoided using the word "Christian" as much as possible until this moment. The disciples of Jesus, both Jews and Hellenists, are first labeled "Christians" in Antioch (11:26), and the Latin ending makes clear the name came from the Roman leaders in the city. A new term was needed because the church in Antioch was comprised of both Jewish and gentile believers, and the term means partisans of Christ. It indicates how Messiah-soaked their beliefs and practices were. Bill Shiell, on the basis of this text, asks an important question for us: The question is "When did you become a Christian?" but he means, "When did your faith become noticeable enough that people thought you were a Christian?" (Shiell, *Acts*, 92–94).

FELLOWSHIP EXPRESSED

Prophets traveled to Antioch, now the second most significant center for the mission. One of them, Agabus by name (Hebrew for "grasshopper"), predicted an empire-wide famine that occurred under the emperor Claudius (11:27–28). Luke's reason for this vignette is not so we will be awed by accurate predictions–occurring probably in 46–47 AD—but so, once again, we see the fellowship of the churches. The word "fellowship" means to "share a common life in Christ as siblings of one another." Antioch Christians broke their piggy banks and sent funds along with Barnabas and Saul for the Jerusalem saints. (Galatians 2:1–10 reports this event as well.)

QUESTIONS FOR REFLECTION AND APPLICATION

1. What is the difference between trying to imitate what the early church did and discerning to follow the Spirit's guidance as they did?

2. Does your church have a focus on mission beyond your own church? If so, how does this shape your view of gospel growth in the world today?

3. What important role does Barnabas play once again? How does his involvement move the story forward?

4. Answer Bill Shiell's question: "When did your faith become noticeable enough that people thought you were a Christian?"

POWERS DEFEATED
IN THE MISSION

Acts 12:1–25

¹ It was about this time that King Herod arrested some who belonged to the church, intending to persecute them. ² He had James, the brother of John, put to death with the sword. ³ When he saw that this met with approval among the Jews, he proceeded to seize Peter also. This happened during the Festival of Unleavened Bread. ⁴ After arresting him, he put him in prison, handing him over to be guarded by four squads of four soldiers each. Herod intended to bring him out for public trial after the Passover.

⁵ So Peter was kept in prison, but the church was earnestly praying to God for him.

⁶ The night before Herod was to bring him to trial, Peter was sleeping between two soldiers, bound with two chains, and sentries stood guard at the entrance. ⁷ Suddenly an angel of the Lord appeared and a light shone in the cell. He struck Peter on the side and woke him up. "Quick, get up!" he said, and the chains fell off Peter's wrists.

⁸ Then the angel said to him, "Put on your clothes and sandals." And Peter did so. "Wrap your cloak around you and follow me," the angel told him. ⁹ Peter followed him out of the prison, but he had no idea that what the angel was doing was really happening; he thought he was seeing a vision. [10] They passed the first and second guards and came to the iron gate leading to the city. It opened for them by itself, and they went through it. When they had walked the length of one street, suddenly the angel left him.

[11] Then Peter came to himself and said, "Now I know without a doubt that the Lord has sent his angel and rescued me from Herod's clutches and from everything the Jewish people were hoping would happen."

[12] When this had dawned on him, he went to the house of Mary the mother of John, also called Mark, where many people had gathered and were praying. [13] Peter knocked at the outer entrance, and a servant named Rhoda came to answer the door. [14] When she recognized Peter's voice, she was so overjoyed she ran back without opening it and exclaimed, "Peter is at the door!"

[15] "You're out of your mind," they told her. When she kept insisting that it was so, they said, "It must be his angel."

[16] But Peter kept on knocking, and when they opened the door and saw him, they were astonished. [17] Peter motioned with his hand for them to be quiet and described how the Lord had brought him out of prison. "Tell James and the other brothers and sisters about this," he said, and then he left for another place.

[18] In the morning, there was no small commotion among the soldiers as to what had become of Peter. [19] After Herod had a thorough search made for him and did not find him, he cross-examined the guards and ordered that they be executed.

Then Herod went from Judea to Caesarea and stayed there. [20] He had been quarreling with the people of Tyre and Sidon; they now joined together and sought an audience with him. After securing the support of Blastus, a trusted personal servant of the king, they asked for peace, because they depended on the king's country for their food supply.

[21] On the appointed day Herod, wearing his royal robes, sat on his throne and delivered a public address to the people. [22] They shouted, "This is the voice of a god, not of a man." [23] Immediately,

because Herod did not give praise to God, an angel of the Lord struck him down, and he was eaten by worms and died.

²⁴ *But the word of God continued to spread and flourish.*

²⁵ *When Barnabas and Saul had finished their mission, they returned from Jerusalem, taking with them John, also called Mark.*

Opposition by the political powers kept up with the gospel's expansion. In chapter twelve we will observe opposition by King Herod Agrippa I to Peter, and then Peter will appear only once more in the Book of Acts. He shows up in Acts 15 as a speaker in the Jerusalem Council (Acts 15:7–11) as the narrative hands the mission off to the ministry of Saul/Paul.

GOD'S MISSION

The best ways to read chapter twelve is, first, to see it as an interlude between 11:30 and 12:25 and, second, to begin with the theme at verse twenty-four. Read it again: "But the word of God continued to spread and flourish." This verse aligns with other progress-mapping verses in Acts (6:1, 7; 9:31; 11:21, 24; 19:20) as well as the obvious successes of Peter in Samaria and the eunuch (8:4–40), Saul's initial evangelism in Antioch (9:19b-31), Peter in Lydda, Joppa, and Caesarea (9:32–11:18), and also in Antioch (11:19–24). What happens in chapter twelve furthers the mission.

God's mission is irresistible. We too often succumb to trusting in the so-called "charisma" of humans, thinking at times that we can't get along without so-and-so. When we take our eyes off God and become intensively impressed with our giftedness, we commit a form of idolatry. And idolatry meets God in the second half of chapter twelve. In the Book of Acts, we are tempted to divide the book into the missions of Peter and Paul. Fair enough, but if in describing it that way we fail to see that it is God's mission with Peter and Paul only as God's agents of God's mission, we fail to read the book right.

POWERS AGAINST GOD

King Herod Agrippa, grandson of Herod the Great, was educated in Rome, was a friend of emperor Claudius, and was granted territory to rule by Claudius. Josephus informs us that he at least saw him as an observant Jew. A later Jewish source makes it clear Agrippa had a questionable Jewish heritage (*Mishnah Sota* 7:8). Observant he may have been, but he decapitated James, apostle and brother of John and son of Zebedee. With his approval ratings soaring, he decided to go next after Peter, imprisoning him, securing him safely behind four squads of four guards and gates in a 1st Century version of maximum security (Jennings, *Acts*, 127), all the while planning a grandstanding trial in public at Passover (Acts 12:1–4; cf. Luke 22:1). His plan to slay Peter on Passover ironically become what Passover was: God's act of liberating the enslaved (Shiell, *Acts*, 98–100). The powers love prisons, but God snaps such powers (Jennings, *Acts*, 129).

Some of the faithful became martyrs while others live to continue as witnesses to Jesus. We will never know why James was killed but Peter lived. We are better off discerning the work of God in what happens and not why something happens.

GOD IS ALL-POWERFUL

Luke concentrates our attention on the miraculous, story-filled account of Peter's release from prison. The church is praying to God for Peter (12:5) and God answers their petitions, leading us all to observe the work of God through an angel. Luke's narrative is spectacular (and a bit fun). Peter's totally wrapped up behind the powers (12:6), and an angel awakens Peter and the "chains fell off" (12:7), which is echoed in the famous hymn by Charles Wesley. If that song sticks in your head today, blame Luke. The angel directs Peter to clothe himself and escorts him straight through the sealed protection of the powers (12:8) and then suddenly Peter was alone on a street in Jerusalem (12:9–10).

So powerful and unrealistic was Peter's experience that not until he "came to himself" (12:11) does he realize this was not a vision (12:9). What to do? It's obvious. He returns to life with the other believers in Jerusalem by knocking on the door of the "house of Mary the mother of John, also called Mark" (12:12). His appearance here prepares us for more (12:25; 13:13; 15:37–39; see also Colossians 4:10; Philemon 24; 2 Timothy 4:11; 1 Peter 5:13). So powerful again is this deliverance that even the servant Rhoda, who answered the door at Mary's house, instead of opening the gate charges back into the home to announce Peter's release. Once the stardust settles, they welcome Peter to hear his account of the power of God defeating the powers in the prison. Peter is careful to attribute the whole thing to God. And he wants them to report this all to James, the brother of Jesus (12:17), who was the major church leader in Jerusalem.

God's work is often obvious. Alice and Randy Mathews worship with us on Sundays. Recently Alice told her story, which had these themes: Randy is the pastor and an extrovert; Alice is the introvert who just wants to be left alone in her study reading and writing; but God had other plans. Alice taught a Sunday School class for a pastor on sabbatical long ago; it went so well they invited her back; it went so well a publisher asked her to convert it into a book and more books (see below); it went so well Alice was invited over and over to speak to groups around the world, and she became a leader among the women's movement about evangelicals.

The underlying theme of her story was this: *only God could have turned me, the introvert, into the author on the platform speaking!* She said this over and over. "It was God."

THE POWERS ARE NOT GOD

Herod can persecute and execute, which Herod does. Once with James and then again with the guards who did not keep Peter contained in prison. Herod persecutes and executes, but God prosecutes. Not only does God give Herod a bit of a glimpse of his power by releasing Peter, but the death of Herod becomes in Luke's narrative the just prosecution of a man who took the place of God. Josephus tells a similar story (*Antiquities* 19:343–352; see Keener, *Acts*, 324).

Again, Herod has power. When the quarreling cities of Tyre and Sidon petition for peace, Herod is called into action (12:19b-20). He wears his purple as a way of showing his power, status, and identity. His speech amazes the audience who, like sycophants, acclaim divine status for Agrippa. Herod soaks it into his ego instead of crediting God. God prosecutes the man and he dies, and with a filip of flavor, Luke says "he was eaten by worms and died" (12:23).

Notice again where we began: "*But* the word of God continued to spread and flourish" (12:24).

QUESTIONS FOR REFLECTION AND APPLICATION

1. Do you tend to see two missions in Acts (Peter and Paul) or see one mission (God's, with Peter and Paul as agents)? What difference does it make when you focus on the second view?

2. How does Herod Agrippa set himself up as a power against God? How does Luke as a narrator handle Herod's story?

3. Observe that God opens the city gate for Peter, but Rhoda at first fails to open the house door for him! Have you ever been so surprised at God's answer to prayer that you failed to "open a door" for God's plan?

4. When has God's work been obvious in your life? What doors has God miraculously opened for you?

5. What are the powers that seem to be thwarting your mission for God? How do you need God to be for you all-powerful in those situations? Take time to pray for his powerful intervention now.

FOR FURTHER READING

Alice Mathews, *A Woman God Can Use: Old Testament Women Help You Make Today's Choices* (Grand Rapids: Discovery House, 2018).

Alice Mathews, *A Woman Jesus Can Teach: New Testament Women Help You Make Today's Choices* (Grand Rapids: Discovery House, 2018).

Alice Mathews, *A Woman God's Spirit Can Guide: New Testament Women Help You Make Today's Choices* (Grand Rapids: Discovery House, 2017).

PATTERNS IN
THE MISSION

Acts 12:25–14:28

²⁵ *When Barnabas and Saul had finished their mission, they re-turned from Jerusalem, taking with them John, also called Mark.*

¹³ᐟ¹ Now in the church at Antioch there were prophets and teachers: Barnabas, Simeon called Niger, Lucius of Cyrene, Manaen (who had been brought up with Herod the tetrarch) and Saul. ² While they were worshiping the Lord and fasting, the Holy Spirit said, "Set apart for me Barnabas and Saul for the work to which I have called them." ³ So after they had fasted and prayed, they placed their hands on them and sent them off.

⁴ The two of them, sent on their way by the Holy Spirit, went down to Seleucia and sailed from there to Cyprus. ⁵ When they arrived at Salamis, they proclaimed the word of God in the Jewish synagogues. John was with them as their helper. ⁶ They traveled through the whole island until they came to Paphos. There they met a Jewish sorcerer and false prophet named Bar-Jesus, ⁷ who was an attendant of the proconsul, Sergius Paulus. The proconsul, an intelligent man, sent for Barnabas and Saul because he wanted to hear the word of God. ⁸ But Elymas the sorcerer (for that is what his name means) opposed them and tried to turn the proconsul from the faith. ⁹ Then Saul, who was also called Paul, filled with the

Holy Spirit, looked straight at Elymas and said, [10] *"You are a child of the devil and an enemy of everything that is right! You are full of all kinds of deceit and trickery. Will you never stop perverting the right ways of the Lord?* [11] *Now the hand of the Lord is against you. You are going to be blind for a time, not even able to see the light of the sun." Immediately mist and darkness came over him, and he groped about, seeking someone to lead him by the hand.* [12] *When the proconsul saw what had happened, he believed, for he was amazed at the teaching about the Lord.*

[13] *From Paphos, Paul and his companions sailed to Perga in Pamphylia, where John left them to return to Jerusalem.* [14] *From Perga they went on to Pisidian Antioch. On the Sabbath they entered the synagogue and sat down.* [15] *After the reading from the Law and the Prophets, the leaders of the synagogue sent word to them, saying, "Brothers, if you have a word of exhortation for the people, please speak."*

[16] *Standing up, Paul motioned with his hand and said:*

Fellow Israelites and you Gentiles who worship God, listen to me! [17] *The God of the people of Israel chose our ancestors; he made the people prosper during their stay in Egypt; with mighty power he led them out of that country;* [18] *for about forty years he endured their conduct in the wilderness;* [19] *and he overthrew seven nations in Canaan, giving their land to his people as their inheritance.* [20] *All this took about 450 years.*

After this, God gave them judges until the time of Samuel the prophet. [21] *Then the people asked for a king, and he gave them Saul son of Kish, of the tribe of Benjamin, who ruled forty years.* [22] *After removing Saul, he made David their king. God testified concerning him: 'I have found David son of Jesse, a man after my own heart; he will do everything I want him to do.'*

[23] *From this man's descendants God has brought to Israel the Savior Jesus, as he promised.* [24] *Before the coming of Jesus, John preached repentance and baptism to all the people of Israel.* [25] *As John was completing his work, he said: 'Who do you suppose I am?*

I am not the one you are looking for. But there is one coming after me whose sandals I am not worthy to untie.'

²⁶ *Fellow children of Abraham and you God-fearing Gentiles, it is to us that this message of salvation has been sent.* ²⁷ *The people of Jerusalem and their rulers did not recognize Jesus, yet in condemning him they fulfilled the words of the prophets that are read every Sabbath.* ²⁸ *Though they found no proper ground for a death sentence, they asked Pilate to have him executed.* ²⁹ *When they had carried out all that was written about him, they took him down from the cross and laid him in a tomb.* ³⁰ *But God raised him from the dead,* ³¹ *and for many days he was seen by those who had traveled with him from Galilee to Jerusalem. They are now his witnesses to our people.*

³² *We tell you the good news: What God promised our ancestors* ³³ *he has fulfilled for us, their children, by raising up Jesus. As it is written in the second Psalm:*

> *" 'You are my son;*
> *today I have become your father.'*

³⁴ *God raised him from the dead so that he will never be subject to decay. As God has said,*

> *" 'I will give you the holy and sure blessings promised to David.'*

³⁵ *So it is also stated elsewhere:*
> *" 'You will not let your holy one see decay.'*

³⁶ *Now when David had served God's purpose in his own generation, he fell asleep; he was buried with his ancestors and his body decayed.* ³⁷ *But the one whom God raised from the dead did not see decay.*

³⁸ *Therefore, my friends, I want you to know that through Jesus the forgiveness of sins is proclaimed to you.* ³⁹ *Through him everyone*

who believes is set free from every sin, a justification you were not able to obtain under the law of Moses. [40] *Take care that what the prophets have said does not happen to you:*

[41] " 'Look, you scoffers,
      wonder and perish,
for I am going to do something in your days
      that you would never believe,
even if someone told you.'"

[42] As Paul and Barnabas were leaving the synagogue, the people invited them to speak further about these things on the next Sabbath. [43] When the congregation was dismissed, many of the Jews and devout converts to Judaism followed Paul and Barnabas, who talked with them and urged them to continue in the grace of God. [44] On the next Sabbath almost the whole city gathered to hear the word of the Lord. [45] When the Jews saw the crowds, they were filled with jealousy. They began to contradict what Paul was saying and heaped abuse on him. [46] Then Paul and Barnabas answered them boldly: "We had to speak the word of God to you first. Since you reject it and do not consider yourselves worthy of eternal life, we now turn to the Gentiles. [47] For this is what the Lord has commanded us:
   " 'I have made you a light for the Gentiles,
   that you may bring salvation to the ends of the earth.'"
[48] When the Gentiles heard this, they were glad and honored the word of the Lord; and all who were appointed for eternal life believed.

[49] The word of the Lord spread through the whole region. [50] But the Jewish leaders incited the God-fearing women of high standing and the leading men of the city. They stirred up persecution against Paul and Barnabas, and expelled them from their region. [51] So they shook the dust off their feet as a warning to them and went to Iconium. [52] And the disciples were filled with joy and with the Holy Spirit.

14:1 At Iconium Paul and Barnabas went as usual into the Jewish synagogue. There they spoke so effectively that a great number of Jews and Greeks believed. *2* But the Jews who refused to believe stirred up the other Gentiles and poisoned their minds against the brothers. *3* So Paul and Barnabas spent considerable time there, speaking boldly for the Lord, who confirmed the message of his grace by enabling them to perform signs and wonders. *4* The people of the city were divided; some sided with the Jews, others with the apostles. *5* There was a plot afoot among both Gentiles and Jews, together with their leaders, to mistreat them and stone them.

6 But they found out about it and fled to the Lycaonian cities of Lystra and Derbe and to the surrounding country, *7* where they continued to preach the gospel. *8* In Lystra there sat a man who was lame. He had been that way from birth and had never walked. *9* He listened to Paul as he was speaking. Paul looked directly at him, saw that he had faith to be healed *10* and called out, "Stand up on your feet!" At that, the man jumped up and began to walk. *11* When the crowd saw what Paul had done, they shouted in the Lycaonian language, "The gods have come down to us in human form!" *12* Barnabas they called Zeus, and Paul they called Hermes because he was the chief speaker. *13* The priest of Zeus, whose temple was just outside the city, brought bulls and wreaths to the city gates because he and the crowd wanted to offer sacrifices to them. *14* But when the apostles Barnabas and Paul heard of this, they tore their clothes and rushed out into the crowd, shouting: *15* "Friends, why are you doing this? We too are only human, like you. We are bringing you good news, telling you to turn from these worthless things to the living God, who made the heavens and the earth and the sea and everything in them. *16* In the past, he let all nations go their own way. *17* Yet he has not left himself without testimony: He has shown kindness by giving you rain from heaven and crops in their seasons; he provides you with plenty of food and fills your hearts with joy." *18* Even with these words, they had difficulty keeping the crowd from sacrificing to them. *19* Then some Jews came from

Antioch and Iconium and won the crowd over. They stoned Paul and dragged him outside the city, thinking he was dead. [20] *But after the disciples had gathered around him, he got up and went back into the city. The next day he and Barnabas left for Derbe.*

[21] *They preached the gospel in that city and won a large number of disciples. Then they returned to Lystra, Iconium and Antioch,* [22] *strengthening the disciples and encouraging them to remain true to the faith. "We must go through many hardships to enter the kingdom of God," they said.* [23] *Paul and Barnabas appointed elders for them in each church and, with prayer and fasting, committed them to the Lord, in whom they had put their trust.* [24] *After going through Pisidia, they came into Pamphylia,* [25] *and when they had preached the word in Perga, they went down to Attalia.* [26] *From Attalia they sailed back to Antioch, where they had been committed to the grace of God for the work they had now completed.* [27] *On arriving there, they gathered the church together and reported all that God had done through them and how he had opened a door of faith to the Gentiles.* [28] *And they stayed there a long time with the disciples.*

PAUL'S MISSION TRIPS

We commonly speak of three mission trips by Paul, and this long passage covers the first of these trips. The first trip starts in Syrian Antioch, sails to Cyprus, sails north to the mainland of Asia Minor or the Anatolia (modern day Turkey) where he launches kingdom work in Pisidian Antioch, Iconium, Lystra and Derbe, from which locations he returned to Syrian Antioch. In Paul's mission trips, we can discern his patterns of mission as well as learn paradigms for our mission work, whether we are heading off to new locations or remaining in our own village. It is important that we not woodenly *imitate* Barnabas and Saul, but we can *learn* from their mission work for our day in our way. Below we will look at six patterns in the gospel mission. We don't, for instance, shake dust off our feet when someone rejects the gospel (13:51).

COMMISSIONED

Some, convinced they are called by God, go out on their own without any sanctioning church and without any confirmation or recognition of the calling. This is unwise. The text of Acts 12:25–13:3 reads as if Barnabas and Saul (notice the order) with three others (a black man named Simeon called Niger, Lucius of Cyrene, and Manaean, who was well connected) were gathered in worship and the Spirit spoke through the "prophets and teachers" in Antioch to commission Barnabas and Saul to mission work. Unlike Jerusalem, this church was more charismatic or Spirit-prompted. Their act of consecration was to lay hands on them and send them off to what we call the first mission trip (13:4–14:28; see map). After their mission was completed, the two returned to their commissioning church in Syrian Antioch and report "all that God had done through them" and how God "had opened a door of faith to the Gentiles" (14:27). They took a furlough for "a long time" (14:28).

Wisdom has grown around commissioning. In many settings, churches wisely require preparation in both ministry and education as well as in cultural learning about the context to which someone is called. Commissioning organizations discern the fit and calling of those who propose their own candidacy. In many contexts the new missionaries will be welcomed by a team of missionaries already at work in that location. Missionary work can be profoundly lonely and demanding; it can lead to depression and family stresses; it challenges every facet of the heart and mind and body and feelings. Wise mission organizations provide pastoral care for missioners, rest and leisure for their health, and fellowship that sustains them. We see no inner revelations of stress about either Barnabas or Saul, though one of their companions from Jerusalem, John Mark, evidently felt enough stress to return home once they landed in Asia Minor (13:13). Wise commissioning organizations can often discern whether or not a couple or family or a single person will fit in the next context. I suspect John Mark was not prepared for the "looseness" of the Pauline mission when it came to gentile converts not needing to observe the Mosaic law.

LOCATION

Where we launch gospel mission matters immensely. That it shifts and changes from one person to the next and how it changes from one moment to the next requires sensitivity to the Spirit to discern where God wants us. There is nothing cookie cutter or programmatic about gospel work. The program is God's and the cookies God cuts are the ones God wants cut.

One of the apostle Paul's repeated lines about his mission work is "first to the Jew, then to the Gentile" (Romans 1:16; 2:9). Luke's account more than confirms this. Four times (13:5, 14, 44; 14:1) we read that Saul/Paul began his mission work in a synagogue. To claim the Galilean man named Jesus was Israel's Messiah required a Jewish story, a Jewish fulfillment, and a Jewish audience. Romans and Greeks had no interest in that Jewish story, and to claim Jesus was the long-expected "Messiah" was to make an irrelevant claim to them. Paul went where he has an audience. Traveling Jewish males were often afforded an opportunity to "share" when they attended a synagogue.

We are not called to go to synagogues (unless we are invited, and even then what Paul did would not be acceptable in our society). What we can learn here is organic gospeling. Athletes share Christ in locker rooms and on airplanes and buses and in small groups, family members in homes, friends in coffee shops and in schools, authors in their writings, pastors in their visitations and sermons and classes, and the list goes on. I perceive in Acts a touchstone approach: where your audience is, there's your starting point.

What about Saul becoming "Paul"? While Barnabas, John Mark, and Saul were on the island of Cyprus, Barnabas' home (Acts 4:36), Luke tells us in a passing comment that Saul was also called Paul (13:9), and he does not explain the name change. But from this point on, two things happen: (1) the name is always Paul and (2) it is no longer Barnabas then Saul but Paul then Barnabas. Saul is a Hebrew name with royal connotations, but in Greek that word (*saulos*) refers to a man who has the gait of a tortoise (a shuffler) or a courtesan (sexy, or perhaps effeminate). Perhaps then Saul becomes Paul as a mission-sensitive name; perhaps he had more than one name.

GOSPELING

We are told numerous times in our passages of Paul's first mission trip that the missioners spread the gospel message

(13:5; 14:3, 7, 14–17). They "proclaimed" (13:5), they spoke boldly (14:3), they preached (14:7), and they gospeled (14:15; NIV has "bringing you good news"). Various words are used in the New Testament for what we call evangelism and each highlights a slightly difference nuance. To gospel is to explain, to declare, to announce, and to proclaim a message about what God has brought to completion in Jesus. Because the term evangelism has acquired numerous barnacles that hide in some ways the crystal clear content of the gospel, namely, Jesus as Messiah, I prefer using "gospel" as a verb as we find in 14:15: they were gospeling.

Speaking of the content, Acts 13's sermon by Paul in the synagogue of Pisidian Antioch is a longish account (for Luke) of the gospel of Paul (13:16–41). Here are its major features, most of which are much like Peter's sermon in Acts 2:

1. Paul told them a specialized version of the story of God's work in Israel's history, beginning with God's election and liberation of the children of Israel from Egypt, the conquest of the land, and the rise of leaders like Saul and especially David.
2. That story finds it fulfillment in the story of Jesus, the Davidic Messiah who was preceded by John the baptizer.
3. He informs both Jews and God-fearing gentiles in the synagogue that the gospel is for their salvation. At this point Paul fills in some lines glossed over so far by
4. explaining that their scriptures announced this all in advance.
5. Paul calls for a decision by promising forgiveness to those who surrender to Jesus in allegiant faith. He says they will be justified. Attached to this promise of redemption for believers is a warning of the consequences of not turning to Jesus as Messiah but

it comes with a glimpse of hope: "I [God] am going to do something in your days that you would never believe" (Acts 13:41, from Habakkuk 1:5).

Here is Paul's gospel: Israel's story about a future Davidic king is fulfilled in King Jesus as Messiah. He is the content of the gospel, and the benefits of the gospel are forgiveness and justification, and these benefits are given only to those who surrender in trusting allegiance to Jesus as Lord and King. That story now fulfilled forms the heart of the gospel.

Paul's gospeling in Lystra complements what he preached in Pisidian Antioch (14:14–17), where we hear him call the gentiles "to turn from these worthless things to the living God" to the Creator of all who in creation gives witness to his kindness. Paul goes into this in part because the Lystrans were convinced he and Barnabas were deities!

We need all over again, as if for the first time, to renew this kind of gospel preaching. That is, gospeling that means telling people about Jesus and who Jesus is and what he does for us and will do for the world. The gospel is God at work in this world in and through Jesus as his agents tell others about him.

OPPOSITION TO THE GOSPEL

Gospel work has its ups and downs, some of it emotional and some of it spiritual and some of it petty jealousies and some of it racist or sexist or classist, and some of it social and some of it physical. Some lose friends, some lose family members, some lose jobs, some lose status and power and money. Of course, the ups include experiencing God's gracious love and the love of one another and fellowship and a sense that one participates in God's good work in this world. Perhaps you have some ups and downs yourself.

Paul and Barnabas did. They witnessed the work of God in their midst but they also encountered daily opposition to their gospel mission. Notice how often the theme appears in our passage.

On Cyprus Bar-Jesus [son of Jesus] Elymas, a Jewish sorcerer and false prophet (13:6) who worked for the proconsul Sergius Paulus, sought to turn the proconsul away from listening to Barnabas and Saul.

In Pisidian Antioch the Jewish opponents of Paul were filled with zeal (NIV has "jealousy"), countered what he was teaching, and abused him verbally (13:45). Near the end of his time in Antioch some leaders in the city "stirred up persecution" against them (13:50).

In Iconium those in the synagogue who didn't believe Jesus was the Messiah discredited Paul and Barnabas (14:2) and even plotted to stone them to death (14:5).

In Lystra Paul was opposed by some who traveled down from the former cities of Paul's mission work. In Lystra their plot to stone him was achieved and they dragged Paul outside the city thinking he was dead (14:19).

It is not macabre to ponder the shape of Paul's body. He will tell the Galatians "I bear on my body the marks of Jesus" (Galatians 6:17). If you read 2 Corinthians 11:23–27, it takes no imagination to wonder about scars, broken bones, and even some disfigurements.

The gospel Paul preached makes a claim on all of one's life, which means the one who hears the gospel is being challenged to convert, to turn from a current way of life, to trust in Jesus as Savior, and to follow Jesus as Lord. The gospel cuts into one's identity, one's status, one's financial comforts, and one's family. For these reasons and others, the gospel mission work was opposed, but the opposition ultimately was opposition to God.

POWER OF GOD

One of the ups that some see in their mission is a display of the power of God. When the sorcerer on the island of Cyprus sought to dissuade the proconsul for listening to the gospel Paul, "filled with the Holy Spirit," seemingly got in his face, accused him of allegiance to the devil and deceit and trickery and then announced the "hand of the Lord" would come upon him in judgment to blind him. Which happened (13:9–11). In Iconium, Paul and Barnabas witnessed God doing "signs and wonders" (14:3). In Lystra, God gave a lame man powers to walk again (14:8–10). So much power attended their mission work that in Lystra those who witnessed the miracle attempted to deify Paul and Barnabas (14:11–13, 18). Their explanations to the Lystrans did not entirely convince.

The response of Paul and Barnabas blows over me as refreshing breezes. Too many on the platforms in our churches today crave celebrity, glory, power and honor–even if they don't admit it and even if they overtly state they don't like that aspect of being on the platform. To be gifted to speak the Word of God, to witness the power of God through preaching or the signs and wonders, and to be given applause by hundreds and thousands, to be known, to be recognized in public, to be given glory are temptations many can't resist. Celebrity is about being famous for being famous but it is also about being put on a pedestal, to be given privileges others don't have, to be excepted from rules and regulations, and to be treated in such a manner that very few can escape its temptations to narcissisms. Celebrity pushes people to believe their press clippings and to be persuaded they are special (McKnight and Barringer, 175–200). They're not. God is. They are but servants of God and they are called, like Jesus, not to be served but to serve (Mark 10:35–45).

Paul and Barnabas, so attuned were they to God's glory

and God's work, that they visibly demonstrated their shock and fear by ripping their clothes. They then declared without mincing words that the powers were God's not theirs.

CONVERSIONS

One doesn't count numbers to establish faithfulness to the gospel mission but numbers at times confirm the power of God at work. But Luke does tell his readers that the gospel converted the lives of many. Sergius Paulus on Cyprus believed (13:12), in Pisidian Antioch "many of the Jews and devout converts to Judaism followed Paul and Barnabas" (13:43), some gentiles in the same city swore allegiance to Jesus (13:48) as the gospel spread "through the whole region" (13:49), in Iconium "a great number of Jews and Greeks believed" (14:1) and in Derbe, their last city in the first mission trip, "they won a large number of disciples" (14:21).

Luke wants us to watch the gospel mission from Jerusalem to Rome. Along the way we have seen gentiles convert, both in Samaria in Acts 8 and in Caesarea in Acts 10. Paul's pattern was to begin in a synagogue where he found his own ethnic group who had natural ties to his scriptures. But synagogues had gentile God-fearers who partly converted to Judaism apart from circumcision. One of the audiences most receptive to the Pauline gospel, and the denial of the necessity of circumcision surely played a role, was gentiles. Smack dab in Pisidian Antioch this is displayed. The Jewish attendees were against Paul so he turned to the gentiles, and the gentiles swarmed to the gospel (13:46–48).

Let's be clear. Conversions are vital to gospel preaching, not so much to establish the success of a preacher or evangelist, but because conversion is what God does. Jesus is the Lord, he wants disciples. The Spirit is at work and wants reception. But there is a sickness at times when it comes to numbers. I remember reading a book some years ago where the major divisions in the book were how many were attending Sunday services. I teach students who at times ask one another "how big is your church?" Sometimes the answer is used to measure a pastor's self-worth. Let's remember this: the average church in the USA is about 70 people (that's before the pandemic). Most people attend small churches. What matters is (1) God's glory and (2) the church's faithfulness to the gospel in both teaching and living.

Conversion in the early church was not just a decision to believe in Jesus, but for Jews it was to absorb their old story with its fulfillment in Jesus, and for gentiles it was to turn from idols and sinful practices to follow Jesus in the purity of love and holiness and righteousness. Not much is said in the Book of Acts beyond the opening evangelistic work but one thing becomes clear from Paul's letters is that discipleship in the way of Jesus became a constant need in the mission churches. We call it today "catechism," which was assigned to the "elders" (14:23). When Paul and Barnabas reversed their path to visit the churches they had planted we are told they were "strengthening the disciples and encouraging them to remain true to the faith" and he revealed to them that persecution may well meet them too (14:21–23). This was catechism.

QUESTIONS FOR REFLECTION AND APPLICATION

1. Think about the commissioning process in your church or denomination for missionaries and ministers. How does it compare with the commissioning of Barnabas and Paul?

2. What is the difference between the content of the gospel and the benefits of the gospel?

3. Look up Acts 12:17; 13:16; 19:33; 21:40; 24:10; 26:1. What do you notice about the gestures of the speakers in these passages?

4. What were the differences between what conversion meant to a Jew and what it meant to a gentile? What did you need to give up and/or take on when you converted?

5. Why does Paul begin his work in most new cities in the synagogue? What could "organic gospeling" look like for you, in your location? Where are you naturally designed to begin witnessing for Jesus?

FOR FURTHER READING

Scot McKnight, Laura Barringer, *A Church called Tov* (Carol Stream: Tyndale Momentum, 2020).

UNITY IN THE MISSION

Acts 15:1–35

[1] *Certain people came down from Judea to Antioch and were teaching the believers: "Unless you are circumcised, according to the custom taught by Moses, you cannot be saved."* [2] *This brought Paul and Barnabas into sharp dispute and debate with them. So Paul and Barnabas were appointed, along with some other believers, to go up to Jerusalem to see the apostles and elders about this question.* [3] *The church sent them on their way, and as they traveled through Phoenicia and Samaria, they told how the Gentiles had been converted. This news made all the believers very glad.*

[4] *When they came to Jerusalem, they were welcomed by the church and the apostles and elders, to whom they reported everything God had done through them.*

[5] *Then some of the believers who belonged to the party of the Pharisees stood up and said, "The Gentiles must be circumcised and required to keep the law of Moses."*

[6] *The apostles and elders met to consider this question.*

[7] *After much discussion, Peter got up and addressed them: "Brothers, you know that some time ago God made a choice among you that the Gentiles might hear from my lips the message of the gospel and believe.* [8] *God, who knows the heart, showed that he*

accepted them by giving the Holy Spirit to them, just as he did to us. [9] He did not discriminate between us and them, for he purified their hearts by faith. [10] Now then, why do you try to test God by putting on the necks of Gentiles a yoke that neither we nor our ancestors have been able to bear? [11] No! We believe it is through the grace of our Lord Jesus that we are saved, just as they are."

[12] The whole assembly became silent as they listened to Barnabas and Paul telling about the signs and wonders God had done among the Gentiles through them.

[13] When they finished, James spoke up. "Brothers," he said, "listen to me. [14] Simon has described to us how God first intervened to choose a people for his name from the Gentiles. [15] The words of the prophets are in agreement with this, as it is written:

> [16] " 'After this I will return
>   and rebuild David's fallen tent.
> Its ruins I will rebuild,
>   and I will restore it,
> [17] that the rest of mankind may seek the Lord,
>   even all the Gentiles who bear my name,
> says the Lord, who does these things'—
> [18] things known from long ago.

[19] "It is my judgment, therefore, that we should not make it difficult for the Gentiles who are turning to God. [20] Instead we should write to them, telling them to abstain from food polluted by idols, from sexual immorality, from the meat of strangled animals and from blood. [21] For the law of Moses has been preached in every city from the earliest times and is read in the synagogues on every Sabbath."

[22] Then the apostles and elders, with the whole church, decided to choose some of their own men and send them to Antioch with Paul and Barnabas. They chose Judas (called Barsabbas) and Silas, men who were leaders among the believers. [23] With them they sent the following letter:

The apostles and elders, your brothers,

To the Gentile believers in Antioch, Syria and Cilicia: Greetings.

24 We have heard that some went out from us without our authorization and disturbed you, troubling your minds by what they said. 25 So we all agreed to choose some men and send them to you with our dear friends Barnabas and Paul—26 men who have risked their lives for the name of our Lord Jesus Christ. 27 Therefore we are sending Judas and Silas to confirm by word of mouth what we are writing. 28 It seemed good to the Holy Spirit and to us not to burden you with anything beyond the following requirements: 29 You are to abstain from food sacrificed to idols, from blood, from the meat of strangled animals and from sexual immorality. You will do well to avoid these things.

Farewell.

30 So the men were sent off and went down to Antioch, where they gathered the church together and delivered the letter. 31 The people read it and were glad for its encouraging message. 32 Judas and Silas, who themselves were prophets, said much to encourage and strengthen the believers. 33 After spending some time there, they were sent off by the believers with the blessing of peace to return to those who had sent them. [34] 35 But Paul and Barnabas remained in Antioch, where they and many others taught and preached the word of the Lord.

Acts 15's congress of the church's leaders works out nothing less than a compromise that preserved unity and prevented a yawning fissure of two different churches, one for gentiles and one for Jews. Unity is easy to propose, difficult to achieve, nearly impossible to maintain. The early church reveals all three dimensions as it seeks to avoid a first century version of segregation, of separate but equal churches. The quest in the early church was for a "fellowship of differents," that is, of people who are not the same but who transcend and celebrate differences by fellowship in Christ (McKnight, *A Fellowship of Differents*).

THE CONTENTION

Some persons, and the text does not say if they are believers or not, have clear enough minds, and deep enough concerns about the mission of Paul and Barnabas, as well as stiff enough commitments to the law of Moses that they choose to travel some 250 miles to go toe-to-toe with the missioners and their sponsoring congregation, the church in Syrian Antioch (15:1). Their belief was that one could not be "saved" unless circumcised. The apostles and elders in Jerusalem will soon say these persons "went out without our authorization" (15:24).

We are looking here at the single most significant point of contention in the first generation of the church: Do gentile believers in Jesus observe the Torah as do the Jewish believers? Their Bible and Paul's stated explicitly that circumcision was the covenant requirement for all, including gentiles, and it was an "everlasting covenant" (Genesis 17:1–14). Furthermore, full converts (proselytes) to Judaism were required to be circumcised, so a clear precedent was already at work. Yet, in neither of the gentile conversion stories told by Luke, the eunuch in Acts 8 and Cornelius in Acts 10, was circumcision required. Think of circumcision as the single act that demonstrated a full commitment. The rite signaled to the Jewish community one's full commitment to Torah observance and that one had crossed the threshold out of paganism into Judaism.

The claim of this traveling group created a "sharp dispute and debate" with Paul and Barnabas (15:2). By the time we have read the entire Book of Acts and all of Paul's letters we will see that gentile Torah observance was a tension point in probably every church in the Pauline mission. We are right to assume that the pattern of opposition to the mission work in the first mission trip was at least in part spurred on by Paul's growing belief in freedom from the Torah for gentile believers.

The decision in Antioch is that the contention has to be resolved, that Antioch was not the place to resolve the issue, and that such an important issue would require a full-scale discussion among the apostles and elders in Jerusalem. The church needed a congress, so they sent Paul and Barnabas to Jerusalem, and on their way they, if I may, barnstormed for the work of God among the gentiles apart from circumcision (15:3). They also gave a full report to the Jerusalem leaders upon arrival.

THE CONGRESS

Some decisions require the presence of prominent experts in the field. Notice that Luke says the Pharisee believers are the ones who leveled the accusation against Paul and Barnabas. Many Christians to this day stereotype them the way H.L. Mencken once stereotyped Puritans: "Puritanism–The haunting fear that someone, somewhere, may be happy." Notice that on trial Paul says he "is" (not "was") a Pharisee (Acts 23:6). Pharisaism and belief in Jesus were compatible for some, including the group lodging these allegations. Instead of here claiming one's salvation was in jeopardy, the accusation is only that gentile converts "must be circumcised and required to keep the law of Moses" (15:5). N.T. Wright's imaginative thinking that they were debating the loyalty of Paul's circle to the covenant is much to the point (Wright, *Paul*, 140). This is what the congress faced, discussed, and resolved. The experts each are given the mic.

First, Peter. He reminds them of his experience of being the first to gospel the gentiles with Cornelius where he and those who turned to Jesus received the Spirit and God "purified their hearts by faith" (15:9), which means without circumcision. Peter pushes even harder against the Pharisee Christian position by stating that none of them had been able to bear the requirements to follow the law of Moses, so why ask the gentile converts to attempt it (15:10). I consider this statement one of the most radical statements one can find in the entire New Testament. Salvation, he tells the congress, is "through the grace of our Lord Jesus" (15:11). His answer then to the Pharisee Christians is "No!"

Second, Barnabas and Paul (notice the order) must have made quite an impression because Luke says "the whole assembly became silent," which is often language used when listening to powerful orators (15:12). In this case, the preeminent troublemakers! They told stories about "signs and wonders God had done among the Gentiles through them" (15:12). Their voice is reduced to one verse.

Third, James, the brother of Jesus and the major leader of the church in Jerusalem. Noticeably, he affirms Simon (Peter), not Barnabas and Paul, whom God used first to gospel the gentiles (15:14). Rhetorically it appears he wants to affirm (1) the gentile mission, (2) Peter as the fountain of that mission, and therefore (3) Paul as simply one who continued that divine initiative. James, too, knows like modern evangelicals that he needs some biblical support, so he appeals to Amos 9:11–12's explicit prediction that in the future God would save gentiles (Acts 15:15–18).

THE COMPROMISE

We must observe the *compromise* James proposes as we also notice that it is James, not Paul or Peter, with the deciding voice. Two sides are in dispute: Paul claims total freedom from the law, and the Pharisee believers claim the necessity of law observance. James proposes (1) to "not make it difficult for the Gentiles who are turning to God" (15:19) and (2) proposes that they be required to observe what gentiles who lived in the land of Israel were to observe. Either James is appealing here to Leviticus 17:8–14, which is built on Genesis 9:4–6, or he is pushing in various ways against idolatry (Gaventa, *Acts*, 221–224). His proposal is then turned into a letter and sent on to Antioch as Jerusalem's decision (15:22–35). His proposal is in some ways quite workable and gives respect both to the Old Testament laws and to the practice of the law in the Land of Israel. He honors his Jewish context while respecting the experience of Peter and the mission theology of Barnabas and Paul. Compromises are often not met with grinning agreements by either side, and one is left to wonder what the locals thought and what Paul would eventually put in place in his mission work. There is more to consider here.

In effect, James, in softening both the Pharisee believer side as well as the Pauline side, has made gentile converts a new category of their own. His compromise degrades the status of gentile converts to partial converts to the Torah. It will have to be left to other study guides in this series to work out how Paul approached this decision, but I will go on record here to say that Paul must have offered a reluctant, or at least a temporary, signature to the decision of the congress. Please read carefully Galatians 2:1–10, where we see Paul's own take of a similar (the same?) public discussion in Jerusalem and where he is far more dismissive of the Pharisee side, and then read 1 Corinthians 9:19–23, where Paul's flexibility in mission comes to the fore. Ask yourself if you think Paul required the Jerusalem congress's decision for his gentile mission churches. We hear not a word of this decision in any letter of Paul's. Furthermore, the Jerusalem church never does seem to get fully on board for the mission of Paul, and perhaps that is indicated in the order of name used in Jerusalem: Barnabas and Paul. Their absence of support for Paul while he is on trial in Caesarea (later in Acts) suggests that they preferred (at least) the James compromise over the Pauline mission stance.

The decision of James is spelled out in detail in the letter sent by the "apostles and elders" (15:23), and this decision is received well in Antioch (15:30–35). Acts 16:4 indicates this decision was also delivered in cities of the first mission trip. Compromises often require further nuancing in the heat of the mission and 1 Corinthians 9:19–23, which we cited above, looks like how Paul worked it out in his mission work. But there's more than this to say. The unity that seems to be the aim of this congress in Jerusalem is not achieved by some theological affirmations of how best to live. No, that unity is a gift of God, not an achievement of human efforts. As the missional theologian John Franke reminds us, "The most significant basis for solidarity in the church is the ongoing presence of Christ and the Holy Spirit in the Christian community" and that unity will not be uniformity but what he calls an "interdependent particularity" (*Missional Theology*, 162, 165). Our unity then is greater than our uniformity.

QUESTIONS FOR REFLECTION AND APPLICATION

1. What was the single most significant point of contention in the early church?

2. Peter, Barnabas and Paul, and James all speak to the council. What are the differences and similarities of their arguments?

3. What is the compromise James suggests? What do you think of his solution?

4. Name the one most important boundary marker in your Christian community. How does your church navigate differences of perspective and practice on this issue?

5. What is the difference between unity and uniformity? Which one does your church value more?

FOR FURTHER READING

John Franke, *Missional Theology: An Introduction* (Grand Rapids: Baker Academic, 2020).
Scot McKnight, *A Fellowship of Differents* (Grand Rapids: Zondervan, 2016).
H.L. Mencken, *A Mencken Chrestomathy* (New York: Alfred A. Knopf, 1949), 624.

PEOPLE IN THE MISSION

Acts 15:36–16:10

36 Some time later Paul said to Barnabas, "Let us go back and visit the believers in all the towns where we preached the word of the Lord and see how they are doing." 37 Barnabas wanted to take John, also called Mark, with them, 38 but Paul did not think it wise to take him, because he had deserted them in Pamphylia and had not continued with them in the work. 39 They had such a sharp disagreement that they parted company. Barnabas took Mark and sailed for Cyprus, 40 but Paul chose Silas and left, commended by the believers to the grace of the Lord. 41 He went through Syria and Cilicia, strengthening the churches.

16:1 Paul came to Derbe and then to Lystra, where a disciple named Timothy lived, whose mother was Jewish and a believer but whose father was a Greek. 2 The believers at Lystra and Iconium spoke well of him. 3 Paul wanted to take him along on the journey, so he circumcised him because of the Jews who lived in that area, for they all knew that his father was a Greek. 4 As they traveled from town to town, they delivered the decisions reached by the apostles and elders in Jerusalem for the people to obey. 5 So the churches were strengthened in the faith and grew daily in numbers.

⁶ Paul and his companions traveled throughout the region of Phrygia and Galatia, having been kept by the Holy Spirit from preaching the word in the province of Asia. ⁷ When they came to the border of Mysia, they tried to enter Bithynia, but the Spirit of Jesus would not allow them to. ⁸ So they passed by Mysia and went down to Troas. ⁹ During the night Paul had a vision of a man of Macedonia standing and begging him, "Come over to Macedonia and help us." ¹⁰ After Paul had seen the vision, we got ready at once to leave for Macedonia, concluding that God had called us to preach the gospel to them.

On one of my social media accounts, I saw someone had listed the top twenty books that had shaped them. I got to wondering and began my own list. But as I was pondering the list the next day on a walk with Kris, another question formed in my head. Not which *books* but which *people* have influenced me the most. That of course begins with parents and siblings and Kris and friends and colleagues, but it led me to ponder people who deeply shaped my career. My German teacher in high school, Herr Kurr, then came my college Bible professor, Joe Crawford, then my two favorite seminary professors, Murray Harris and Grant Osborne, and then I was deeply influenced by James D.G. Dunn, my doctoral supervisor. I am who I am because of these *people* even more than by the books I have read.

People matter, and in this passage we look at several people who are connected to Paul during his second mission trip. They are (1) Barnabas, (2) John Mark, (3) Silas, (4) Timothy, and (5) "a man of Macedonia." It is easy to stereotype, and I don't want to do that, but we can see something true about each of these. One of the sorts of friendships needed reconciliation, another was about working for the gospel together, and the other was used by the Spirit to lead Paul and Silas to a brand new ministry. Relationships shape our mission work.

BARNABAS AND JOHN MARK: RECONCILIATIONS

We have been observing Barnabas, a Levite from the island of Cyprus, who was known from the beginning as a "son of encouragement" (Acts 4:36). It was he who paved the way for the recent convert Saul to be welcomed in Jerusalem (9:27), and who was the lead minister in the early mission work with Saul (11:22–30; 12:25; chapter 13). Barnabas was a fan of John Mark even though John had abandoned the mission, perhaps over law observance of gentile converts (13:13), and Paul must have felt betrayed by Barnabas (a not uncommon experience in relationships). Barnabas pressed Paul to take John Mark on the second mission trip but Paul refused (15:37–38) so the two early missioners, Barnabas and Paul, split the mission (15:39–40). If one reads between the lines at 1 Corinthians 9:6, we can infer Barnabas and Paul reconciled. The same occurs with John Mark. In Colossians 4:10, we read that John Mark, now with Paul, sends greetings, and the same is said in Philemon 24. Later Paul will make it clear that John Mark has been of good help in the mission (2 Timothy 4:11).

Even the best of relationships require some patching up at times because of the "jagged edges of working with people" (Jennings, *Acts*, 150). Paul and Barnabas, Paul and Peter, and Paul and John Mark each had their disagreements. That these relationships are siblings-in-Christ relationships summons them not only to friendship and fellowship but also at times to forgiveness and reconciliation. We dare not idealize the apostle Paul as always right, either. Barnabas appears to have gotten it right about John Mark.

SILAS AND TIMOTHY: NEW CO-WORKERS

I have been teaching, preaching, and writing for almost four decades, and some of Kris' and my best friendships are tied to the ministries I have been given. Whether it is my pastors or my colleagues or my author friends or my students, most of my relationships are what Paul would call "co-workers" in gospel mission. Friendships often emerge out of co-working.

Paul was too hard on John Mark, perhaps, but that does not discount the valuable role Silas, who replaced Barnabas, will play in Paul's mission (Acts 15:40–41). Silas, who is a prophet (Acts 15:32), will accompany Paul on the second mission trip (cf. 15:22, 27, 40; he appears in Acts 16, 17 and 18). Paul calls him by his Latin name, Silvanus, in his letters (1 Thessalonians 1:1; 2 Thessalonians 1:1; 2 Corinthians 1:19), as he is a Roman citizen (Acts 16:37).

On the second trip Paul encounters the young convert Timothy, who, in effect, seems to replace John Mark. Timothy becomes Paul's Associate Apostle, and I would call him Paul's closest friend. He accompanies Paul for the rest of Paul's life. Timothy presents Paul with a challenge to the mission. His father is a gentile, his mother Jewish, which makes him Jewish in that day. But he was not circumcised, which meant he was out of line as a Jew, and therefore some did not accept his Jewish status. Paul had enough tensions with both Jewish believers and non-believers so he regulated his status, having him circumcised (Acts 16:1–3).

A few observations of the many that could be offered about Timothy:

1. Paul seemed to need him (17:15),
2. He cared about Timothy (1 Corinthians 16:10; 2 Timothy 4:9, 21),
3. Paul mentored him (1 Timothy 6:20), and loved him (Philemon 1),
4. He represented Paul at times (Acts 17:14; 19:22; 1 Thessalonians 3:2, 6),
5. He was Paul's closest dialogue partner as *they* taught (Acts 17:4–5) and wrote letters (1 Thessalonians 1:1; Colossians 1:1; Philemon 1; 2 Corinthians 1:1; Romans 16:21; Philippians 1:1).

Timothy gets almost no credit for the contribution he made to Paul's letters even though Paul often includes him as a co-author. Our bad.

The "Man from Macedonia": Spirit-led into a New Ministry

The cohort of missioners covered the area of the first mission and began to look a bit west and north to new territories to preach the gospel about Jesus. The mission's next major step was to enter into what we call Europe or Greece, which in our passage is called Macedonia (Acts 17:6–10). This fits the plan of Acts 1:8 to get to the ends of the earth.

God somehow prevented them from preaching in Asia (16:6) so they journeyed on to "the border of Mysia" where they "tried to enter Bithynia." But again the "Spirit of Jesus would not allow them to" (16:7). Clearly Luke had heard Paul tell this story: they tried and tried but the Lord prevented them so they traveled to the coastal city of Troas where they had a vision of "a man from Macedonia" summoning them to do the gospel mission there. That vision led Paul to conclude that God had prevented them in one area in order to call then to another area (16:10).

QUESTIONS FOR REFLECTION AND APPLICATION

1. Who are the people who have most shaped your life and your mission?

2. Which important relationships have you had to reconcile? How did God help smooth the jagged edges?

3. What are some of the important roles Timothy played in Paul's life? Do you have any long-term co-workers in ministry who are close with you in the same way?

4. Have you ever sensed that God was prohibiting your opportunities for ministry, similar to the way Paul sensed that the Spirit would not let him go to Asia? What did that block ultimately make possible for you?

5. Think about your Christian relationships. Who are the people you most want to co-labor with for the gospel? What concrete steps can you take to deepen those bonds?

FOR FURTHER READING

Scot McKnight, *Pastor Paul*, 31–78.

HOUSEHOLD CONVERSIONS IN THE MISSION

Acts 16:11–40

[11] *From Troas we put out to sea and sailed straight for Samothrace, and the next day we went on to Neapolis.* [12] *From there we traveled to Philippi, a Roman colony and the leading city of that district of Macedonia. And we stayed there several days.*

[13] *On the Sabbath we went outside the city gate to the river, where we expected to find a place of prayer. We sat down and began to speak to the women who had gathered there.* [14] *One of those listening was a woman from the city of Thyatira named Lydia, a dealer in purple cloth. She was a worshiper of God. The Lord opened her heart to respond to Paul's message.* [15] *When she and the members of her household were baptized, she invited us to her home. "If you consider me a believer in the Lord," she said, "come and stay at my house." And she persuaded us.*

[16] *Once when we were going to the place of prayer, we were met by a female slave who had a spirit by which she predicted the future. She earned a great deal of money for her owners by fortune-telling.* [17] *She followed Paul and the rest of us, shouting, "These men are servants of the Most High God, who are telling you the way to be saved."* [18] *She kept this up for many days. Finally Paul became*

so annoyed that he turned around and said to the spirit, "In the name of Jesus Christ I command you to come out of her!" At that moment the spirit left her.

¹⁹ When her owners realized that their hope of making money was gone, they seized Paul and Silas and dragged them into the marketplace to face the authorities. ²⁰ They brought them before the magistrates and said, "These men are Jews, and are throwing our city into an uproar ²¹ by advocating customs unlawful for us Romans to accept or practice."

²² The crowd joined in the attack against Paul and Silas, and the magistrates ordered them to be stripped and beaten with rods. ²³ After they had been severely flogged, they were thrown into prison, and the jailer was commanded to guard them carefully. ²⁴ When he received these orders, he put them in the inner cell and fastened their feet in the stocks.

²⁵ About midnight Paul and Silas were praying and singing hymns to God, and the other prisoners were listening to them. ²⁶ Suddenly there was such a violent earthquake that the foundations of the prison were shaken. At once all the prison doors flew open, and everyone's chains came loose. ²⁷ The jailer woke up, and when he saw the prison doors open, he drew his sword and was about to kill himself because he thought the prisoners had escaped. ²⁸ But Paul shouted, "Don't harm yourself! We are all here!"

²⁹ The jailer called for lights, rushed in and fell trembling before Paul and Silas. ³⁰ He then brought them out and asked, "Sirs, what must I do to be saved?"

³¹ They replied, "Believe in the Lord Jesus, and you will be saved—you and your household." ³² Then they spoke the word of the Lord to him and to all the others in his house. ³³ At that hour of the night the jailer took them and washed their wounds; then immediately he and all his household were baptized. ³⁴ The jailer brought them into his house and set a meal before them; he was filled with joy because he had come to believe in God—he and his whole household.

³⁵ *When it was daylight, the magistrates sent their officers to the jailer with the order: "Release those men."* ³⁶ *The jailer told Paul, "The magistrates have ordered that you and Silas be released. Now you can leave. Go in peace."*

³⁷ *But Paul said to the officers: "They beat us publicly without a trial, even though we are Roman citizens, and threw us into prison. And now do they want to get rid of us quietly? No! Let them come themselves and escort us out."*

³⁸ *The officers reported this to the magistrates, and when they heard that Paul and Silas were Roman citizens, they were alarmed.* ³⁹ *They came to appease them and escorted them from the prison, requesting them to leave the city.* ⁴⁰ *After Paul and Silas came out of the prison, they went to Lydia's house, where they met with the brothers and sisters and encouraged them. Then they left.*

God's mission through redemption in Christ and the power of the Spirit, advanced as it was through humans like Philip, Peter, and Paul, transformed humans from God-resisting to God-receiving. At times these conversions transformed entire households as in Acts 16. Before we take another step, I ask you to sit down for a brief word. People in the ancient world no more "chose" their religion than, to move back a century or so, the Irish chose to be Catholic, Danes chose to be Lutherans, and the Dutch chose to be Reformed. Ancient Romans and Jews were nurtured from birth into a faith, which was as national and ethnic as it was religious and spiritual. God required ancient Israelites to nurture their children into the faith, which is what the Shema (Deuteronomy 6:4–9) revealed. To be Jewish was to be in the covenant.

Household conversion surprised exactly no one in Philippi, a Roman colony on the famous Egnatian Way that connected Rome to Byzantium. If the head of the household, in one case a woman named Lydia and in another case the jailor, was converted to king Jesus, the whole house was as well.

LYDIA'S HOUSEHOLD

God's summons through the man from Macedonia–no one knows who this was, but the guessing is fun–gets Paul and Silas and Luke (notice "we" in our passage) across the Aegean into Macedonia (modern Greece) to the beautiful colony Philippi (16:11–12). Jews often built their houses of prayer, a common term for a synagogue outside the Land of Israel, near water to facilitate their many ritual lustrations, and near that body of water these missioners meet women, one named Lydia (16:13–14). She was from Asia Minor's Thyatira and had a business trading purple cloth. Lynn Cohick observes that this business put her among the elite of Philippi (Cohick, 241). She had sufficient space and resources to house and feed Paul and his companions. Noticeably, she was a one-God-worshiper, which means she was a Godfearer or partial convert to Judaism.

The God who called Paul to Macedonia "opened her heart" to what Paul was teaching (16:14). Her reception of the gospel led to two practices in her life: (1) baptism with her entire household and (2) distribution of her wealth in open table hospitality (16:15; Shiell, *Acts*, 129). Her logic should be forgotten because it too often has been: "If you consider me a believer," or "If you judge me faithful," then "come and stay at my house." I translate, "She urged us." The emphasis here is on her compelling rhetoric. She was, after all, a business dealer. It is very likely, too, that she becomes Paul's benefactor for his time in Philippi, and thus became the bridge to leaders in Philippi (as Barnabas had done for Paul in Jerusalem).

A Jailor's Household

Near the "place of prayer," Paul encountered a "female slave" controlled by some kind of evil spirit, not unlike the nearby oracle of Delphi (Keener, *Acts*, 396–397), by the power of which she offered prophecies for profit (16:16). The power of God at work through Paul exposed her to God's Spirit, prompting her to become an unintended evangelist for Jesus (16:17). Her use of "Most High God" may simply make Paul's God one among many, which Paul then confronts with the one-and-only God. Luke observed Paul's annoyance, which led Paul to exorcise the demon and eliminate the profit (16:18–19), which led to the arrests of Paul and Silas. They were accused of illegal activities.

The men, at least due in part to xenophobia (16:20; Keener, *Acts*, 404–406) as well as economic power being pulled down, are put on public display, no doubt near the forum. Once again Paul's body was physically abused (see too Philippians 1:27–30). The graphics of the description include "stripped" and "beaten with rods" and "severely flogged" (Acts 16:22–23). Prisons embody power, and in this case, power corrupted by toxicity and idolatry. The foundations will be shaken by God, namely, that true power is in God's hands and in his Messiah Jesus. Like Peter (12:4–6), Paul and Silas were under heavy guard. Acts again shows this is God's mission when the earthquake strikes, opens the doors, and unshackles the prisoners (Keener, *Miracles Today*). The jailor in Philippi knew he was cooked, so he prepares to commit suicide, Paul interrupts him with the good news that no one has escaped–and then proceeds to give him the good news about Jesus. But only after the jailor, who had heard Paul and Silas praising God and witnessing to Jesus, asks "What must I do to be saved?" (16:30).

They informed him to believe that Jesus is the Lord–please

pause here long enough to see this as a challenge to Caesar (Rowe)–so he could be saved with his household (16:31), which led to a brief course in the faith (16:32), to washing the wounds of the beaten missioners, to the baptisms of the jailor and his household, and–just as with Lydia–to hospitality. Luke observes the whole household believed in the Lord Jesus (16:33–34).

The authorities wanted Paul and Silas set free. But, Paul says, not without justice. He demands an apology because they were both Roman citizens who never should have been subjected to such treatment without a trial. The authorities give them an apology, lead them to the edge of the city, and ask them to get out of Dodge. Instead Paul and Silas go to Lydia's, say their thank yous and goodbyes and are off to Thessalonica, which is entering into an even more powerful city.

QUESTIONS FOR REFLECTION AND APPLICATION

1. Which of the details about Lydia and her life most stand out to you? Why?

2. What have you observed so far about persecution and opposition to the gospel in Acts?

3. Notice prominent women in Paul's mission. Lydia is the earliest one mentioned: Phoebe (Rom 16:1–2), Priscilla (Rom 16:3–4; Acts 18:2–3, 26), Junia (Rom 16:7), and Nympha (Col 4:15). Notice, too, Eudoia and Syntyche in Philippians 4:2–3. What does God's inclusion of leading women in the mission say to you?

4. Household conversions are not a thing of the past. Many teens convert their parents and their siblings, and many parents nurture their children into the faith. Sometimes a household conversion can be witnessed when we see a family sitting in church together. Was your family involved in your conversion?

5. Lydia and the jailer both respond to the gospel message with household baptisms and then opening their homes in hospitality. Many churches baptize new converts as a mark of conversion, but not as many see hospitality as a sign of conversion. What could you do to incorporate more practices of hospitality into your Christian life?

FOR FURTHER READING

Lynn Cohick, *Women in the World of the Earliest Christians: Illuminating Ancient Ways of Life* (Grand Rapids: BakerAcademic, 2009).

Craig S. Keener, *Miracles Today* (Grand Rapids: BakerAcademic, 2021).

C. Kavin Rowe, *World Upside Down* (New York: Oxford University Press, 2009), 24–27.

LAUNCHING
THE MISSION

Acts 17:1–34

¹ When Paul and his companions had passed through Amphipolis and Apollonia, they came to Thessalonica, where there was a Jewish synagogue. ² As was his custom, Paul went into the synagogue, and on three Sabbath days he reasoned with them from the Scriptures, ³ explaining and proving that the Messiah had to suffer and rise from the dead. "This Jesus I am proclaiming to you is the Messiah," he said. ⁴ Some of the Jews were persuaded and joined Paul and Silas, as did a large number of God-fearing Greeks and quite a few prominent women.

⁵ But other Jews were jealous; so they rounded up some bad characters from the marketplace, formed a mob and started a riot in the city. They rushed to Jason's house in search of Paul and Silas in order to bring them out to the crowd. ⁶ But when they did not find them, they dragged Jason and some other believers before the city officials, shouting: "These men who have caused trouble all over the world have now come here, ⁷ and Jason has welcomed them into his house. They are all defying Caesar's decrees, saying that there is another king, one called Jesus." ⁸ When they heard this, the crowd and the city officials were thrown into turmoil. ⁹ Then they made Jason and the others post bond and let them go.

[10] *As soon as it was night, the believers sent Paul and Silas away to Berea. On arriving there, they went to the Jewish synagogue.* [11] *Now the Berean Jews were of more noble character than those in Thessalonica, for they received the message with great eagerness and examined the Scriptures every day to see if what Paul said was true.* [12] *As a result, many of them believed, as did also a number of prominent Greek women and many Greek men.*

[13] *But when the Jews in Thessalonica learned that Paul was preaching the word of God at Berea, some of them went there too, agitating the crowds and stirring them up.* [14] *The believers immediately sent Paul to the coast, but Silas and Timothy stayed at Berea.* [15] *Those who escorted Paul brought him to Athens and then left with instructions for Silas and Timothy to join him as soon as possible.*

[16] *While Paul was waiting for them in Athens, he was greatly distressed to see that the city was full of idols.* [17] *So he reasoned in the synagogue with both Jews and God-fearing Greeks, as well as in the marketplace day by day with those who happened to be there.* [18] *A group of Epicurean and Stoic philosophers began to debate with him. Some of them asked, "What is this babbler trying to say?" Others remarked, "He seems to be advocating foreign gods." They said this because Paul was preaching the good news about Jesus and the resurrection.* [19] *Then they took him and brought him to a meeting of the Areopagus, where they said to him, "May we know what this new teaching is that you are presenting?* [20] *You are bringing some strange ideas to our ears, and we would like to know what they mean."* [21] *(All the Athenians and the foreigners who lived there spent their time doing nothing but talking about and listening to the latest ideas.)*

[22] *Paul then stood up in the meeting of the Areopagus and said: "People of Athens! I see that in every way you are very religious.* [23] *For as I walked around and looked carefully at your objects of worship, I even found an altar with this inscription: TO AN UNKNOWN GOD. So you are ignorant of the very thing you worship—and this is what I am going to proclaim to you.*

24 The God who made the world and everything in it is the Lord of heaven and earth and does not live in temples built by human hands. 25 And he is not served by human hands, as if he needed anything. Rather, he himself gives everyone life and breath and everything else. 26 From one man he made all the nations, that they should inhabit the whole earth; and he marked out their appointed times in history and the boundaries of their lands. 27 God did this so that they would seek him and perhaps reach out for him and find him, though he is not far from any one of us. 28 'For in him we live and move and have our being.' As some of your own poets have said, 'We are his offspring.' 29 Therefore since we are God's offspring, we should not think that the divine being is like gold or silver or stone—an image made by human design and skill. 30 In the past God overlooked such ignorance, but now he commands all people everywhere to repent. 31 For he has set a day when he will judge the world with justice by the man he has appointed. He has given proof of this to everyone by raising him from the dead.

32 When they heard about the resurrection of the dead, some of them sneered, but others said, "We want to hear you again on this subject." 33 At that, Paul left the Council. 34 Some of the people became followers of Paul and believed. Among them was Dionysius, a member of the Areopagus, also a woman named Damaris, and a number of others.

There is a tendency to think we need to imitate Paul if we want to have Paul's success. Imitation needs reconsideration. In our passage some have said, "Paul's mission concentrated on cities, so we need to begin our mission work in cities." Well, not exactly. Paul *launched* his mission work in synagogues. He did not begin in cities because they were cities–as if he had a city strategy–but in synagogues, which happened to be in cities. Paul launched his churches in the most comfortable setting he knew–Jewish synagogues. There he would find fellow Jews, and Scripture being read and explained, and most importantly he knew he would hear a story about Israel.

If we want to imitate Paul then we would launch ministries precisely where our gifts and that location match. Think about it. If everyone imitates Paul's city missions what would happen to the vast expanse of rural communities in the USA? Or to the sprawling suburbs surrounding those major cities? When some attach the divine plan to city-centrism in mission, as some do in saying we must imitate Paul in launching ministries in cities first, we fail our rural communities as we also fail the divine plan for the gospel to go to everyone. No location is more important than any other. What we need is missioners finding their own sweet spot for launching mission work. Lawyers with lawyers, farmers with farmers, journalists with journalists, teachers with teachers, and neighbors with neighbors.

LAUNCHING MISSION
IN THESSALONICA

Paul and Silas headed straight for the synagogue and, once again, took advantage of the opportunity for visitors to offer a word. His word was "This [had-to-suffer] Jesus I am proclaiming to you is the Messiah" (17:3). He tells them about Jesus. He deliberated, discussed, and debated this for three successive weeks in the Sabbath service (17:2). His explanations convinced some to convert, that is, "some Jews" as well as "a large number" among the "God-fearing Greeks" and "prominent women" (17:4).

To launch a mission in the heart of a synagogue is to court opposition by those who were not convinced. In Thessalonica some of his opponents were zealously against what he was doing so they incited a populist insurrection against Paul and

Silas but they found, not Paul or Silas, but only Jason and other believers in the home. So they dragged them into the public with a hyperbolic accusation that they are turning the world upside down (17:6) and with yet another ironic announcement of the gospel: "They are all defying Caesar's decrees, saying there is another king, one called Jesus" (17:7). The only word that fits this message is "confrontation." Whether direct or not, Jesus-as-Lord means Caesar-is-not (Rowe). The story ends without much resolution. The authorities release Jason and the others and at night they urge Paul and Silas to move on (17:9–10). This experience is reflected as well in Paul and Silas and Timothy's first letter back to the Thessalonians (cf. chps. 1–2).

It is not inevitable in every context but this can be said without wavering. The lordship or kingship of Jesus challenges the human heart to surrender, and many humans don't surrender until their last weapon has been exhausted.

LAUNCHING MISSION IN BEREA

Repeat: straight to the synagogue to launch his mission. Change: instead of a potent opposition that led to being chased from the city, in Berea, Paul's Jewish audience responded differently. They listened to Paul, they surely asked him plenty of questions, but they probed the scriptures to see if Paul's message lined up with the Bible. I have studied Jewish conversions to Jesus as Messiah (McKnight, Ondrey). The average convert requires seven years to reconsider, and consider, and then reconsider some more. They study and ask questions and probe the scriptures, but it takes a long while of intense investigation for a Jewish person to come to the conclusion that Jesus of the Christians is in fact Israel's Messiah. The fundamental challenge, and why it takes so long to convert, is about Jewish identity, about one's tradition and family and community and culture, and about reforming a Messianic Jewish identity with a new tradition, family, community, and culture.

Paul experienced opposition from the Thessalonicans all the way down in Berea (17:13) and once again they sent Paul off to the next location (17:14–15). Noticeably, Silas and Timothy were safe enough to remain in Berea for deeper catechism in the faith. It is not unknown to many that the majority (perhaps 90%) of Jewish converts to Jesus return to their former faith and abandon faith in Jesus. What also can be said is that these conversions are most unlike the gospel many hear today. Jews are not looking for their sins to be forgiven because their high holiday, Yom Kippur, takes care of that. No, they convert to Jesus as the Messiah and only then discover forgiveness in Jesus.

LAUNCHING MISSION IN ATHENS

The Berean leaders escorted Paul all the way to Athens (17:15) and here Paul actually does what is today called city ministry. He was vexed by the idolatries of this once-dominant Athens, the queen of Greek cities with its history of politics and war and academics. Paul launched his mission once again in the synagogue but also in the public marketplace (17:17). He was there long enough to have formed his own tentmaking business, which was also a place for conversation and gospeling the locals. Some Epicurean (a philosophy about happiness and pleasure) and Stoic (a philosophy about harmony with nature and reason) philosophers, the two most common forms of public philosophy at the time, thought Paul was a bit whacky in his gospel "about Jesus and the resurrection" (17:18)[1] so they

---

1. It is possible "the resurrection" is understood by the Athenians as a female goddess, that is, The Resurrection.

invited him to a public lecture at one of Athens' famed legal locations: the Areopagus (17:19–20). In those days, with no TV and only occasional public theater and sports in the offing, one could find regular public speakers traveling through to give speeches in public places. Going to a public speech was 1st Century entertainment!

For the first time in Acts, Paul took his message into the public sphere of intellectual debate, setting the context for public Christian intellectuals. Notice the following elements of this public address which seems to have a "seeker-friendly" tone to it while it shows awareness as well of current philosophies:

First, Paul's driving problem is the idolatry of Athens, that there is one true God, and that God cannot be contained in temples and shrines (17:16, 22–25, 29–30).

Second, he does what he can to make positive connections with his audience. He speaks of their being religious (17:22), of one of their known authors (17:28), and he makes use of their theology ("we are God's offspring": 17:29).

Third, he courageously labels their idolatries and sins. He speaks of their being "ignorant" (17:23, 30) and that their religious practices are wrong (17:24–25, 29).

Fourth, he sets in place bridges from their world to the world of Israel's story completed in Jesus as Messiah when he says "I am going to proclaim to you" what you do not know (17:23), when he speaks of God being invisible and omnipresent and not locked down to one place (17:24–25, 29), when he speaks of the unity of all humans (17:26), and when he says this God can be known by all humans (17:27–28).

Finally, Paul directly states the Athenians are accountable to God, that God will judge all humans, and that the judge is the one who was raised from among the dead (17:31).

We need to appreciate the significance of this location. It's a bit like combining the Supreme Court and the Congress in one location. In that location Paul subordinates explicit identification of Jesus to a more general belief in God. He has created a bridge to further conversation but we are not unfair to wonder if Luke's speech reflects a Paul who did not say enough. Bill Shiell's terse reminder says it all: "The only place we know of where Paul visited but did not establish a church was Athens" (Shiell, *Acts*, 139).

What intrigued the audience was this bit about the resurrection, so Paul later was able to explain himself. Unlike the previous missions with a "large number" (17:4) and "many" (17:12), we learn of only some conversions in Athens, including two named converts. One, an Areopagus member named Dionysius, and another a woman named Damaris, and Luke–ever the recorder of what he has learned–adds "others with them" (17:34, my translation).

Paul's gospel missions were launched not in cities as cities but in synagogues in cities. His interactions with the city authorities are problematic enough to say that Paul was a failure when it came to influencing cities as cities. God's work through Paul (and Silas and Timothy) showed power in his synagogue preaching, the conversations that flowed out of that preaching, and the catechisms of converts that followed.

QUESTIONS FOR REFLECTION AND APPLICATION

1. Paul often took advantage of the chance synagogues offered to visitors to share a message and used it to tell about Jesus. If you were Paul with your own gifts, where would you launch a church?

2. How was the response of the Bereans to Paul's message different from responses he had encountered elsewhere?

3. What are some techniques Paul uses in his sermon at Areopagus?

4. McKnight writes, "Many humans don't surrender until their last weapon has been exhausted." What was the "last weapon" you held onto before surrendering to Jesus?

5. What is your "sweet spot" for mission? Urban, rural, suburban environments, or somewhere else? What can you do to increase your ministry there?

FOR FURTHER READING

Scot McKnight, Hauna Ondrey, *Finding Faith, Losing Faith* (Waco, Texas: Baylor University Press, 2008), 65–122.

C. Kavin Rowe, *World Upside Down* (New York: Oxford, 2009).

GOD'S EPISODES
IN THE MISSION

Acts 18:1–23

[1] After this, Paul left Athens and went to Corinth. [2] There he met a Jew named Aquila, a native of Pontus, who had recently come from Italy with his wife Priscilla, because Claudius had ordered all Jews to leave Rome. Paul went to see them, [3] and because he was a tentmaker as they were, he stayed and worked with them. [4] Every Sabbath he reasoned in the synagogue, trying to persuade Jews and Greeks.

[5] When Silas and Timothy came from Macedonia, Paul devoted himself exclusively to preaching, testifying to the Jews that Jesus was the Messiah. [6] But when they opposed Paul and became abusive, he shook out his clothes in protest and said to them, "Your blood be on your own heads! I am innocent of it. From now on I will go to the Gentiles."

[7] Then Paul left the synagogue and went next door to the house of Titius Justus, a worshiper of God. [8] Crispus, the synagogue leader, and his entire household believed in the Lord; and many of the Corinthians who heard Paul believed and were baptized.

[9] One night the Lord spoke to Paul in a vision: "Do not be afraid; keep on speaking, do not be silent. [10] For I am with you, and no one is going to attack and harm you, because I have many

people in this city." ¹¹ So Paul stayed in Corinth for a year and a half, teaching them the word of God.

¹² While Gallio was proconsul of Achaia, the Jews of Corinth made a united attack on Paul and brought him to the place of judgment. ¹³ "This man," they charged, "is persuading the people to worship God in ways contrary to the law."

¹⁴ Just as Paul was about to speak, Gallio said to them, "If you Jews were making a complaint about some misdemeanor or serious crime, it would be reasonable for me to listen to you. ¹⁵ But since it involves questions about words and names and your own law— settle the matter yourselves. I will not be a judge of such things." ¹⁶ So he drove them off. ¹⁷ Then the crowd there turned on Sosthenes the synagogue leader and beat him in front of the proconsul; and Gallio showed no concern whatever.

¹⁸ Paul stayed on in Corinth for some time. Then he left the brothers and sisters and sailed for Syria, accompanied by Priscilla and Aquila. Before he sailed, he had his hair cut off at Cenchreae because of a vow he had taken. ¹⁹ They arrived at Ephesus, where Paul left Priscilla and Aquila. He himself went into the synagogue and reasoned with the Jews. ²⁰ When they asked him to spend more time with them, he declined. ²¹ But as he left, he promised, "I will come back if it is God's will." Then he set sail from Ephesus. ²² When he landed at Caesarea, he went up to Jerusalem and greeted the church and then went down to Antioch. ²³ After spending some time in Antioch, Paul set out from there and traveled from place to place throughout the region of Galatia and Phrygia, strengthening all the disciples.

Ministry in the mission of God in this world comprises daily activities, sometimes filled with drudgery, as well of episodes of creation and redemption that take us to the heights of joy. Honesty requires that I say more of the former than the latter. We prefer to report the latter. Ministry and parenting mirror one another. Parenting involves love and joy and arguments and missteps and budgets and planning and cooking and hauling kids to sports activities and attending parent-teacher conferences and dusting and cleaning and washing, washing, washing clothes and, well, not a lot of thank yous and affirmations. But if you ask a parent about a child you are likely to hear something like, "She got elected to student council" or "She scored her first goal in the last game." Without the daily routines and activities there is no parenting, but without the episodes life lacks sparkle. There's no promise to think every day will be filled with fun while everything in life improves (Bowler). If it does for you, could you write up your formula in a book so we can all read it?

Daily routines cracked by problems and redemptions filled out the schedule for God's mission with Paul in the second mission trip. In Luke's plan to get us from Jerusalem to Rome, we now pick up the story with the man leaving Athens to arrive in the well-known city of Corinth, where we hear about both daily routines and activities as well as some moments of God's redemption.

DAILY ACTIVITIES IN THE MISSION

Read Acts 18:1–4 for a window opened on the daily life of Paul. It involved travel, which at times meant by boat through some ferocious winds and boat-endangering waves and at other times by foot for miles and miles in the heat and cold (18:1, 18–19, 22–23). It is not far from Athens to Corinth, but by the end of this chapter Paul will be on the road and waves (for months). He mentored, learned from, and worked with others, and in our passage we learn about Aquila and Priscilla, who as Jews were kicked out of Rome by the emperor Claudius in 49AD. Those expelled were the leaders of the troubles, and some say he removed Jewish Christians and their leading non-Christian Jewish opponents. These became some of his closest friends.

They too were tentmakers, which is just as likely to be a term for leather working as it is for making tents from linen (well-known in Tarsus). Elites and teachers despised manual labor; Paul chose to do manual labor to relieve any burden from his house churches and to fund his co-workers. It meant he had tough and strong hands; it meant renting space; it meant hard work in the heat of the day; it meant his shop became a place for conversations and conversions; it meant meeting people in Corinth. His daily life was shaped by weekly Sabbath services where Paul "reasoned in the synagogue," and Luke clarifies that Paul was persuading Jews and Greeks that Jesus was the Messiah and Lord (18:4–5). (The NIV's "trying" is an interpretation.) And he got to concentrate even more on his preaching gifts when Silas and Timothy arrived from Macedonia (18:5), which, once he had been removed from the synagogue to the home of someone named Titius Justus, lasted for 18 months (18:7, 11).

His daily activities also involved, as we have already observed, opposition to God's mission (18:6, 12–17). It sure seems Paul got used to this part of the mission, and he also never failed to see it as co-suffering with Christ himself. What he didn't get used to were the tensions *within the churches* in Corinth. We will see in 1 Corinthians a revelation of problems and in 2 Corinthians 10–13 will be able to cull out a long list of charges made by the Corinthians against Paul himself. His 18 months in that city surely began to percolate into some of these charges. What many of us in our own mission work experience simply adds local color to the common pattern of Paul's own mission: hassles from without and problems from within.

Episodes in the Mission

The grind of daily life forms the person, but redemptive episodes are reported. First, he formed a special relationship with Aquila and Priscilla, and you can find more information in 1 Corinthians 16:19; Romans 16:3–4; 2 Timothy 4:19. They do gospel work as a married couple. That her name precedes his at times either indicates her greater giftedness or her higher social status (cf. Acts 18:18). Relationships sustained the apostle Paul. Second, he experienced abusive power from Jews who opposed his gospel, and Paul rashly uttered a curse on them (18:6; Shiell, *Acts*, 148). Third, the "synagogue leader" and his "entire household" converted to king Jesus (18:8), and Christians have always gloated a bit in the conversion of the well-known. Fourth, God spoke one night in a vision to Paul that he was going to survive the oppositions, which led Paul to stay for a long time in Corinth (18:9–11). The beautiful words God says to Paul, "I am with you," evoke God's abiding presence with the Israelites in the wilderness, in the temple, in God with them in Jesus, and in the Spirit of God (see Pinter, *Acts*, 423–424). And fifth, his Jewish opponents in Corinth "made a united attack" or opposed him "with shared passion," and hauled him before the judgment seat (*bēma* in Greek; which still stands in Corinth today), accusing him of being a lawbreaker (18:13). Gallio, a proconsul in 51AD in Corinth, dismissed their allegations as something they have to settle in-house (18:12–16), but this only led the accusers to turn on Sosthenes, the replacement synagogue leader (18:17) who may well also have been a convert (1 Corinthians 1:1). That Gallio seemed not to care sent a warning up the pole to the believers. Violence at the hands of Rome did not require just cause.

Our ordinary routines in life are pock-marked by pain

and broken relationships. But they are buoyed by moments of God's redemptive work. We often try to control it all, but life's rough edges routinely remind us that ours is to be faithful in the midst of the chaos. Come what may.

QUESTIONS FOR REFLECTION AND APPLICATION

1. In what ways are ministry and the drudgery of daily life similar?

2. What do you notice or learn about Paul's daily life in this lesson?

3. What are some of the key redemptive episodes in this part of Paul's life?

4. How does God's promise to Paul to be with him also encourage you that God will be with you in the ups and downs of life?

5. In what areas of your life do you most need God's presence?

FOR FURTHER READING

Kate Bowler, *Everything Happens for a Reason (And Other Lives I've Loved)* (New York: Random House, 2018).

Kate Bowler, *No Cure for Being Human (And Other Truths I Need to Hear)* (New York: Random House, 2021).

THE HUB OF
THE MISSION

Acts 18:24–19:41

²⁴ *Meanwhile a Jew named Apollos, a native of Alexandria, came to Ephesus. He was a learned man, with a thorough knowledge of the Scriptures.* ²⁵ *He had been instructed in the way of the Lord, and he spoke with great fervor and taught about Jesus accurately, though he knew only the baptism of John.* ²⁶ *He began to speak boldly in the synagogue. When Priscilla and Aquila heard him, they invited him to their home and explained to him the way of God more adequately.* ²⁷ *When Apollos wanted to go to Achaia, the brothers and sisters encouraged him and wrote to the disciples there to welcome him. When he arrived, he was a great help to those who by grace had believed.* ²⁸ *For he vigorously refuted his Jewish opponents in public debate, proving from the Scriptures that Jesus was the Messiah.*

¹⁹:¹ *While Apollos was at Corinth, Paul took the road through the interior and arrived at Ephesus. There he found some disciples* ² *and asked them, "Did you receive the Holy Spirit when you believed?" They answered, "No, we have not even heard that there is a Holy Spirit."* ³ *So Paul asked, "Then what baptism did you receive?" "John's baptism," they replied.* ⁴ *Paul said, "John's baptism was a baptism of repentance. He told the people to believe in the one coming after him, that is, in Jesus."* ⁵ *On hearing this, they*

were baptized in the name of the Lord Jesus. ⁶ *When Paul placed his hands on them, the Holy Spirit came on them, and they spoke in tongues and prophesied.* ⁷ *There were about twelve men in all.*

⁸ *Paul entered the synagogue and spoke boldly there for three months, arguing persuasively about the kingdom of God.* ⁹ *But some of them became obstinate; they refused to believe and publicly maligned the Way. So Paul left them. He took the disciples with him and had discussions daily in the lecture hall of Tyrannus.* ¹⁰ *This went on for two years, so that all the Jews and Greeks who lived in the province of Asia heard the word of the Lord.* ¹¹ *God did extraordinary miracles through Paul,* ¹² *so that even handkerchiefs and aprons that had touched him were taken to the sick, and their illnesses were cured and the evil spirits left them.*

¹³ *Some Jews who went around driving out evil spirits tried to invoke the name of the Lord Jesus over those who were demon-possessed. They would say, "In the name of the Jesus whom Paul preaches, I command you to come out."* ¹⁴ *Seven sons of Sceva, a Jewish chief priest, were doing this.* ¹⁵ *One day the evil spirit answered them, "Jesus I know, and Paul I know about, but who are you?"* ¹⁶ *Then the man who had the evil spirit jumped on them and overpowered them all. He gave them such a beating that they ran out of the house naked and bleeding.* ¹⁷ *When this became known to the Jews and Greeks living in Ephesus, they were all seized with fear, and the name of the Lord Jesus was held in high honor.* ¹⁸ *Many of those who believed now came and openly confessed what they had done.* ¹⁹ *A number who had practiced sorcery brought their scrolls together and burned them publicly. When they calculated the value of the scrolls, the total came to fifty thousand drachmas.* ²⁰ *In this way the word of the Lord spread widely and grew in power.*

²¹ *After all this had happened, Paul decided to go to Jerusalem, passing through Macedonia and Achaia. "After I have been there,"* *he said, "I must visit Rome also."* ²² *He sent two of his helpers, Timothy and Erastus, to Macedonia, while he stayed in the province of Asia a little longer.*

^{23} About that time there arose a great disturbance about the Way. ^{24} A silversmith named Demetrius, who made silver shrines of Artemis, brought in a lot of business for the craftsmen there. ^{25} He called them together, along with the workers in related trades, and said: "You know, my friends, that we receive a good income from this business. ^{26} And you see and hear how this fellow Paul has convinced and led astray large numbers of people here in Ephesus and in practically the whole province of Asia. He says that gods made by human hands are no gods at all. ^{27} There is danger not only that our trade will lose its good name, but also that the temple of the great goddess Artemis will be discredited; and the goddess herself, who is worshiped throughout the province of Asia and the world, will be robbed of her divine majesty." ^{28} When they heard this, they were furious and began shouting: "Great is Artemis of the Ephesians!" ^{29} Soon the whole city was in an uproar. The people seized Gaius and Aristarchus, Paul's traveling companions from Macedonia, and all of them rushed into the theater together. ^{30} Paul wanted to appear before the crowd, but the disciples would not let him. ^{31} Even some of the officials of the province, friends of Paul, sent him a message begging him not to venture into the theater. ^{32} The assembly was in confusion: Some were shouting one thing, some another. Most of the people did not even know why they were there. ^{33} The Jews in the crowd pushed Alexander to the front, and they shouted instructions to him. He motioned for silence in order to make a defense before the people. ^{34} But when they realized he was a Jew, they all shouted in unison for about two hours: "Great is Artemis of the Ephesians!" ^{35} The city clerk quieted the crowd and said: "Fellow Ephesians, doesn't all the world know that the city of Ephesus is the guardian of the temple of the great Artemis and of her image, which fell from heaven? ^{36} Therefore, since these facts are undeniable, you ought to calm down and not do anything rash. ^{37} You have brought these men here, though they have neither robbed temples nor blasphemed our goddess. ^{38} If, then, Demetrius and his fellow *craftsmen have a grievance against anybody, the courts are open and there are proconsuls. They can press charges.* [39] *If there is anything further you want to bring up, it must be settled in a legal assembly.* [40] *As it is, we are in danger of being charged with rioting because of what happened today. In that case we would not be able to account for this commotion, since there is no reason for it."* [41] *After he had said this, he dismissed the assembly.*

The hub of God's mission through Paul (and others) was Ephesus. Cities and synagogues around Ephesus were gospeled by Paul and his companions (cf. Colossians 4:12–13; Revelation 2–3). Paul seemed to have left Ephesus behind when he went to Jerusalem, but that's only because Luke told us about his trip to Jerusalem and then on to Rome, but Rome never became the center of the mission in Acts. Paul planned, according to his letters to Timothy, to return to Ephesus, the hub of his mission. Our tour guide in Turkey always loves to hear this about his beloved country. Ephesus was to the Pauline mission what Grand Rapids is to the Dutch Reformed, Wheaton to evangelicals, Nashville to Southern Baptists, Canterbury to the Anglicans . . . you get the idea. It was the hub of his mission. All his trips now seem to start from there and end there.

Most days for those around Paul must have been "What's-gonna-happen-today-with Paul?" days. Luke gives us three snapshots of God's mission in Ephesus in our passage: (1) Updating conversions, (2) God's amazing power, and (3) the ire of the economic powers. Notice the daily invasion of unanticipated variety in the reality of mission work. There is spiritual formation, there is the mountain top experience of miracles, and there are the crushing fears of intense opposition, all topped off with a surprising defense by the political authorities of Ephesus. Who knew?!

Updating Conversions

Everybody grows in the faith, but the kind of growth we see here can only be seen as updating conversions, however clumsy some might feel with this expression. We find two incidents in Ephesus of converts to Jesus who had not yet been schooled in the fullness of the gospel. These two stories compare with the growth in faith we see in both Mary and Peter in the Gospels. They responded positively to Jesus, but as Jesus' ministry becomes more and more clear, they had to respond to fresh revelations (McKnight, *Turning to Jesus*).

The new guy, a Jew named Apollos (a very common name in Egypt) with an impressive resumé, arrives. He was "learned" in that he had a "thorough knowledge of the Scriptures" (18:24). He was a follower of John the Baptist, who preached repentance and the coming of the Messiah, and we could translate that he was also "zesty in the Spirit" (18:25). Apollos arrived from a mission at work in Alexandria that reflected only the "baptism of John" (18:25). He was a skilled speaker, which was no small compliment in the 1st Century. Like Paul he took advantage of the opportunity to speak about Jesus in the synagogue. Two of Paul's closest missioners, Priscilla and Aquila (note the order again), take him aside to update him on the fuller story of the life of Jesus (18:26). Apollos moves in this passage, I infer, from a Jesus who was a contemporary of John the Baptist to a crucified-and-raised Jesus and a Pentecost faith. His conversion was intensified as his gifts were baptized. Apollos' immediate desire then was full gospel mission work in Achaia, which turns out to be Corinth (not Athens; 19:1), and there he became a noticeable apologist for Jesus *as the Messiah* (18:27–28). The Corinthian concern about Paul's weak speaking skills may derive from comparing him to the strong skills of this apologist from Alexandria.

As Priscilla and Aquila found an Apollos whose gospel faith needed updating, so Paul finds about a dozen men like Apollos but not as far along in the journey. For Paul, reception of the Spirit is the threshold for full conversion (cf. 1 Corinthians 12:13; Romans 8:9). In Ephesus there are "disciples" (19:1) with a faith without the completion of Jesus' life and death and resurrection and Pentecost. These men admit they have never even heard of "a Holy Spirit" and knew only the repentance-baptism of John the Baptist (19:2–3). They were persuaded by Paul's explanations and turn to Jesus, they got baptized and, after Paul laid his hands on them, they received the gift of the Holy Spirit, spoke in tongues and prophesied (19:6).

Conversion isn't a single moment in time even if many have a single life-transforming moment. Most conversions occur over time, and they also unfold throughout one's life as believers learn and deepen their faith. That deepening has moments of intensification. I grew up in a kind of faith that had little to no emphasis on the Holy Spirit, but as a seventeen year old, at a church camp, I learned (for the first time?) about the Holy Spirit. I confessed my sin and asked the Spirit to fill me, I experienced a power I had never known, and from that moment under a large oak tree in the middle of Iowa I was launched into the very thing I'm doing as I type this sentence. That was half a century ago. I had already prayed to receive Christ once and had "rededicated" my life numerous times, but the camp experience updated my conversion.

GOD'S AMAZING POWER

The pattern in the first Pauline mission (Acts 12:25–14:20) is briefed again when Paul arrives for the second time (cf. 18:19) in Ephesus. For three months he "spoke boldly" but this time Luke summarizes his message as "the kingdom of God" (19:8). With his many opportunities to expound the kingdom, Paul explained (1) the God and Lord of the kingdom, (2) the redemption and lordship of the kingdom, (3) the people of the kingdom, (4) the ethic of the kingdom, as well as (5) the ever-expanding territory of the kingdom (McKnight, *Kingdom Conspiracy*). Of course, true to the pattern, the message that Jesus is the king over all does not sit well with some, which forces Paul to withdraw to lecture at "the hall of Tyrannus" for two years. So compelling were Paul's lectures that Luke hyperbolizes only slightly when he says "all the Jews and Greeks . . . in the province of Asia heard the word of the Lord" (19:9–10).

The first sign of God's amazing power then is Paul's preaching. The second was God's miracles done through him, which included handkerchiefs becoming effective in healing and exorcisms (19:11–12).

The third demonstration of God's gospel power is what God does about the Jewish exorcists aping Paul's formula of invoking the "name of the Lord Jesus" (19:13). It backfires when a possessed man jumps on the so-called exorcists. This wondrous act of power turns many to Jesus as the true Lord over the spirits (19:14–20). God's power led to some confessing their sins and turning in their magic potion books to be burned. Luke tells us the value of the books was 50,000 drachmas (19:19). The power of God here enters into the deepest resources of society.

THE IRE OF THE ECONOMIC POWERS

You know the weight of God's power when it impacts the economy with very serious losses. If Jesus is Lord, he is Lord over all, and if over all, he is Lord over the economy. It cost converts the value of the magical potion books, and we read in the next episode in Acts 19 about a lucrative business of making shrines for Artemis that was in danger of bankruptcy because of losses to those finding the gospel. The bucket-list temple of Artemis in Ephesus was one of the world's wonders with its 127 marble columns, some of which were overlaid with gold. Shrines of terra cotta and silver, cheap and expensive, were available in abundance in this city filled with religions and cults. The gospel was cutting into the profits of the producers of small statues.

Demetrius leads the craft guild, admits the compelling power of Paul's gospeling in Ephesus, recognizes that his gospel denies their gods as hollow idols, and then subtly shifts into legitimating his financial concerns by appealing to how this gospel degrades the worship of Artemis. He is not the only person whose pecuniary ambitions are justified by appeal to religion. Every president in the USA has appealed to the masses with affirmations of the Christian faith, and many preachers and church leaders have returned the favor (Redding).

The workers turn into a mob of religionists openly confessing the greatness of their own local religion: "Great is Artemis *of the Ephesians!*" (19:28). The mob seizes two of Paul's companions, Gaius and Aristarchus, and drags then into the theater, which could have been the small theater at the top of the city or the colossal theater off the forum. Paul wants to be "in the room where it happens" but his close friends close the doors on that (19:30–31). Some suggested that a Jew of high respect, Alexander, could speak to the issue, but the mob wanted no part of anyone remotely connected to this Jewish Messiah Jesus to control the story (19:33–34).

Once again a Rome-based political authority, the "city clerk" (19:35), pacifies the crowd by combining his political position with a call to follow the law. Ironically he makes it clear these men have done nothing wrong. They have neither called into question the superiority of Ephesus nor its goddess Artemis so the only legitimate and face-saving approach is to calm down and, if need be, go to court for a ruling (19:35–41).

Sometimes the law favors the Christian and sometimes it does not. This time it did, though only by silencing the mob. Those early Christians learned not to trust the system even if it at times gave them shelter. In the meantime we see the routines of daily life, the downs of opposition and the ups of God's redemptive work. Such is the life of the one on mission.

QUESTIONS FOR REFLECTION AND APPLICATION

1. What part did Ephesus play in God's gentile mission?

2. What does "updating conversions" mean in this lesson, and why is it an important idea?

3. What demonstrations of God's power accompanied Paul's work?

4. How have you seen the gospel disrupt economics as it causes people to tackle the idols in their lives?

5. Has anything crept into your heart as an idol that you might need to confront?

FOR FURTHER READING

Scot McKnight, *Kingdom Conspiracy* (Grand Rapids: Brazos, 2014).

Scot McKnight, *Turning to Jesus* (Louisville, Kent.: Westminster John Knox, 2002), 1–48.

Jonathan D. Redding, *One Nation Under Graham* (Waco, Texas: Baylor University Press, 2021).

TRAVEL IN THE MISSION

Acts 19:1, 21–22; 20:1–16

¹ While Apollos was at Corinth, Paul took the road through the interior and arrived at Ephesus. There he found some disciples

²¹ After all this had happened, Paul decided to go to Jerusalem, passing through Macedonia and Achaia. "After I have been there," he said, "I must visit Rome also." ²² He sent two of his helpers, Timothy and Erastus, to Macedonia, while he stayed in the province of Asia a little longer.

²⁰:¹ When the uproar had ended, Paul sent for the disciples and, after encouraging them, said goodbye and set out for Macedonia. ² He traveled through that area, speaking many words of encouragement to the people, and finally arrived in Greece, ³ where he stayed three months. Because some Jews had plotted against him just as he was about to sail for Syria, he decided to go back through Macedonia. ⁴ He was accompanied by Sopater son of Pyrrhus from Berea, Aristarchus and Secundus from Thessalonica, Gaius from Derbe, Timothy also, and Tychicus and Trophimus from the province of Asia. ⁵ These men went on ahead and waited for us at Troas. ⁶ But we sailed from Philippi after the Festival of Unleavened Bread, and five days later joined the others at Troas, where we stayed seven days.

7 On the first day of the week we came together to break bread. Paul spoke to the people and, because he intended to leave the next day, kept on talking until midnight. 8 There were many lamps in the upstairs room where we were meeting. 9 Seated in a window was a young man named Eutychus, who was sinking into a deep sleep as Paul talked on and on. When he was sound asleep, he fell to the ground from the third story and was picked up dead. 10 Paul went down, threw himself on the young man and put his arms around him. "Don't be alarmed," he said. "He's alive!" 11 Then he went upstairs again and broke bread and ate. After talking until daylight, he left. 12 The people took the young man home alive and were greatly comforted.

13 We went on ahead to the ship and sailed for Assos, where we were going to take Paul aboard. He had made this arrangement because he was going there on foot. 14 When he met us at Assos, we took him aboard and went on to Mitylene. 15 The next day we set sail from there and arrived off Chios. The day after that we crossed over to Samos, and on the following day arrived at Miletus. 16 Paul had decided to sail past Ephesus to avoid spending time in the province of Asia, for he was in a hurry to reach Jerusalem, if possible, by the day of Pentecost.

Estimates vary, but the apostle Paul traveled approximately 10–12,000 miles on mission (see Keener, *Acts*, 332). In the text above I combined two notes about travel from chapter nineteen with the opening to chapter twenty because they tie the travel narrative together. From Corinth by land Paul traveled up the coast of Greece and down Western Asia Minor to Ephesus, with plans to reverse the path on his way to Jerusalem, after which he intended to travel to Rome. He leaves Ephesus for Macedonia in 20:1 to arrive eventually in Greece (Corinth), where he spent three months, during which time he wrote Romans. His plan was to go to Syria (Antioch) and down to Jerusalem by boat, but he caught wind of a plot to kill him, so he traveled by land up Greece and took a boat across to Troas. Then on to Ephesus on his way to Jerusalem.

RISKS IN TRAVEL

Travel entailed many risks. Paul's own words count some of the risks, and I ask you to read this text slowly as your imagination takes you back to the real world of Paul's travels on mission.

1. Three times I was beaten with rods, once I was pelted with stones,
2. three times I was shipwrecked,
3. I spent a night and a day in the open sea,
4. I have been constantly on the move.
5. I have been in danger from rivers,
6. in danger from bandits,
7. in danger from my fellow Jews,
8. in danger from Gentiles;
9. in danger in the city,
10. in danger in the country,
11. in danger at sea;
12. and in danger from false believers.
13. I have labored and toiled and have often gone without sleep;
14. I have known hunger and thirst and have often gone without food;
15. I have been cold and naked (2 Corinthians 11:25–27).

His risks involved persecution wherever he preached the message about Jesus, but also the risks of his mission work involved travel dangers.

Road weariness must have accompanied Paul's life. Ministry during the pandemic has bewildered many in their own mission work. I have heard from pastor friends that as many as 50% of pastors considered resigning during the pandemic. The restless nights of anxiety, the endless complications of technology for the streaming of services, the extra time required just to do ordinary tasks, the back and forth with the CDC and governmental bodies about regulations, the irritations and anger and frustrations and loud words of those who refuse the masks and those who insist on the masks, and behind and under and through it all the absence of bodies in worship services or the presence of only some of those bodies, and the wondering how many have actually "left" haunt our pastors. Paul's weariness was not unlike those in the heat of pandemic ministries.

Travel in Paul's day took lots of time and involved, beside endless delays, learning to find provisions and places to spend overnight. Walkers could cover 20 miles in a day and on a good day boats could cover 100 miles. It is unlikely Paul rode a horse or could afford a chariot. There were measured stops on Roman roads. Mediterranean weather could be brutally hot while winter evenings could be cold. We must reckon as well with the intense dangers of shipwrecks and drownings. Plus, Paul seemed to change his travel plans quite often, as we see in 1 Corinthians 16:1–12, and in our passage, he intends to sail past Ephesus but ends up overnighting (Acts 20:16).

MINISTRY DURING TRAVEL

Travel involved lots of chatting and praying and mentoring. Paul's companions for his trip to Jerusalem are listed here (20:4) though Luke does not mention what mattered intensely to Paul, namely, the collection of funds for the poor saints in Jerusalem (Romans 15:25–28). Nor does Luke care to mention all the trouble Paul had with the Corinthian Christians.

REDEMPTION IN THE TRAVEL

One of the most charming stories told about Paul, a story too unusual not to be true, occurs in Troas on Sunday. The well-known "we" appears in 20:5 and stays with the trip all the way to Jerusalem and then on to Rome. It concerns a man named "Good Luck" (Eutychus) who fell asleep during a seemingly endless back-and-forth dialogue with Paul. The sleeper fell three stories. Everyone was alarmed so they scurried down to find him dead, but when Paul arrives he says his life is in him, but this language might indicate that God was about to work a miracle (Luke 7:14–15; 8:54–55; Acts 9:40; cf. 2 Kings 4:32–37). And God does raise Eutychus. Without missing a beat, they went back to the apartment, ate a meal or partook in eucharist, Paul talked until daybreak, and then left. Travel involves endless accounts of great and small experiences.

QUESTIONS FOR REFLECTION AND APPLICATION

1. When you look at Paul's travel troubles all laid out in the quote from 2 Corinthians, how do you feel? What do you imagine it was like for him to travel 10,000 miles under such conditions?

2. Which details about the cultural context of Paul's travels most stand out to you?

3. Who traveled with Paul on this particular section of his journey?

4. Have you had especially wearying seasons of life or ministry? What sustained you?

5. Has serving God ever taken you traveling? How have your travels troubled you?

WITNESS IN THE MISSION

Acts 20:17–38

¹⁷ From Miletus, Paul sent to Ephesus for the elders of the church.
¹⁸ When they arrived, he said to them:

You know how I lived the whole time I was with you, from the first day I came into the province of Asia. ¹⁹ I served the Lord with great humility and with tears and in the midst of severe testing by the plots of my Jewish opponents. ²⁰ You know that I have not hesitated to preach anything that would be helpful to you but have taught you publicly and from house to house. ²¹ I have declared to both Jews and Greeks that they must turn to God in repentance and have faith in our Lord Jesus.

²² And now, compelled by the Spirit, I am going to Jerusalem, not knowing what will happen to me there. ²³ I only know that in every city the Holy Spirit warns me that prison and hardships are facing me. ²⁴ However, I consider my life worth nothing to me; my only aim is to finish the race and complete the task the Lord Jesus has given me—the task of testifying to the good news of God's grace.

²⁵ Now I know that none of you among whom I have gone about preaching the kingdom will ever see me again. ²⁶ Therefore, I declare to you today that I am innocent of the blood of any of

you. [27] For I have not hesitated to proclaim to you the whole will of God.

[28] Keep watch over yourselves and all the flock of which the Holy Spirit has made you overseers. Be shepherds of the church of God, which he bought with his own blood. [29] I know that after I leave, savage wolves will come in among you and will not spare the flock. [30] Even from your own number men will arise and distort the truth in order to draw away disciples after them. [31] So be on your guard! Remember that for three years I never stopped warning each of you night and day with tears.

[32] Now I commit you to God and to the word of his grace, which can build you up and give you an inheritance among all those who are sanctified. [33] I have not coveted anyone's silver or gold or clothing. [34] You yourselves know that these hands of mine have supplied my own needs and the needs of my companions. [35] In everything I did, I showed you that by this kind of hard work we must help the weak, remembering the words the Lord Jesus himself said: 'It is more blessed to give than to receive.

[36] When Paul had finished speaking, he knelt down with all of them and prayed. [37] They all wept as they embraced him and kissed him. [38] What grieved them most was his statement that they would never see his face again. Then they accompanied him to the ship.

The emotional farewell by Paul given to the elders, overseers, or pastors (20:17, 28) in Ephesus is Paul's witness to God's mission. Paul does not depict himself as a hero even if he affirms his faithfulness in this speech. In fact, in this passage he calls himself a slave of God (20:19: "served" or better yet "slaved"), which was the lowest of all stations in society. In the Bible honest self-affirmations like these by Paul are abundant, however much they discomfort us and make us think of bragging.

A RESILIENT WITNESS

Here's Paul summarizing his faithfulness in Ephesus (20:18–21, 25–27). He was humble, he cried often, he was opposed time and time again, yet he remained faithful. He taught them what they needed in public and made regular pastoral visits to homes. He called all people to turn to the Lord Jesus and God's grace and away from sin (evangelism), and he courageously taught them all that he knew to be true to the gospel (catechism).

Paul was resilient, but resilience is more than hanging on, and in some ways more than what we normally mean by faithfulness. What we see in Paul is a gospel commitment that flexed and adjusted and grew as he learned. We dare not think Paul was perfect; he could be abrasive at times. But he learned, and he grew from his failures.

A READY WITNESS

His resilience formed into a courage to face an inevitable martyrdom (20:22–25). He takes that path because he is "compelled by the Spirit." The Spirit has revealed opposition awaiting him. This readiness to go to Jerusalem where he knows he will experience the stiffest opposition he has seen so far is rooted not only in the Spirit but in his self-denying cruciform way of life: "I consider my life worth nothing to me." And, all that matters is to "complete the task the Lord Jesus has given" to him (20:24). What Jesus said is Paul's motto:

"Whoever wants to be my disciple must deny themselves and take up their cross daily and follow me. For whoever wants to save their life will lose it, but whoever loses their life for me will save it" (Luke 9:23–24).

Maybe we need to ask ourselves more often, "Am I ready to go if God calls?"

Paul turns from witness to his own martyrdom to urge the elders to:

1. maintain their personal spiritual life,
2. to pastor the Christians of Ephesus who have been redeemed by Christ's blood,
3. to watch out for those intent on destroying God's mission,
4. to guard against supposed believers who will "distort the truth" and "draw away disciples after them, and
5. to remember his own example (20:28–31).

All of these are found in the terms Paul uses here for ministries: elders who offer wisdom, overseers who watch and protect the flock well, and pastors who tend to people with loving care.

Paul's readiness to face the ultimate challenge reminds me of Dietrich Bonhoeffer's end. Arrested and interrogated, he was held in constant suspense of what might happen next. Then one day he was removed from his prison cell and taken from one holding cell to another, eventually taken to Flossenbürg where he was executed. An English officer wrote of him that "He was one of the very few persons I have ever met for whom God was real and always near." On a Sunday on the 8th of April, 1945, Bonhoeffer conducted a worship service for the prisoners who were with him in Schönberg. His text that morning was from Isaiah 53:5, which reads "by his wounds we are healed," and from 1 Peter 1:3, which speaks of a "living hope through the resurrection of Jesus from the dead." That officer said, "He had hardly ended his last prayer when the door opened and two civilians entered." Then he "took me aside" to say, "This is the end, but for me it is the beginning of life." A day later, after being taken to Flossenbürg, before removing his prison garb, Bonhoeffer was observed kneeling in prayer. At the gallows, he prayed once again. He was hanged at the order of Hitler on a Monday. (*Life Together*, 13; E. Bethge, *Dietrich Bonhoeffer*, 926–928).

Like Paul, he was read to be a witness in life or death and a pastor to others when it mattered most.

A Relieving Witness

Unlike so many today, Paul was scrupulous about working with his own hands in manual labor so he could both not be a burden to his churches as well as provide for his co-workers and the poor (1 Thessalonians 2:9; 1 Corinthians 4:12; 9:15–18). He relieved others from providing by providing for his circle of workers. He quoted Jesus to finish his talk that day, reminding them that it is more blessed to provide for others, which is what he did from his funds, than to receive (20:32–35). His parting from Ephesus was painful both in saying farewell and especially because Paul had indicated they'd never seen him again (20:36–38).

What Paul wanted them to remember was what he perceived to be the truth of his own life–it was a faithul witness to the redemptive work of God in Christ, and he was chosen by God to participate in God's mission.

Questions for Reflection and Application

1. What are the distinctions given here between evangelism and catechism?

2. How did Paul live out the stern warnings about the difficulty of disciple-life Jesus gave in Luke 9?

3. How does Paul's pastoring till a faithful end compare with Bonhoeffer's similar actions?

4. Dean Pinter, in his *Acts* (p. 468), says Paul's speech "reflects humility and humanity, tears and trials, service and suffering." Find these traits in the passage and mark them. How would you describe Paul's character coming through in this passage?

5. If you had to give an end-of-ministry goodbye speech to beloved co-workers, what would you say to leave them with?

FOR FURTHER READING

Eberhard Bethge, *Dietrich Bonhoeffer: A Biography* (rev. ed.; Minneapolis: Fortress, 2000), 926–928.
Dietrich Bonhoeffer, *Life Together* (trans. John Doberstein; San Francisco: Harper & Row, 1954).

DETERMINATION
IN THE MISSION

Acts 21:1–16

¹ After we had torn ourselves away from them, we put out to sea and sailed straight to Kos. The next day we went to Rhodes and from there to Patara. ² We found a ship crossing over to Phoenicia, went on board and set sail. ³ After sighting Cyprus and passing to the south of it, we sailed on to Syria. We landed at Tyre, where our ship was to unload its cargo. ⁴ We sought out the disciples there and stayed with them seven days. Through the Spirit they urged Paul not to go on to Jerusalem. ⁵ When it was time to leave, we left and continued on our way. All of them, including wives and children, accompanied us out of the city, and there on the beach we knelt to pray. ⁶ After saying goodbye to each other, we went aboard the ship, and they returned home.

⁷ We continued our voyage from Tyre and landed at Ptolemais, where we greeted the brothers and sisters and stayed with them for a day. ⁸ Leaving the next day, we reached Caesarea and stayed at the house of Philip the evangelist, one of the Seven. ⁹ He had four unmarried daughters who prophesied.

¹⁰ After we had been there a number of days, a prophet named Agabus came down from Judea. ¹¹ Coming over to us, he took Paul's belt, tied his own hands and feet with it and said, "The

Holy Spirit says, 'In this way the Jewish leaders in Jerusalem will bind the owner of this belt and will hand him over to the Gentiles.' " ¹² When we heard this, we and the people there pleaded with Paul not to go up to Jerusalem. ¹³ Then Paul answered, "Why are you weeping and breaking my heart? I am ready not only to be bound, but also to die in Jerusalem for the name of the Lord Jesus." ¹⁴ When he would not be dissuaded, we gave up and said, "The Lord's will be done."

¹⁵ After this, we started on our way up to Jerusalem. ¹⁶ Some of the disciples from Caesarea accompanied us and brought us to the home of Mnason, where we were to stay. He was a man from Cyprus and one of the early disciples.

Only in going to Jerusalem will Luke get Paul to Rome (Acts 1:8). It's not a simple travel plan, and they have to shift transportation at times. Willie James Jennings considers Paul and friends as "an order of hitchhikers" (Jennings, *Acts*, 196). The crooked paths he traveled eventually get him to Rome to preach the gospel according to the divine plan.

SPIRIT-INSPIRED PREDICTIONS

There is a noticeable theme at work in our passage, namely, the determination of Paul to go to Jerusalem that is matched by warnings for him not to go because of the intense opposition to Paul:

1. In Tyre. Acts 21:4: "Through the Spirit they urged Paul not to go on to Jerusalem."
2. In Caesarea. Acts 21:10–12: Agabus, a Christian prophet, used a prophetic symbol (cf. Jeremiah 13; 19:1–15; 27:2) and said, "The Holy Spirit says . . . the Jewish leaders . . . will bind" Paul and "hand him

over to the Gentiles." The people there pleaded with
Paul not to go to Jerusalem. (On "bind" compare
Acts 20:22.)

3. They sought to persuade him to change his mind
and simply surrendered his decision to the will of
God (21:14).

The first two warnings are prophetic-inspired words from
the Holy Spirit, and the third a clear window onto the back-
and-forth between Paul and those trying to prevent Paul.

Agabus is mentioned as a prophet but so too are the four
unmarried daughters of Philip (21:9). "Woman" does not
cancel out "prophet" in spite of how the church has oper-
ated for most of its history. The Old Testament knows of
women prophets as well. A prophet is someone who hears
from God to speak to the people of God a message from God.
Philip's daughters did this routinely. I translate 21:9 "This
man's four virgin daughters were prophesying." We must not
forget Priscilla taught Apollos (18:26), Junia was an apostle
(Romans 16:7), and Paul knew of other women prophets (1
Corinthians 11:5; Cohick; McKnight, *Blue Parakeet*).

SPIRIT-INSPIRED DETERMINATIONS

Paul's response is first anticipated in the very words of Agabus
and then restated by Paul. Agabus (cf. Acts 11:28) expressly
connects what will happen to Paul with words Luke had used
before for Jesus' own fate in Jerusalem. (Compare Acts 21:11
with Luke 18:32.) Agabus is saying, "What will happen to
you will be just like Jesus." Paul's response shows his stubborn determination. First, in his certainty of his calling he
deflects their emotional response with "Why are you weeping and breaking my heart?" (21:13). Second, like Polycarp
in the second century, Paul says he's more than willing and

ready not only to get arrested but even to die in Jerusalem. He sees his fate as participating in the fate of Jesus. (Compare Acts 19:21; 20:3, 16 with Luke 9:51, 53; 13:33; 18:31.) Third, no matter how hard they tried, Paul was unpersuadable about what he senses is his calling.

Was Paul inspired by the Spirit with courage, like Jesus, to poke his head into the mouth of the lion, or was he stubborn or even reckless? Luke does not overtly disapprove of Paul's decision unless you want to take the juxtaposition of these two warnings as Luke's way of criticizing his companion Paul. Remember, Luke shaped this book as a narrative from Jerusalem to Rome (Acts 1:8) and by the time the book is done, Luke records Paul preaching the gospel in Rome. This makes me think Luke was on Paul's side. Notice too that his arrest led to a number of opportunities to give his witness before the gentiles, something Luke explicitly makes part of Paul's mission (Acts 9:15–16). Jimmy Dunn put this all into a compact statement when he wrote that "Paul's journey to Jerusalem has the same outcome as that of Jesus–rejected by his people and left to the mercy of the Roman authorities" (Dunn, *Acts*, 280). The Spirit-prompted warnings then are predictions not prohibitions.

Furthermore, many of us have gone face-to-face and even toe-to-toe with some mighty determined fierceness on the part of someone certain about what they knew God wanted them to do. We can learn in these situations to surrender such persons to their convictions while we have our druthers. Discernments of the mind of God, no matter how open we are to them, are not certainties. As Shiell says it, "God's will is not a road map . . . [but] a journey based on the presence of the risen Christ in the believer's life" (Shiell, *Acts*, 181). As he observes, we often don't know the will of God until we can look back on it after time.

The decision was made. Paul headed to Jerusalem, a three

day walk, and found hospitality with Mnason, a Cypriot disciple of Jesus, who was "one of the early disciples" (21:16).

QUESTIONS FOR REFLECTION AND APPLICATION

1. Consider the three warnings given to Paul about going to Jerusalem. Seeing them together, what do you guess about the intensity of his determination, that he could overcome them all?

2. Do you think Paul was stubborn, reckless, or courageous in going to Jerusalem? Why?

3. What do you think Paul knew about what would happen to him in Jerusalem? Do you think God revealed to him what the cost of his obedience would be?

4. Look at the passage again and mark instances of others attempting to prevent Paul from going to Jerusalem.

5. Do you have a sense of a call for your life from God? What are some missions God has given you in line with that call? How would you rate your level of determination to accomplish that call in the face of obstacles?

FOR FURTHER READING

Lynn Cohick, *Women in the World of the Earliest Christians* (Grand Rapids: Baker Academic, 2009). Scot McKnight, *Blue Parakeet* (2d ed.; Grand Rapids: Zondervan, 2018).

ACTS IN THE MISSION

Acts 21:17–36

[17] When we arrived at Jerusalem, the brothers and sisters received us warmly. [18] The next day Paul and the rest of us went to see James, and all the elders were present. [19] Paul greeted them and reported in detail what God had done among the Gentiles through his ministry. [20] When they heard this, they praised God.

Then they said to Paul: "You see, brother, how many thousands of Jews have believed, and all of them are zealous for the law. [21] They have been informed that you teach all the Jews who live among the Gentiles to turn away from Moses, telling them not to circumcise their children or live according to our customs. [22] What shall we do? They will certainly hear that you have come, [23] so do what we tell you. There are four men with us who have made a vow. [24] Take these men, join in their purification rites and pay their expenses, so that they can have their heads shaved. Then everyone will know there is no truth in these reports about you, but that you yourself are living in obedience to the law. [25] As for the Gentile believers, we have written to them our decision that they should abstain from food sacrificed to idols, from blood, from the meat of strangled animals and from sexual immorality." [26] The next day Paul took the men and purified himself along with them. Then he went to the temple to give notice of the date *when the days of purification would end and the offering would be made for each of them.*

27 When the seven days were nearly over, some Jews from the province of Asia saw Paul at the temple. They stirred up the whole crowd and seized him, 28 shouting, "Fellow Israelites, help us! This is the man who teaches everyone everywhere against our people and our law and this place. And besides, he has brought Greeks into the temple and defiled this holy place." 29 (They had previously seen Trophimus the Ephesian in the city with Paul and assumed that Paul had brought him into the temple.) 30 The whole city was aroused, and the people came running from all directions. Seizing Paul, they dragged him from the temple, and immediately the gates were shut. 31 While they were trying to kill him, news reached the commander of the Roman troops that the whole city of Jerusalem was in an uproar. 32 He at once took some officers and soldiers and ran down to the crowd. When the rioters saw the commander and his soldiers, they stopped beating Paul. 33 The commander came up and arrested him and ordered him to be bound with two chains. Then he asked who he was and what he had done. 34 Some in the crowd shouted one thing and some another, and since the commander could not get at the truth because of the uproar, he ordered that Paul be taken into the barracks. 35 When Paul reached the steps, the violence of the mob was so great he had to be carried by the soldiers. 36 The crowd that followed kept shouting, "Get rid of him!"

Acts embody ideas that transcend words, just as music takes words to a higher level. In this passage we see three actions that embody more than words can tell. Actions can be intended for one thing while others interpret them another way. The best of intentions, then, can sometimes backfire.

THE OMISSION

Tension between Paul and the leaders of the church in Jerusalem can be sensed in this passage, and the Jerusalem leaders decide *actions* can make Paul's message and intentions clear. In fact, this tension was roiling the whole time of Paul's mission work though he seems oblivious to it because Luke says nothing of problems brewing in Jerusalem.

However, the act that is *omitted* may be the most glaring fact of all. Paul spent much of his mission raising funds for the poor saints in Jerusalem. Some think it wasn't so much a career-long fundraiser as something he did twice, early and then later in his tours. I suspect fundraising was a career-long practice. Paul saw the *act* of delivering funds from the gentile mission churches as a visible, trumpet-like announcement of his support and respect for Jerusalem and the mother church. For Paul's own accounts, read 1 Corinthians 16:1–4, Romans 15:14–32, and 2 Corinthians 8–9.

Paul had an intense desire to hand over these funds when he got to Jerusalem. Luke says not a word. Or does he? In the first three verses of our passage nothing is said. Perhaps "received us warmly" indicates they accepted the funds. In Acts 24:17, Paul himself said he brought "gifts for the poor" to Jerusalem. Why did Luke say nothing? I suggest the Jerusalem church leaders did not accept the funds because it imperiled their own safety. Paul was well aware of the possibility of their rejection of his gift before he got to Jerusalem (Romans 15:31). Regardless of whether one sees the omission or not, what was so obsessively important to Paul does not merit a direct mention by Luke. Perhaps Paul used the funds to pay for the four men who took a vow (21:24), in which case the leaders in Jerusalem saw it as a way to convince others that Paul was observant of the law. Paul's originally planned act was perhaps shifted by them to another *act* designed to deliver a different message.

Lots of perhapses here because of Luke's omission.

THE COMMISSION

The gospel impacted Jerusalem so much the elders inform Paul that "thousands of Jews have believed," but they add a noteworthy feature of their faith: "all of them are zealous for the law" (21:20). In Jerusalem, Jewish believers not only followed Jesus, but they also observed the Torah. They were hearing that Paul taught *Jews* in the diaspora "to turn away from Moses," which rejection was symbolized in not circumcising and not following rules about food and Sabbath (21:21).

Their recommendation was an *action*. The action was for Paul to fund the Nazirite vows (Numbers 6:1–21) and temple performance of those vows of four men in order to show the Jewish believers and non-believers that Paul was safe. Was this not some kind of division in the church? Was this not something like "separate but equal"? Or are they repeating hyperbole? Did Paul actually encourage Jewish believers *not* to observe Jewish laws? Paul does not respond to these accusations, but 1 Corinthians 9:19–23 was Paul's mission motto, and at times he must have crossed some boundary markers. Gentile believers, the elders repeat, are to follow the guidelines set forth in the Jerusalem Conference (Acts 15:1–29; cf. 21:25). Paul seems to be in a no-win corner of conformity (Jennings, *Acts*, 199–201). Paul was a square peg for their round holes.

Paul complies with their recommendations and registers the vows and the date of their offering to finish off their time of purification (21:26–27). Their *act* intended to say one thing but others aren't convinced. The recommendation of the elders, like many compromises, didn't achieve the result desired. An act intending to communicate one thing (support of the poor saints in Jerusalem or the unity of the church) can be interpreted another way or even totally ignored as hypocrisy. What Paul did caused a great commotion despite his (or the leaders') intention.

THE COMMOTION

Rhetorical exaggeration draws a crowd, whether in Jerusalem in Paul's day or on Twitter in ours. "Jews from Asia," which suggests some Jews from Ephesus, spot Paul in the temple (21:27) and publicly accuse him of the following:

1. He is teaching everywhere against the people,
2. He is against the law,
3. He is against the temple,
4. He violated temple purity by escorting a gentile into the temple, and
5. He has violated this holy place (temple) (21:28).

The accusations are exaggerated and mistaken (cf. Acts 16:3; 18:18; 20:6, 16), though we need to have some sympathy. Most religions have markers that intensely clarify boundaries and even teasing with them can provoke heated reactions. A commotion about Paul ensues over temple purity, violations of temple purity, and there could even be seen some scapegoating of Paul for the tensions at work in Jerusalem over gentile impurities and Roman domination. So intense is the tension that Luke tells us they attempted to kill Paul, who must now be thinking Agabus got it right! The Roman authorities put a halt to the mob scene and save Paul's life. Once again, saved by the Romans in Jerusalem as in Ephesus. As with the mob scene around Jesus, so with Paul in their cries "Away with him!" (cf. Acts 19:35–41; Luke 23:18, 21).

Only two ideas need to be kept in mind: Luke wants to get Paul to Rome and the way to Rome will be full of surprises and tensions, including false allegations and trumped up charges of apostasy. Paul's path was crooked and filled with dangers, but he will get there because God's mission is to get Paul there.

QUESTIONS FOR REFLECTION AND APPLICATION

1. Which theories about the gift for the poor of Jerusalem do you find most compelling?

2. Why do you think the act of paying for the vows didn't have the impact Paul hoped for?

3. Which of the false allegations against Paul do you find most grievous?

4. What boundary markers in your church community can provoke a response this intense?

5. Have you even been misunderstood regarding your intentions? How did you handle the situation?

WITNESSING TO
THE AUTHORITIES
IN THE MISSION

Acts 21:37–22:29

37 As the soldiers were about to take Paul into the barracks, he asked the commander, "May I say something to you?" "Do you speak Greek?" he replied. 38 "Aren't you the Egyptian who started a revolt and led four thousand terrorists out into the wilderness some time ago?"

39 Paul answered, "I am a Jew, from Tarsus in Cilicia, a citizen of no ordinary city. Please let me speak to the people."

40 After receiving the commander's permission, Paul stood on the steps and motioned to the crowd. When they were all silent, he said to them in Aramaic: 22:1 "Brothers and fathers, listen now to my defense." 2 When they heard him speak to them in Aramaic, they became very quiet. Then Paul said:

3 I am a Jew, born in Tarsus of Cilicia, but brought up in this city. I studied under Gamaliel and was thoroughly trained in the law of our ancestors. I was just as zealous for God as any of you are today. 4 I persecuted the followers of this Way to their death, arresting both men and women and throwing them into prison, 5 as the high priest and all the Council can themselves testify. I even obtained letters from them to their associates in Damascus, and went there to bring these people as prisoners to Jerusalem to be punished. [6] About noon as I came near Damascus, suddenly a bright light from heaven flashed around me. [7] I fell to the ground and heard a voice say to me, 'Saul! Saul! Why do you persecute me?'

[8] 'Who are you, Lord?' I asked. 'I am Jesus of Nazareth, whom you are persecuting,' he replied. [9] My companions saw the light, but they did not understand the voice of him who was speaking to me. [10] 'What shall I do, Lord?' I asked. 'Get up,' the Lord said, 'and go into Damascus. There you will be told all that you have been assigned to do.'

[11] 'My companions led me by the hand into Damascus, because the brilliance of the light had blinded me. [12] A man named Ananias came to see me. He was a devout observer of the law and highly respected by all the Jews living there. [13] He stood beside me and said, 'Brother Saul, receive your sight!' And at that very moment I was able to see him. [14] Then he said: 'The God of our ancestors has chosen you to know his will and to see the Righteous One and to hear words from his mouth. [15] You will be his witness to all people of what you have seen and heard. [16] And now what are you waiting for? Get up, be baptized and wash your sins away, calling on his name.'

[17] When I returned to Jerusalem and was praying at the temple, I fell into a trance [18] and saw the Lord speaking to me. 'Quick!' he said. 'Leave Jerusalem immediately, because the people here will not accept your testimony about me.' [19] 'Lord,' I replied, 'these people know that I went from one synagogue to another to imprison and beat those who believe in you. [20] And when the blood of your martyr Stephen was shed, I stood there giving my approval and guarding the clothes of those who were killing him.' [21] Then the Lord said to me, 'Go; I will send you far away to the Gentiles.'

[22] The crowd listened to Paul until he said this. Then they raised their voices and shouted, "Rid the earth of him! He's not fit to live!" [23] As they were shouting and throwing off their cloaks and flinging dust into the air, [24] the commander ordered that Paul be taken into

the barracks. He directed that he be flogged and interrogated in order to find out why the people were shouting at him like this.

²⁵ As they stretched him out to flog him, Paul said to the centurion standing there, "Is it legal for you to flog a Roman citizen who hasn't even been found guilty?" ²⁶ When the centurion heard this, he went to the commander and reported it. "What are you going to do?" he asked. "This man is a Roman citizen." ²⁷ The commander went to Paul and asked, "Tell me, are you a Roman citizen?" "Yes, I am," he answered. ²⁸ Then the commander said, "I had to pay a lot of money for my citizenship." "But I was born a citizen," Paul replied. ²⁹ Those who were about to interrogate him withdrew immediately. The commander himself was alarmed when he realized that he had put Paul, a Roman citizen, in chains.

In the Lukan narrative, the aim is to witness to the gospel about Jesus "to the ends of the earth" (Acts 1:8), and one dimension of the witness was revealed to Ananias when Paul was converted to Jesus and to a new mission from God. In 9:15–16, the Lord revealed to Ananias that Paul "is my chosen instrument to proclaim my name to the Gentiles and their kings and to the people of Israel," and in that witness he would also suffer. Each element of this revelation occurs in the passage we are now considering (cf. 22:15, 21). Paul is called here to "carry" (NIV has "proclaim"), as in a prophetic burden, the "name" to the world. His mission work did that and in our passage he begins his witness to the upper echelon of Rome.

One Way to Tell Your Story

Luke himself described Saul's conversion and commission to the gentiles in Acts 9, but in this passage Paul does the telling, and he will do it again in chapter twenty-six. The accounts remain the same, but new details arise in each new report. In particular, the "Paul's Past" section below is entirely new in Paul's own narrative. There are four elements to Paul's autobiography, which can easily become a framework for anyone's conversion story: one's past, one's encounter, one's commission, and some will have supernatural experiences of revelation as well (see Pinter, *Acts*, 502–506).

Paul's opportunity to tell his story begins with a tribune hauling him into prison, with Paul telling the man he had something to say, the man asking Paul if he could speak Greek though he had confused him with another rebel, and Paul informing the tribune that he was a Jew. He begged the tribune for a chance to address the mob in defense of himself (22:1), which Paul then does by telling his story in Aramaic (a dialect of Hebrew) (21:37–40). The gesture Paul uses, Shiell tells us, would have been the thumb, index and middle fingers extended with the fourth and fifth fingers folded into the palm (Shiell, *Acts*, 187). Roman orators practiced their gestures.

PAUL'S PAST

Paul is defending himself in a form of address called an "apology" or "defense" (22:1), but to do that he doesn't lay out a logical argument. Rather he tells his story. To tell a good story one needs to create tension. Paul does this by describing his past persecution of believers, a zeal he had because of his radical commitment to the purity of people, temple, and law. He begins by creating connection with his Jewish audience in Jerusalem: "I am a Jew" (22:3), born in Tarsus but nurtured in Jerusalem under its leading rabbi, Gamaliel. Furthermore, he was a blueblood when it came to Torah observance in that he zealously followed strict interpretation (22:3). To illustrate his zeal he explains how he opposed the very movement he is now part of when he says, "I persecuted . . . this Way to their death" (NIV adds "followers of"), imprisoning them (22:4) with the permission of Jerusalem's major leaders (22:5).

Step back to see what he has said, namely, that *there is nothing in his past that made him susceptible to becoming a follower of Jesus as Israel's Messiah.* I've heard this narrative a thousand times when people tell their conversion stories. But many grow up under wonderful Christian nurture that makes their conversion, unlike Paul's, more than likely. My grandparents on both sides were Christians, my parents were both Christians, Kris and I are both Christians, and our two children are both Christians.

Not all conversion stories are alike, and neither can we expect two different people to tell someone's story the same way. In fact, the same person might adjust their own story to different audiences.

PAUL'S ENCOUNTER WITH JESUS

That not-all-inevitable-Jesus-following past was shattered when Jesus appeared to him on the road to persecute Christians in Damascus. Paul's account here is nearly identical to what is found in Acts 9:3–9, though in chapter 22 Ananias becomes "a devout observer of the law and highly respected by all the Jews living there" (22:12). Now where are we in Paul's narrative? *The only thing that can explain my conversion to the Way of Jesus is an act of God because I saw things exactly as you did*–he tells them–*before my trip to Damascus where I met Jesus personally.*

A person's encounter with Jesus, sometimes in a sudden life-shattering encounter and other times with gentle nods of the soul over time, turns a personal story from "BC" to "AC" days, from Before Christ to After Christ.

PAUL'S COMMISSION

Of course, not everyone's commission is Paul's (thank God), but in our conversion to Jesus we have a new way of life, a commission to become Christlike and to do what God has gifted us to do. God's mission through Paul begins with Paul knowing God's will (22:14), "to see the Righteous One and to hear words from his mouth" (22:14), and then much more like Acts 9 he is called to "be his witness to all people" (22:15; cf. 9:15–16). The big picture is identical: Paul is called to be a witness to the gentiles, which is the story Acts 13–28 narrates.

PAUL'S REVELATION

Acts 9:29 informed us that, now back in Jerusalem after his conversion, it was learned there was a plot to kill Paul, so the brothers escorted him down to Caesarea where he then traveled back home to Tarsus. When Paul gives his account of that departure from Jerusalem in Acts 22 we hear a different version. He's in the temple, in a trance, and the Lord revealed the plot to kill him. The reason for their plot was they refused his witness to the gospel about Jesus as Messiah (22:17–18). Paul, zealous to gospel his fellow Jews in Jerusalem, negotiates with the Lord by reminding the Lord that these fellow Jews know his zeal for the Torah (22:19–20). Sorry the Lord says, "Go; I will send you far away to the Gentiles" (22:21).

Paul's public witness has two parts. The first part emphasizes that he's safe because he's always been zealous for the Lord and for the Torah. The second part is that his conversion is not some radical nonsense but something that comes from a revelation from God. Which means, to resist the mission of God to the gentiles is to resist God! Here he goes again, putting his audience into a corner for decision.

Like Diaspora, Like Jerusalem

Which is why the totally unconvinced mob explodes in 22:22–23. Their response was nothing Paul hadn't already seen dozens of times in the mission. Any suggestion that Paul's vision, no matter how badly misunderstood by the mob, was a God-given vision that told him to minister to gentiles was absurd. This provoked his audience beyond toleration. The tension is thick, and it dissipates from an unlikely source.

The "commander" (22:24; Greek *chiliarch*, a military post; 23:26 tells us it is Claudius Lysias) orders Paul into the "barracks" of the Antonia fortress where he was to be interrogated under torture (22:24). But the decision by the empire's powers to torture meets a response that removes more tension. Even the Roman powers have to bow to their own laws about the rights of citizenship. Paul asks—and you decide what tone he used in the question, but it's the ultimate trump card—if it is "legal" to torture an untried, uncondemned Roman *citizen* (22:25). The "centurion" stops dead in his tracks and reports Paul's status to the commander who then asked Paul if it's true. Paul affirms his citizenship. A man-game of power and status is now played. The commander, puffy chested, declares how much he paid for his citizenship and Paul one-ups him with, "I was born a citizen" (22:28).

Game, set, match.

The next move will not be to release the man nor will it be to torture Paul but to put him before the Jewish authorities in Jerusalem (22:30–23:10). Paul's precise location in the social hierarchy has become a mystery to everyone: the Romans must treat a citizen well, but he's in trouble with his fellow Jews; his fellow Jews, however, do not accept his mission to gentiles; and all the while Paul makes it clear he's every part the Jew and Roman they are! "Can someone be

Jewish, observant, Roman citizen, and Christian?" was the question on the mind of many. The Romans will leave this discussion, at least for starters, with the Jewish authorities.

No matter how one answers that question, a Lukan reality is at work: Paul is given the opportunity to witness about Jesus every step of the way to Rome.

QUESTIONS FOR REFLECTION AND APPLICATION

1. How does this passage fulfill God's prophetic message about Paul to Ananias back in Luke 9?

2. What does Paul emphasize about himself in telling his own story, and how does it differ from the way Luke tells his story?

3. Why do you think Peter's sermon on Pentecost (Acts 2) was so much more effective than Paul's here in Acts 22?

4. Willie James Jennings writes of Paul's appeal to citizenship: "This is in fact the only kind of citizenship for a disciple of Jesus. It is one that plays the game of the state, working with its identity politics to defeat its use of violence" (Jennings, *Acts*, 206). What are some of your privileges that you can use to defeat the state at its own game?

5. Consider the four elements of Paul's autobiography listed here and use the framework to tell your own story: past, encounter, commission, supernatural experiences.

APOLOGIES AND PROVOCATIONS IN THE MISSION

Acts 22:30–23:11

³⁰ *The commander wanted to find out exactly why Paul was being accused by the Jews. So the next day he released him and ordered the chief priests and all the members of the Sanhedrin to assemble. Then he brought Paul and had him stand before them.*

^{23:1} *Paul looked straight at the Sanhedrin and said, "My brothers, I have fulfilled my duty to God in all good conscience to this day."* ² *At this the high priest Ananias ordered those standing near Paul to strike him on the mouth.* ³ *Then Paul said to him, "God will strike you, you whitewashed wall! You sit there to judge me according to the law, yet you yourself violate the law by commanding that I be struck!"* ⁴ *Those who were standing near Paul said, "How dare you insult God's high priest!"* ⁵ *Paul replied, "Brothers, I did not realize that he was the high priest; for it is written: 'Do not speak evil about the ruler of your people.'"*

⁶ *Then Paul, knowing that some of them were Sadducees and the others Pharisees, called out in the Sanhedrin, "My brothers, I am a Pharisee, descended from Pharisees. I stand on trial because of the hope of the resurrection of the dead."* ⁷ *When he said this, a dispute broke out between the Pharisees and the Sadducees, and*

the assembly was divided. ⁸ (The Sadducees say that there is no resurrection, and that there are neither angels nor spirits, but the Pharisees believe all these things.) ⁹ There was a great uproar, and some of the teachers of the law who were Pharisees stood up and argued vigorously. "We find nothing wrong with this man," they said. "What if a spirit or an angel has spoken to him?" ¹⁰ The dispute became so violent that the commander was afraid Paul would be torn to pieces by them. He ordered the troops to go down and take him away from them by force and bring him into the barracks.

¹¹ The following night the Lord stood near Paul and said, "Take courage! As you have testified about me in Jerusalem, so you must also testify in Rome."

It is difficult to know what to make of our passage. The Roman authority wants Paul to face Jewish authorities in order to clarify the cause of the furor about him (22:30). When he does, Paul calls the high priest a name (23:1–5), only to admit his wrong for doing so, and then he provocatively turns the two parties against one another (23:6–9). And then the Roman commander once again protects Paul from his fellow Jews (23:10). The Lord assures Paul that he will witness to Jesus in Rome (23:11).

There's a time to pacify and a time to provoke. Paul chose the latter.

SOMETIMES YOU HAVE TO APOLOGIZE

Paul was unafraid of the legal authorities in Jerusalem so he "looked straight" at them. They comprised some of the Sanhedrin. He is also unafraid to affirm publicly his "good conscience" in his life as a citizen (23:1) but, because of what he was accused of already in his brief time in Jerusalem, this strikes the high priest as hubris. Paul's response goes too far as he name-calls Ananias, a volatile high priest from 47–58 AD, a "whitewashed wall" and calls him out for violating the law by commanding him to be struck (23:3). When someone informs Paul that the man so name-called is the high priest, Paul confesses by quoting scripture that denounces such behavior (23:4–5).

Truth tellers admit failure. False narratives are not the way of Christ. Paul could have spun the story to emphasize ignorance but instead he pulls from his memory a scripture that denounces his own words (from Exodus 22:28). Christian leaders and pastors, as many of us have witnessed over the last decade, have been caught in sin and, instead of telling the truth on themselves, have blamed and denied and spun the story (McKnight and Barringer, 55–80). Paul provides for them a better way, the way of truth telling. If they don't learn from Paul, they may have to learn from whistleblowers on social media.

SOMETIMES YOU HAVE TO USE YOUR SMARTS

Abruptly Luke opens a curtain to another stage, one with both Pharisees and Sadducees listening to Paul's case. Paul, realizing he's got no chance of a fair hearing, splits the council by aligning himself with one side, the Pharisees. "I am a Pharisee" is not deceit, for Paul's own Torah observance was consistent with Pharisaism. We are prone in too many Christian circles to demean Pharisees as picayune, policing legalists out to make sure everyone toes the line. This is exactly wrong. Yes, Jesus had run-ins with them, not because they were legalistic but because their practice of the Torah was unlike his, which was (no doubt) more liberal. But the

Pharisees were popular with ordinary people, and their goal was to make the law do-able for all. Jesus and Paul's "version" of Judaism was a variant of the Pharisees, not a flat-out opposition of Pharisaism in all ways. Paul steps into this difference and deepens the division by claiming he is being called in for his belief in resurrection of the body, which, as Tom Wright says, "put the cat among the pigeons" (Wright, *Paul*, 358). Belief in the resurrection makes him entirely Jewish and entirely Christian at the same time. The Sadducees pitch a fit over this because, as Luke briefly sketches, they deny resurrection, angels, and spirits, all of which the Pharisees embrace. You can almost hear the clamor.

Paul chose the way of provocation, though in doing so he could not have known how it would turn out. What did turn out was protection and a word of assurance from the Lord. It is wise for us to look back on what has happened in life, even when we did something foolish, to see how the Lord has guided our path to where we are now—in spite of ourselves!

One Step Closer to Rome

When Paul enters into the cultural war between the two major power blocs, the Pharisees favor Paul, and the tumult draws the attention of the Roman authorities. Just as Paul had done near the end of chapter twenty-one. He is led to safety in the "barracks."

The irony thickens: protected by the Romans so Paul can be led down to Caesarea to witness to more Roman authorities so they in turn can send him off to Rome to witness to more Roman authorities, all to fulfill the plan of Luke to get the gospel to the end of the world (Acts 1:8; 28:14–31). Roman protection from Paul's opponents so Paul can get a free trip to Rome intensifies the irony.

QUESTIONS FOR REFLECTION AND APPLICATION

1. This Paul is the same man who wrote, " If it is possible, as far as it depends on you, live at peace with everyone" (Romans 12:18). Why do you think that in this circumstance he chose provocation over peace?

2. How do the Romans function to actually further Paul's gospel mission?

3. Note the nuances of the Pharisees explained here. How did Jesus and Paul both fit and not-fit in with the Pharisees?

4. What can you learn from Paul's example of humility and apology when he realized he was in the wrong?

5. Has anyone's work against you actually served to further God's plans for you? What happened?

FOR FURTHER READING

Scot McKnight, Laura Barringer, *A Church called Tov* (Carol Stream, Ill.: Tyndale Momentum, 2020).

PLOTS AND ESCAPES
IN THE MISSION

Acts 23:12–35

[12] The next morning some Jews formed a conspiracy and bound themselves with an oath not to eat or drink until they had killed Paul. [13] More than forty men were involved in this plot. [14] They went to the chief priests and the elders and said, "We have taken a solemn oath not to eat anything until we have killed Paul. [15] Now then, you and the Sanhedrin petition the commander to bring him before you on the pretext of wanting more accurate information about his case. We are ready to kill him before he gets here."

[16] But when the son of Paul's sister heard of this plot, he went into the barracks and told Paul. [17] Then Paul called one of the centurions and said, "Take this young man to the commander; he has something to tell him." [18] So he took him to the commander. The centurion said, "Paul, the prisoner, sent for me and asked me to bring this young man to you because he has something to tell you." [19] The commander took the young man by the hand, drew him aside and asked, "What is it you want to tell me?" [20] He said: "Some Jews have agreed to ask you to bring Paul before the Sanhedrin tomorrow on the pretext of wanting more accurate information about him. [21] Don't give in to them, because more than forty of them are waiting in ambush for him. They have taken an oath not to eat or drink until

they have killed him. They are ready now, waiting for your consent to their request." ²² *The commander dismissed the young man with this warning: "Don't tell anyone that you have reported this to me."* ²³ *Then he called two of his centurions and ordered them, "Get ready a detachment of two hundred soldiers, seventy horsemen and two hundred spearmen to go to Caesarea at nine tonight.* ²⁴ *Provide horses for Paul so that he may be taken safely to Governor Felix."*

²⁵ *He wrote a letter as follows:*

²⁶ *Claudius Lysias,*
To His Excellency, Governor Felix:

Greetings.
      ²⁷ *This man was seized by the Jews and they were about to kill him, but I came with my troops and rescued him, for I had learned that he is a Roman citizen.* ²⁸ *I wanted to know why they were accusing him, so I brought him to their Sanhedrin.* ²⁹ *I found that the accusation had to do with questions about their law, but there was no charge against him that deserved death or imprisonment.* ³⁰ *When I was informed of a plot to be carried out against the man, I sent him to you at once. I also ordered his accusers to present to you their case against him.*

³¹ *So the soldiers, carrying out their orders, took Paul with them during the night and brought him as far as Antipatris.* ³² *The next day they let the cavalry go on with him, while they returned to the barracks.* ³³ *When the cavalry arrived in Caesarea, they delivered the letter to the governor and handed Paul over to him.* ³⁴ *The governor read the letter and asked what province he was from. Learning that he was from Cilicia,* ³⁵ *he said, "I will hear your case when your accusers get here." Then he ordered that Paul be kept under guard in Herod's palace.*

Closer to the end of his life the apostle Paul will write that "everyone who wants to live a godly life in Christ Jesus *will be persecuted*" (2 Timothy 3:12). Before he had even arrived in Caesarea and watched Agabus perform a prophetic symbol of the apostle's fate in Jerusalem, Paul was convinced of those words he would eventually write. His own experience everywhere proved it. Paul did not take this personally, for he saw opposition to himself as opposition to God and his Messiah Jesus.

Persecution stories are best narrated rather than dissected. Comparing one to another is helpful too, and Paul's experience parallels Jesus' own experience. If we back up just a bit to watch all this scene unfold, we may be struck by a legal system that can become so unjust and corruptible.

OPPOSING THE WORK OF GOD

Opponents of the gospel appropriate various forms for their attacks, from family disappointments and pleading and stonewalling, to neighborhood exclusion, to community condescension and constrictions, to social injustices, to physical harm and imprisonment and torture, and then to murder and martyrdom. There are Christian news cycles designed to report recent persecutions of the church and there are famous books cataloguing one horrific story after another. (Frend; Wikipedia has a lengthy account.)

Not every report of "persecution" is true, for some Christians think every questionable look is opposition to the gospel, every decision to hire someone else persecution, and every legal decision that is against their political party opposes the gospel (while other Christians have fought for the other side). Because persecution is valorized in the church, many want in on the valor for the slightest of reasons.

We need to learn to dignify genuine accounts of persecution, and Paul's is one of those. In this text, the form of persecution gets no further than a plot by Saul-like zealous Jews, perhaps a group called the "sicarii," or nationalistic assassins (21:38), to assassinate him on his trip to Caesarea. Planning such a plot is tantamount to murder and violates Jewish law. The plot was sizable, resolute, and detailed. Forty men went on hunger strike until they killed him. (One doubts they follow through when their plot falls apart.) Once again, in an act of resolute disregard of the law, they conspired with "chief priests and elders" (23:14; cf. Luke 9:22; Acts 4:5, 8, 23) and the "council" to arrange one more meeting with Paul so they could nab him in transit (23:12–15). That the council agreed to terms with them is a profound injustice. The would-be assassins bribed the federal court. The plot is discovered by Paul's nephew (son of Paul's sister who lives in Jerusalem; cf. 22:3), and he informs Paul who then requests the commander to listen to his nephew's account; he listens and decides to protect Paul (23:16–22). Again, a Roman protects Paul while his fellow Jews are willing to break the law in murdering him.

ESCAPING THE OPPOSITION

At times Christians have escaped plots (cf. Acts 9:23–24; 20:3, 19). At times they haven't. I remember being regaled by a story of a denomination president giving an account of his harrowing, narrow escape from an ambush of machine gun fire in an African village. When he was done telling me the story, he pulled out from his desk drawer a brick from the building behind which he hid as the gunfire ricocheted all around him. He was visibly moved telling the story for the umpteenth time.

Paul escapes because the Romans protect him because he's a Roman citizen, and the tensions in Jerusalem are a bit too high. Lysias instructs two centurions to leave Jerusalem at 9 pm with two hundred soldiers, seventy horsemen, and two hundred right-handers (or spearmen)–yikes, all for one guy with forty zealots wanting his death and the customary bandits on many roads–surrounding Paul to escort him to the governor in Caesarea, Felix. About half way they overnighted and returned, with Paul going on to Caesarea. Lysias wrote a letter describing the basics of the situation we have already read in Acts 21:27–23:10. His finding was that the Jews wanted to kill him, but their accusation pertained to the inner workings of their own laws, none of which in this case had to do with capital punishment. He adds a new wrinkle at the end of his letter: "I also ordered his accusers to present to you their case against him" (23:30). The situation in Jerusalem was both so volatile and seemingly incapable of being rendered with justice that he requires the prosecutors to appear before the Roman governor Felix in a safer location. Felix, who ruled from 53–59 AD, receives Paul, reads the letter aloud before Paul, discovers he's from Cilicia, and informs Paul his case will be heard once Paul's accusers make their case before him (23:35). Paul stays in "Herod's palace" in Caesarea (23:35), the ruins of which exist today. I love to stand there peering out into the Mediterranean thinking about what Paul was doing in custody.

Rome may protect here but it cannot be trusted to protect Paul or the gospel.

QUESTIONS FOR REFLECTION AND APPLICATION

1. What are some forms persecution and gospel-opposition can take in our world?

2. What happens to the plot to murder Paul?

3. Paul's sister is referenced here. What does that stir you to imagine about his family and his life before the Damascus road? Do you think Paul's nephew or sister were believers?

4. Have you ever been involved in a church conflict, where different interpretations of the Bible or church polity or life were taken to a court of law? How did that "friendly fire" impact you?

5. The next time you see a church battle brewing, how might you be able to act to work toward unity?

FOR FURTHER READING

W.H.C. Frend, *Martyrdom and Persecution in the Early Church* (New York: Oxford University Press, 1965).
Persecution of Christians at Wikipedia: https://en .wikipedia.org/wiki/Persecution_of_Christians

IN COURT BEFORE ROMAN POWER IN THE MISSION (1)

Acts 24:1–25:12

[1] *Five days later the high priest Ananias went down to Caesarea with some of the elders and a lawyer named Tertullus, and they brought their charges against Paul before the governor.* [2] *When Paul was called in, Tertullus presented his case before Felix:*

We have enjoyed a long period of peace under you, and your foresight has brought about reforms in this nation. [3] *Everywhere and in every way, most excellent Felix, we acknowledge this with profound gratitude.* [4] *But in order not to weary you further, I would request that you be kind enough to hear us briefly.* [5] *We have found this man to be a troublemaker, stirring up riots among the Jews all over the world. He is a ringleader of the Nazarene sect* [6] *and even tried to desecrate the temple; so we seized him.*[7] [8] *By examining him yourself you will be able to learn the truth about all these charges we are bringing against him.*

[9] *The other Jews joined in the accusation, asserting that these things were true.* [10] *When the governor motioned for him to speak, Paul replied:*

I know that for a number of years you have been a judge over this nation; so I gladly make my defense. [11] *You can easily verify* that no more than twelve days ago I went up to Jerusalem to worship. [12] My accusers did not find me arguing with anyone at the temple, or stirring up a crowd in the synagogues or anywhere else in the city. [13] And they cannot prove to you the charges they are now making against me. [14] However, I admit that I worship the God of our ancestors as a follower of the Way, which they call a sect. I believe everything that is in accordance with the Law and that is written in the Prophets, [15] and I have the same hope in God as these men themselves have, that there will be a resurrection of both the righteous and the wicked. [16] So I strive always to keep my conscience clear before God and man. [17] After an absence of several years, I came to Jerusalem to bring my people gifts for the poor and to present offerings. [18] I was ceremonially clean when they found me in the temple courts doing this. There was no crowd with me, nor was I involved in any disturbance. [19] But there are some Jews from the province of Asia, who ought to be here before you and bring charges if they have anything against me. [20] Or these who are here should state what crime they found in me when I stood before the Sanhedrin—[21] unless it was this one thing I shouted as I stood in their presence: "It is concerning the resurrection of the dead that I am on trial before you today."

[22] Then Felix, who was well acquainted with the Way, adjourned the proceedings.

"When Lysias the commander comes," he said, "I will decide your case."

[23] He ordered the centurion to keep Paul under guard but to give him some freedom and permit his friends to take care of his needs. [24] Several days later Felix came with his wife Drusilla, who was Jewish. He sent for Paul and listened to him as he spoke about faith in Christ Jesus. [25] As Paul talked about righteousness, self-control and the judgment to come, Felix was afraid and said, "That's enough for now! You may leave. When I find it convenient, I will send for you." [26] At the same time he was hoping that Paul would offer him a bribe, so he sent for him frequently and talked with him.

²⁷ When two years had passed, Felix was succeeded by Porcius Festus, but because Felix wanted to grant a favor to the Jews, he left Paul in prison.

²⁵:¹ Three days after arriving in the province, Festus went up from Caesarea to Jerusalem, ² where the chief priests and the Jewish leaders appeared before him and presented the charges against Paul. ³ They requested Festus, as a favor to them, to have Paul transferred to Jerusalem, for they were preparing an ambush to kill him along the way. ⁴ Festus answered, "Paul is being held at Caesarea, and I myself am going there soon. ⁵ Let some of your leaders come with me, and if the man has done anything wrong, they can press charges against him there."

⁶ After spending eight or ten days with them, Festus went down to Caesarea. The next day he convened the court and ordered that Paul be brought before him. ⁷ When Paul came in, the Jews who had come down from Jerusalem stood around him. They brought many serious charges against him, but they could not prove them.

⁸ Then Paul made his defense:

I have done nothing wrong against the Jewish law or against the temple or against Caesar.

⁹ Festus, wishing to do the Jews a favor, said to Paul,

Are you willing to go up to Jerusalem and stand trial before me there on these charges?

¹⁰ Paul answered:

I am now standing before Caesar's court, where I ought to be tried. I have not done any wrong to the Jews, as you yourself know very well. ¹¹ If, however, I am guilty of doing anything deserving death, I do not refuse to die. But if the charges brought against me by these Jews are not true, no one has the right to hand me over to them. I appeal to Caesar!

¹² After Festus had conferred with his council, he declared:

You have appealed to Caesar. To Caesar you will go!

Proper trials involve legal accusations made by prosecutors and legal defense made by the defense lawyers. In our two passages, Paul appears before Felix (57–59 AD) then Festus (59–60 AD). In each case, we catch the rudiments of official hearings, and they are quite unlike the commotion and chaos experienced in the previous chapters when Paul was rescued from a mob by a Roman commander, when he appeared before the council, and when he escaped the plot to assassinate him. Readers need to remember that the "Jews" of these scenes are not *all* Jews but instead a very small group of zealous patriots who, as Paul himself was, saw the messianic movement around Jesus and Paul to be a very serious threat to their way of life.

Two Sides to Every Story

We may be more than ready to side with Paul. I know I am. But hearing the prosecution's charges is not only required on the part of anyone who cares about justice, but it's also important for anyone who wants to minister to people on opposing sides. Their charges, lodged by the lawyer Tertullus against Paul (reformatted from 24:5–6 as an outline), don't take much imagination to rethink how each of these points would have been expounded by the speakers:

1. We have found this man to be a troublemaker, stirring up riots among the Jews all over the world.
2. He is a ringleader of the Nazarene sect.
3. He even tried to desecrate the temple.

I think they are mostly right (from their perspective). Everywhere Paul went on mission, as we have seen time and time again, turbulence emerged and sometimes with a furor. And in their favor, making someone a troublemaker, a disturber of the peace as we might say, leads the charges into clear violation of the way of the empire at a time when turbulence is on the rise in Judea. Yes, too, he was a "ringleader" of what they call the "Nazarene sect," a reference to Jesus of Nazareth. But, no, he didn't even try to "desecrate the temple." The charge was false that he ushered a gentile beyond the wall that demarcated the Jewish from the gentile areas of the temple. Again, temple disturbance would have been a well-known public offense. By exaggerating something (cf. 21:29) or making something up the prosecution team diminishes the truthfulness of their case and gives to Paul an opening for a serious challenge.

Felix and his team were required to listen carefully to these charges, to give Paul ample time to defend himself, and then to render a judgment. Luke at least permits us to hear a precis of what occurred in this trial. Paul's side now. Like the prosecutors, he strokes the ego of Felix. Paul's defense includes:

1. What happened is recent enough that Felix can check Paul's claims.
2. He was not arguing with anyone at the temple.
3. He was not stirring up the crowds in synagogue or in the city.
4. They have no proof.

Paul now goes on the offense, framing his next words as a confession of sort, and uses his opportunity to establish that he's a good Jew:

1. He worships the God of Israel.
2. He does so "as a follower of the Way."

3. Their calling it a "sect" is inaccurate.
4. He trusts the Law and the Prophets.
5. He believes in the resurrection of "both the righteous and the wicked."
6. He tries to keep his conscience clear of offenses.
7. He brought gifts "for the poor" to temple.
8. He did so in a state of purity.

Back to a defense:

1. Again, he was not with a crowd and didn't create a disturbance.
2. He contends the ones who ought to be present are from Ephesus and not some orator-lawyer.
3. He contends Tertullus and buddies need to state the crime against Roman law he has broken.
4. If it's about the resurrection–he's gospeling–then they could say so. (He knows this is a frivolous lawsuit for Romans and a respectable claim for Paul as one of the Pharisees.)

The governor, now informed of the Way of Jesus, decides as many judges have done to wait for Lysias the commander to arrive before he can render a judgment. Paul is to be kept under guard but with access to his own people (not "friends" as in the NIV)(24:23).

An interesting cameo appearance occurs with Felix's wife, Drusilla, who is Jewish and the youngest and now twice-married daughter of Herod Agrippa I (12:20–23). Paul is requested to appear before them. Which Paul does, and it's no surprise that he gospels them: "he spoke about faith in Christ Jesus" (24:24). He expounds teachings that go back and forth between Judaism and the Roman world, namely, "righteousness, self-control and the judgment to come."

Evidently his teachings, perhaps especially the self-control part but perhaps the judgment theme, penetrated the conscience of Felix so he dismissed Paul (24:25).

That dismissal entailed a hope by Felix, stuck as he was in "empire politics" (Jennings, *Acts*, 217). Awaiting an NDA-like buyout wasted time (24:26). So Paul sat in custody in Caesarea Maritima for two years where prisoners have many times learned to do something when nothing was happening. Just as Nelson Mandela or Martin Luther King Jr. wrote what they did while in prison when a so-called "nothing was happening" was happening. What Paul did not do was give in to the way of Felix and the empire. Felix drags his feet as a favor to his zealous opponents until the governor changed. Leadership transitioned from Felix, upon his recall, to a more honest and just Festus (24:27). Which meant another court scene not unlike the previous one.

ROUND AND ROUND

Justice for a marginalized Jew like Paul does not take direct steps to the court and back home. Instead, his case can be delayed and postponed and interrupted. Paul has made his case; the previous governor feared what would happen in Jerusalem if he found in favor of Paul. He knows Paul is in the right, but the governor is afraid of rendering that judgment. So he waits and passes the buck to the next governor, Porcius Festus.

To undo bad relations and to open up good relations with Jerusalem, Festus goes up to Jerusalem right away where once again accusations of illegal activity are lodged against Paul. The authorities in Jerusalem ask for Paul to be escorted back to Jerusalem for a proper trial in their courts, all the while knowing the assassins (who evidently had not yet died!) were ready. As if a broken record, once again it is the Roman leader who protects Paul from the illegal activity of the assassins. So Festus instructs his accusers to come down to the palace and lodge their accusations before his court.

Again, Paul appears before a Roman court. Luke tells us those zealous Jews (not from Ephesus, remember) lodge their accusations but nothing sticks. Paul's defense is summarized quickly: "I have done nothing wrong against the Jewish law or against the temple or against Caesar" (25:8). All over again, round and round we go. Festus asks Paul the question Paul must have anticipated and for which he had a trump card of a response. The question:

Are you willing to go up to Jerusalem and stand trial before me there on these charges?

Paul's ready response and defense is that that the case has been shifted from Jerusalem's council to a Roman court in Caesarea so there is no reason to back up and move downward in the chain of power. So, he says:

1. I am now standing before Caesar's court, where I ought to be tried.
2. I have not done any wrong to the Jews, as you yourself know very well.
3. If, however, I am guilty of doing anything deserving death, I do not refuse to die.
4. But if the charges brought against me by these Jews are not true, no one has the right to hand me over to them.
5. (Maybe he's thinking now that there is only one way for me to get to Rome to witness about Jesus to the highest level, to the emperor of Rome.)
6. I appeal to Caesar!

Hashtag Boom! If Paul's appeal to his citizenship showstopped the chaos in the temple courts, his appeal as a citizen to be tried before Nero is the ultimate show-stopper. For his trial, Paul chooses Rome over Jerusalem, which says more than we may like to hear.

Luke's writing mission is to get the mission of God to the ends of the earth (Acts 1:8). Once again, it is mapped on crooked roads and over windy waters, but he's now got the final piece of the plan to get the apostle Paul to the middle of the world where the gospel can spread.

Nero's court.

QUESTIONS FOR REFLECTION AND APPLICATION

1. Do you see any "zealous patriots" in the church today who seem to be opposing the work of Jesus because it threatens their way of life? Who are those groups, and what are their contentions?

2. Does seeing the "prosecution" and "defense" laid out here in a format more similar to our modern trials give you insight into the scene? What do you notice?

3. What do you make of the total absence of Jewish believers from Jerusalem attending to Paul?

4. Do you think Paul should have appealed to Caesar? Could he have appealed to be heard in Caesarea but not Jerusalem? What would have happened if he had appealed only to Festus to hear his case?

5. How does following the injustice and delays in the trial of Paul increase your empathy for unjustly imprisoned people today? What are some steps you can take to learn more about the injustice in criminal justice systems?

IN COURT BEFORE ROMAN POWER IN THE MISSION (2)

Acts 25:13–26:32

[13] *A few days later King Agrippa and Bernice arrived at Caesarea to pay their respects to Festus.* [14] *Since they were spending many days there, Festus discussed Paul's case with the king. He said: "There is a man here whom Felix left as a prisoner.* [15] *When I went to Jerusalem, the chief priests and the elders of the Jews brought charges against him and asked that he be condemned.* [16] *I told them that it is not the Roman custom to hand over anyone before they have faced their accusers and have had an opportunity to defend themselves against the charges.* [17] *When they came here with me, I did not delay the case, but convened the court the next day and ordered the man to be brought in.* [18] *When his accusers got up to speak, they did not charge him with any of the crimes I had expected.* [19] *Instead, they had some points of dispute with him about their own religion and about a dead man named Jesus who Paul claimed was alive.* [20] *I was at a loss how to investigate such matters; so I asked if he would be willing to go to Jerusalem and stand trial there on these charges.* [21] *But when Paul made his appeal to be held over for the Emperor's decision, I ordered him held until I could send him to Caesar.*

²² Then Agrippa said to Festus, "I would like to hear this man myself." He replied, "Tomorrow you will hear him." ²³ The next day Agrippa and Bernice came with great pomp and entered the audience room with the high-ranking military officers and the prominent men of the city. At the command of Festus, Paul was brought in. ²⁴ Festus said: "King Agrippa, and all who are present with us, you see this man! The whole Jewish community has petitioned me about him in Jerusalem and here in Caesarea, shouting that he ought not to live any longer. ²⁵ I found he had done nothing deserving of death, but because he made his appeal to the Emperor I decided to send him to Rome. ²⁶ But I have nothing definite to write to His Majesty about him. Therefore I have brought him before all of you, and especially before you, King Agrippa, so that as a result of this investigation I may have something to write. ²⁷ For I think it is unreasonable to send a prisoner on to Rome without specifying the charges against him."

²⁶:¹ Then Agrippa said to Paul, "You have permission to speak for yourself."

So Paul motioned with his hand and began his defense:

² King Agrippa, I consider myself fortunate to stand before you today as I make my defense against all the accusations of the Jews, ³ and especially so because you are well acquainted with all the Jewish customs and controversies. Therefore, I beg you to listen to me patiently. ⁴ The Jewish people all know the way I have lived ever since I was a child, from the beginning of my life in my own country, and also in Jerusalem. ⁵ They have known me for a long time and can testify, if they are willing, that I conformed to the strictest sect of our religion, living as a Pharisee. ⁶ And now it is because of my hope in what God has promised our ancestors that I am on trial today. ⁷ This is the promise our twelve tribes are hoping to see fulfilled as they earnestly serve God day and night. King Agrippa, it is because of this hope that these Jews are accusing me. ⁸ Why should any of you consider it incredible that God raises the dead? ⁹ I too was convinced that I ought to do all that was possible

to oppose the name of Jesus of Nazareth. [10] And that is just what I did in Jerusalem. On the authority of the chief priests I put many of the Lord's people in prison, and when they were put to death, I cast my vote against them. [11] Many a time I went from one synagogue to another to have them punished, and I tried to force them to blaspheme. I was so obsessed with persecuting them that I even hunted them down in foreign cities. [12] On one of these journeys I was going to Damascus with the authority and commission of the chief priests. [13] About noon, King Agrippa, as I was on the road, I saw a light from heaven, brighter than the sun, blazing around me and my companions. [14] We all fell to the ground, and I heard a voice saying to me in Aramaic, 'Saul, Saul, why do you persecute me? It is hard for you to kick against the goads.' [15] Then I asked, 'Who are you, Lord?' 'I am Jesus, whom you are persecuting,' the Lord replied. [16] 'Now get up and stand on your feet. I have appeared to you to appoint you as a servant and as a witness of what you have seen and will see of me. [17] I will rescue you from your own people and from the Gentiles. I am sending you to them [18] to open their eyes and turn them from darkness to light, and from the power of Satan to God, so that they may receive forgiveness of sins and a place among those who are sanctified by faith in me.'

[19] So then, King Agrippa, I was not disobedient to the vision from heaven. [20] First to those in Damascus, then to those in Jerusalem and in all Judea, and then to the Gentiles, I preached that they should repent and turn to God and demonstrate their repentance by their deeds. [21] That is why some Jews seized me in the temple courts and tried to kill me. [22] But God has helped me to this very day; so I stand here and testify to small and great alike. I am saying nothing beyond what the prophets and Moses said would happen—[23] that the Messiah would suffer and, as the first to rise from the dead, would bring the message of light to his own people and to the Gentiles.

[24] At this point Festus interrupted Paul's defense. "You are out of your mind, Paul!" he shouted. "Your great learning is driving you insane."

[25] "I am not insane, most excellent Festus," Paul replied. "What I am saying is true and reasonable. [26] The king is familiar with these things, and I can speak freely to him. I am convinced that none of this has escaped his notice, because it was not done in a corner. [27] King Agrippa, do you believe the prophets? I know you do."

[28] Then Agrippa said to Paul, "Do you think that in such a short time you can persuade me to be a Christian?"

[29] Paul replied, "Short time or long—I pray to God that not only you but all who are listening to me today may become what I am, except for these chains."

[30] The king rose, and with him the governor and Bernice and those sitting with them. [31] After they left the room, they began saying to one another, "This man is not doing anything that deserves death or imprisonment."

[32] Agrippa said to Festus, "This man could have been set free if he had not appealed to Caesar."

Agrippa concludes Paul could have been set free had he not appealed to Nero as his judge. Doesn't that set your mind to wondering what would have happened to Paul had he been released by Agrippa, or even by Festus before Agrippa? It does mine. Thinking like that, which is called "counterfactual" thinking, is fun but does not take us to the real world that actually occurred. Paul will be sent to Rome to appear before Nero, and to our disadvantage, Luke does not tell that story or its aftermath, though some think Paul was beheaded by Nero while others think he was released and then eventually re-arrested and martyred. Either way, Luke accomplishes his mission of getting the gospel to Rome. In our passage, he creates suspense by slowing down the narrative in order to get his readers and hearers to anticipate a final decision on the fate of Paul. Read this passage as the climactic scene of Acts 21–26, this one before a full gallery of notables.

Real world mission work occurs while others are making decisions about the people God has chosen for that mission work. Here Paul will appear before Herod Agrippa II, whose palace was in Caesarea Philippi (not Caesarea Maritima where he hears about Paul) and who ruled over various areas for up to fifty years. Paul's fate is determined by the decisions of Felix, Festus, and Agrippa II. His life is in the hands of others. Ironically, being in the hands of others turns Paul into a witness to yet another Roman authority.

DECISIONS IN THE HANDS OF OTHERS

Festus, wise to consult with Agrippa because of his knowledge of the Jewish laws, explains what has already been reported in the previous episodes. His judgment was that the accusations against Paul were not what he had expected but were more about Judaism's proper beliefs and about "a dead man named Jesus who Paul claimed was alive" (25:19). Festus explained that Paul appealed to Caesar. Intrigued, Agrippa says he'd like to "hear this man myself" (25:22). Our passage then is a hearing, not a trial.

We may be tempted to read these scenes from Acts 21:27 on in the comfort of our own homes where we are more or less in control of our own lives. The imprisoned have no control, and there is often no requirement to keep them informed of any news or decisions about their case. When I read the story about Nelson Mandela, *The Long Walk to Freedom*, I was struck both by his total ignorance of all that was occurring and by the control the authorities had of what he learned (and didn't learn). Even in our world, when lawyers can negotiate for us with the authorities, there is much the imprisoned don't know because the authorities make decisions behind closed doors. The imprisoned have lost control.

In such situations the imprisoned are driven to make sense of life on their own, and they often turn to prayer, to reading, to as much outside communication as is permitted, and especially to imagination of justice when they are set free. Think of Gandhi, Dietrich Bonhoeffer, Solzhenitsyn, and Martin Luther King Jr.—all in prison formulating ideas and plots that have reshaped our world.

Stories in the Hands of Others

I know numerous women abused by Christian leaders, pastors, and authorities. Most of them have been asked and even required to tell their story many times. Sometimes to poker-faced and seemingly unbelieving "listeners" sitting around a table. Sometimes to people who empathize in tears. Nearly every person who has told me such stories have said two things. First, that each time their story was told it was re-wounding. Second, nothing happened time and time again. More than one woman has told me they felt like their audiences were voyeurs.

I say this because it's more than likely, in spite of his seeming courage and even bravado, each time Paul told his story he re-experienced the trauma of his near-death mob scene and the potential of assassination. Paul did not walk away from any of his persecutions saying, "Hey guys, when's the next one?" Luke told us Paul's story, but Paul told Felix and probably also Festus. He now tells Agrippa II, well known for his knowledge and support of Jewish law, the same story all over again in Acts 26:1–23.

This time he tells his story to Agrippa and his wife Bernice, who enter into the palace to great fanfare with a solid introduction of the facts by Festus (25:24–27). Festus states, "I found he had done nothing deserving of death" and therefore he had no solid case to present against him in Nero's court (25:25–27). By the time the next chapter is tied shut, Agrippa will agree (26:32).

Beverly Gaventa provides a compelling outline of this speech that shows it moves to a middle and then reverses itself. The technical term for such an ordering of phrases is "chiasm" (Gaventa, *Acts*, 339).

Paul is faithful to tradition (6–8)
Paul persecuted others (9–11)
Paul sent as a witness (12–18)
Paul served as a witness (19–20)
Paul was persecuted (21)
Paul is faith to tradition (22–23)

One more time Paul does not provide a point-by-point refutation but instead tells his story. Stories have a way of compelling listeners and readers.

Opening with an orator's gesture (Acts 12:17; 13:16; 19:33; 21:40; 24:10; 26:1), which is two fingers extended, two against the palm, and an upraised thumb (Shiell, *Acts*, 106), Paul repeats what he said to Felix but with a few adjustments, all designed to show that his mission is the result of a revelation from God (look at v. 19) and his mission is consistent with Judaism's own beliefs. In fact, Paul effectively demonstrates that his opponents opposed the vision of their own scriptures to include gentiles in the mission of God (Dunn, *Acts*, 324). As others have said (Pinter, *Acts*, 569–570), Paul turns this supposed "defense" into something else, nothing less than an offense.

First, he affirms the intelligence of Agrippa about Jewish customs, and some would say this is as much proper as it is flattery (26:2–3).

Second, he announces his own faithful observance as an approved Jew, a Pharisee (26:4–5).

Third, he dives right into the heart of the gospel, the resurrection of Jesus (26:6–8), and asks a loaded but seemingly naïve question: What's so hard to believe Jesus was raised from the dead with a God like ours?!

Fourth, he poses his present life against his former life of persecuting those who believed Jesus was Messiah (26:9–11). He admits his sinfulness here.

But fifth, his former life was interrupted by an appearance of the Lord Jesus, an appearance that converted him and turned him into a mission agent for Jesus (26:12–20). In this section Paul explains his mission: "to open their [gentile's] eyes and turn them from darkness to light, and from the power of Satan to God, so that they may receive forgiveness of sins and a place among those who are sanctified by faith in me" (26:18). So he became an obedient-to-God agent (26:19–20).

Which led, sixth, to persecution in Jerusalem (26:21).

Finally, Paul says he stands there as one helped by God to witness to what the "prophets and Moses said would happen," which was to send the Messiah who would suffer and rise from the dead and "bring the message of light to his own people" but also "to the Gentiles" (26:23).

As is done rudely and constantly on current major network news "conversations," Festus barges into Paul's story with, "You are out of your mind" (26:24), which, Paul, never afraid to speak his mind, denies outright (26:25). Then he cleverly backs up to give context for all he's saying only to push Agrippa to answer a telling question: "Do you believe the prophets?" (26:27). Not to put too fine a point on it, Paul then softens that question by saying "I know you do." That is one potent rhetoric burst, which Agrippa answers with a question about Paul attempting to convert him to becoming a Christian (26:28). Whether he means "in such a short argument" or "in such a short time" is not clear. All the Greek text has is "in little." "Of course!" Paul all but says.

DECISIONS IN THE
HANDS OF OTHERS

The question and defense suddenly end as Luke has given us what he wants his readers to know. The authorities get up and leave, seemingly leaving Paul sitting there in the dock. In leaving they chat with one another that (1) Paul has done nothing to deserve death and (2) that he could be set free had he not appealed to Nero.

So, mistaken appeal or not, to Nero he must go.

QUESTIONS FOR REFLECTION
AND APPLICATION

1. What do you think might have happened to Paul if he had not appealed to Caesar?

2. What do you see happening as a result of Gaventa's chiasm suggestion for the order of Paul's speech? Where is the emphasis?

3. How does Paul turn his defense into an offense?

4. Have you ever had to tell a traumatizing story over and over again? Or have you listened while a friend shared their traumatic story with you? How can that experience give you empathetic insight into Paul's mindset in these scenes?

5. Have you ever had major decisions for your life held in the hands of others? How did that feel?

FOR FURTHER READING

Nelson Mandela, *The Long Walk to Freedom* (Boston: Little, Brown, 1994).

PROMPTINGS IN THE MISSION

Acts 27:1–28:13

[1] *When it was decided that we would sail for Italy, Paul and some other prisoners were handed over to a centurion named Julius, who belonged to the Imperial Regiment.* [2] *We boarded a ship from Adramyttium about to sail for ports along the coast of the province of Asia, and we put out to sea. Aristarchus, a Macedonian from Thessalonica, was with us.*

[3] *The next day we landed at Sidon; and Julius, in kindness to Paul, allowed him to go to his friends so they might provide for his needs.* [4] *From there we put out to sea again and passed to the lee of Cyprus because the winds were against us.* [5] *When we had sailed across the open sea off the coast of Cilicia and Pamphylia, we landed at Myra in Lycia.* [6] *There the centurion found an Alexandrian ship sailing for Italy and put us on board.* [7] *We made slow headway for many days and had difficulty arriving off Cnidus. When the wind did not allow us to hold our course, we sailed to the lee of Crete, opposite Salmone.* [8] *We moved along the coast with difficulty and came to a place called Fair Havens, near the town of Lasea.*

[9] *Much time had been lost, and sailing had already become dangerous because by now it was after the Day of Atonement. So Paul warned them,* [10] *"Men, I can see that our voyage is going to*

be disastrous and bring great loss to ship and cargo, and to our own lives also." ¹¹ But the centurion, instead of listening to what Paul said, followed the advice of the pilot and of the owner of the ship. ¹² Since the harbor was unsuitable to winter in, the majority decided that we should sail on, hoping to reach Phoenix and winter there. This was a harbor in Crete, facing both southwest and northwest.

¹³ When a gentle south wind began to blow, they saw their opportunity; so they weighed anchor and sailed along the shore of Crete. ¹⁴ Before very long, a wind of hurricane force, called the Northeaster, swept down from the island. ¹⁵ The ship was caught by the storm and could not head into the wind; so we gave way to it and were driven along. ¹⁶ As we passed to the lee of a small island called Cauda, we were hardly able to make the lifeboat secure, ¹⁷ so the men hoisted it aboard. Then they passed ropes under the ship itself to hold it together. Because they were afraid they would run aground on the sandbars of Syrtis, they lowered the sea anchor and let the ship be driven along. ¹⁸ We took such a violent battering from the storm that the next day they began to throw the cargo overboard. ¹⁹ On the third day, they threw the ship's tackle overboard with their own hands. ²⁰ When neither sun nor stars appeared for many days and the storm continued raging, we finally gave up all hope of being saved.

²¹ After they had gone a long time without food, Paul stood up before them and said: "Men, you should have taken my advice not to sail from Crete; then you would have spared yourselves this damage and loss. ²² But now I urge you to keep up your courage, because not one of you will be lost; only the ship will be destroyed. ²³ Last night an angel of the God to whom I belong and whom I serve stood beside me ²⁴ and said, 'Do not be afraid, Paul. You must stand trial before Caesar; and God has graciously given you the lives of all who sail with you.' ²⁵ So keep up your courage, men, for I have faith in God that it will happen just as he told me. ²⁶ Nevertheless, we must run aground on some island."

²⁷ On the fourteenth night we were still being driven across the Adriatic Sea, when about midnight the sailors sensed they were approaching land. ²⁸ They took soundings and found that the water was a hundred and twenty feet deep. A short time later they took soundings again and found it was ninety feet deep. ²⁹ Fearing that we would be dashed against the rocks, they dropped four anchors from the stern and prayed for daylight. ³⁰ In an attempt to escape from the ship, the sailors let the lifeboat down into the sea, pretending they were going to lower some anchors from the bow. ³¹ Then Paul said to the centurion and the soldiers, "Unless these men stay with the ship, you cannot be saved." ³² So the soldiers cut the ropes that held the lifeboat and let it drift away.

³³ Just before dawn Paul urged them all to eat. "For the last fourteen days," he said, "you have been in constant suspense and have gone without food—you haven't eaten anything. ³⁴ Now I urge you to take some food. You need it to survive. Not one of you will lose a single hair from his head." ³⁵ After he said this, he took some bread and gave thanks to God in front of them all. Then he broke it and began to eat. ³⁶ They were all encouraged and ate some food themselves. ³⁷ Altogether there were 276 of us on board. ³⁸ When they had eaten as much as they wanted, they lightened the ship by throwing the grain into the sea.

³⁹ When daylight came, they did not recognize the land, but they saw a bay with a sandy beach, where they decided to run the ship aground if they could. ⁴⁰ Cutting loose the anchors, they left them in the sea and at the same time untied the ropes that held the rudders. Then they hoisted the foresail to the wind and made for the beach. ⁴¹ But the ship struck a sandbar and ran aground. The bow stuck fast and would not move, and the stern was broken to pieces by the pounding of the surf.

⁴² The soldiers planned to kill the prisoners to prevent any of them from swimming away and escaping. ⁴³ But the centurion wanted to spare Paul's life and kept them from carrying out their plan. He ordered those who could swim to jump overboard first and

get to land. *44 The rest were to get there on planks or on other pieces of the ship. In this way everyone reached land safely.*

28:1 Once safely on shore, we found out that the island was called Malta. 2 The islanders showed us unusual kindness. They built a fire and welcomed us all because it was raining and cold. 3 Paul gathered a pile of brushwood and, as he put it on the fire, a viper, driven out by the heat, fastened itself on his hand. 4 When the islanders saw the snake hanging from his hand, they said to each other, "This man must be a murderer; for though he escaped from the sea, the goddess Justice has not allowed him to live." 5 But Paul shook the snake off into the fire and suffered no ill effects. 6 The people expected him to swell up or suddenly fall dead; but after waiting a long time and seeing nothing unusual happen to him, they changed their minds and said he was a god.

7 There was an estate nearby that belonged to Publius, the chief official of the island. He welcomed us to his home and showed us generous hospitality for three days. 8 His father was sick in bed, suffering from fever and dysentery. Paul went in to see him and, after prayer, placed his hands on him and healed him. 9 When this had happened, the rest of the sick on the island came and were cured. 10 They honored us in many ways; and when we were ready to sail, they furnished us with the supplies we needed.

11 After three months we put out to sea in a ship that had wintered in the island—it was an Alexandrian ship with the figurehead of the twin gods Castor and Pollux. 12 We put in at Syracuse and stayed there three days. 13 From there we set sail and arrived at Rhegium. The next day the south wind came up, and on the following day we reached Puteoli.

Luke's report—notice the "we" of our passage—of Paul's trip from Caesarea across the Mediterranean to Italy's coast and then by road to Rome is one of the ancient world's best descriptions of the reality that we know about ancient travel.

What strikes many of us in reading it is perhaps the question I have myself asked, "Why do we have so many details about the trip itself?" I've also wondered, "Why not some details about the conversations between all these people?" We have what we have because Luke wanted to focus on the trip, and sea trips were often told in that world to the delight of hearers. (Remember these texts were read aloud.)

Wherever we find ourselves, if we have ears to hear and eyes to see, we will discover what God is doing and what God wants done. What we will also discover are promptings from God that push us out of our boats of comfort into the windy seas of ministry. In our obedience to the promptings, we will find ourselves overjoyed with what God grants us to do.

All of this occurs in a narrative of Luke to get this "captive witness" (Gaventa, *Acts*, 349) about Jesus in the City of Rome to the emperor himself. Acts 1:8 is now on the homestretch. Which is to say, in the big mission of God, many little ministries flourish. Paul, remember, is in the hands of Rome, and now we'll find him in the hands of the winds, but Paul knows he's in the hands of God, and God's plan cannot be thwarted.

PROMPTED TO SPEAK WHERE YOU ARE

They're headed for Rome, but the moment you get in a ship you are at the mercy of the winds, especially sailing late in the sailing season as they are, and sometimes the winds take you where they, not you, want to go. It was smooth sailing from Caesarea to Crete ("Fair Havens, near the town of Lasea"; 27:8). Until you choose not to listen to an apostle with a prophetic word. If you were at the mercy of winds which would you listen to? An experienced pilot or the imprisoned prophet? Right, the former. At least I would.

Paul was a veteran of shipwrecks (2 Corinthians 11:25–26) and wind-driven boats. Tom Wright says Paul comes off here as "bossy" (Wright, *Paul*, 375), a bit like the way people with Googled medical knowledge like to diagnose friends' conditions.

Off the southern coast of Crete, Paul predicted the trip would be "disastrous and bring great loss to ship and cargo, and to our own lives also" (27:10), but the centurion took his bearings from the "pilot" and "owner of the ship" and the "majority," which led them into a "wind of hurricane force" (27:11). What Paul said happened. They surrendered the boat to the winds, held the boat together with ropes, slowed it down by the drop-and-drag method of lowering the anchor, and tossed cargo and tackle into the sea. They gave up hope. But Paul's God delivers him from "storm, shipwreck, and snake bite" (Keener, *Acts*, 593).

It didn't help that Paul reminded them that they failed to listen to a prophet instead of a pilot on how to manage a boat on the sea (27:21). It did help that he assured them that an angel revealed to him no one of the 276 of them would be lost by the storm even if the boat would be destroyed (27:22–26). Again not paying sufficient attention to Paul, the crew panicked until Paul told him if they left they'd die (27:31–32). Paul then urged them all to break their fasts and to eat. He prayed before them all and thanked God. Then they tossed the extra grains into the sea. One morning they strike a sandbar and the boat is shattered into pieces. The Roman escorts of Paul wanted all the prisoners put to death for fear of their escape. Once again an agent of Rome, the centurion, wants to protect Paul's (the citizen's) life so they instruct them all to get to the shore on Malta, an island south of Sicily. Some swam and some floated on planks from the boat.

We should have listened to the prophet.

Prompted to Minister
Where You Are

When the stories about power corruptions and sexual abuse of women came to the front page of Christian news, I was comfortably resting in writing and speaking projects. I was intensely interested in the women's stories because I teach pastors and future church workers, but I had no plans to work on those stories or to write about them. My daughter, Laura Barringer, was also intensely interested and also intensely certain I needed to speak up about the injustices and become an advocate for the women. Which I resisted. In fact, she was a downright "pest" about it. Lo and behold, she won the argument. We wrote about it. Our book, *A Church Called Tov*, has called both of us out of our accustomed routines and life into a new ministry. We have spent the major part of the last two years writing, speaking, and podcasting ("tov-casting" I call it) about that very topic. Our story is not uncommon. Plans can easily be derailed by realities that prompt us into altogether new ministries. We are followers here in the ways of Paul (who was himself following Jesus), who on his trip to Rome had four ministerial interruptions.

On the boat just south of Crete, Paul has a prophetic word that is ignored because the decision was made to follow the wisdom of the pilot and the owner of the boat (27:10–11). Paul is no pilot, one can understand why they would listen to an experienced pilot, but contact with God who knows more than pilots puts Paul in the superior position. That doesn't mean people listen. What it does mean is that those gifted by God are to use their gifts whether recognized or not.

On the boat again, this time during the wind-blown tossing of the boat, Paul has another prophetic word (27:21–26). This time they do listen and latch on to his contact with God. After all, they were desperate and Paul, or rather God, was right the first time. Paul would no doubt rather be planting churches, or defending his mission to the gentiles in synagogues, or defending his genuine Jewishness to his Jewish and Roman audiences. But reality strikes, and Paul finds himself in the midst of a hurricane speaking words from God about weather, and thus the apostle-prophet illustrates one of my favorite lines from Conrad, that "one can't live with one's finger everlastingly on one's pulse" (Conrad, *The Heart of Darkness*, 58).

On Malta a semi-miracle occurs, at least I'm not sure how else to describe it. A viper jumps out of a fire being built, strikes Paul, and latches onto his hand. Paul shakes it off and carries on and stuns the Maltese. Waiting for him to swell up and die at the hand of a shipwreck-indicating divine punishment, they realize something unusual has occurred and change their judgment. God made him immune to the poison. Instead of thinking he's a murder and getting his divine comeuppance, they now say "he was a god" (28:6). He's neither a murderer nor a god.

On Malta the "chief official of the island" (a title), Publius, was hospitable to Paul. In his home Paul healed Publius's father of a fever and dysentery, which story ran through the island and the next thing you know Paul is like Jesus in Capernaum. People standing in the doorway uttering petitions for healing, and Luke tells us they were all "cured" (28:10). The generous Publius formed a culture of generosity, and so when Paul and the others left three months later "they furnished us with the supplies we needed" (28:10).

Here's what we can note: Those filled with the Spirit are not locked down to one gift or one ministry. Instead, they are prompted by the Spirit to bring redemption to all sorts of problems. What we can learn is that we can be looking *for what God wants done in a location rather than what we feel called to do or would rather do.*

QUESTIONS FOR REFLECTION
AND APPLICATION

1. What do you think of Luke's sea voyage story, as a story?

2. What might have happened if the centurion had listened to Paul?

3. What are the ministerial interruptions to Paul's trip?

4. Have you ever had the ministry you thought you were called to interrupted by other ministry opportunities you weren't expecting? What happened?

5. McKnight writes, "those gifted by God are to use their gifts whether recognized or not." What gifts has God given you that you need to be practicing, whether or not people recognize them, listen to them, or give you a title?

FOR FURTHER READING

Joseph Conrad, *The Heart of Darkness* (Everyman's Library; New York: A.A. Knopf, 1993).

MISSION ACCOMPLISHED IN THE MISSION

Acts 28:14–31

14 There we found some brothers and sisters who invited us to spend a week with them. And so we came to Rome. 15 The brothers and sisters there had heard that we were coming, and they traveled as far as the Forum of Appius and the Three Taverns to meet us. At the sight of these people Paul thanked God and was encouraged. 16 When we got to Rome, Paul was allowed to live by himself, with a soldier to guard him.

17 Three days later he called together the local Jewish leaders. When they had assembled, Paul said to them: "My brothers, although I have done nothing against our people or against the customs of our ancestors, I was arrested in Jerusalem and handed over to the Romans. 18 They examined me and wanted to release me, because I was not guilty of any crime deserving death. 19 The Jews objected, so I was compelled to make an appeal to Caesar. I certainly did not intend to bring any charge against my own people. 20 For this reason I have asked to see you and talk with you. It is because of the hope of Israel that I am bound with this chain."

21 They replied, "We have not received any letters from Judea concerning you, and none of our people who have come from there has reported or said anything bad about you. 22 But we want to hear what your views are, for we know that people everywhere are talking against this sect."

23 They arranged to meet Paul on a certain day, and came in even larger numbers to the place where he was staying. He witnessed to them from morning till evening, explaining about the kingdom of God, and from the Law of Moses and from the Prophets he tried to persuade them about Jesus. 24 Some were convinced by what he said, but others would not believe. 25 They disagreed among themselves and began to leave after Paul had made this final statement:

The Holy Spirit spoke the truth to your ancestors when he said through Isaiah the prophet:

> 26 Go to this people and say,
> You will be ever hearing but never understanding;
>   you will be ever seeing but never perceiving."
> 27 For this people's heart has become calloused;
>   they hardly hear with their ears,
>   and they have closed their eyes.
> Otherwise they might see with their eyes,
>   hear with their ears,
>   understand with their hearts
> and turn, and I would heal them.'

28 Therefore I want you to know that God's salvation has been sent to the Gentiles, and they will listen!" [29]

30 For two whole years Paul stayed there in his own rented house and welcomed all who came to see him. 31 He proclaimed the kingdom of God and taught about the Lord Jesus Christ—with all boldness and without hindrance!

Acts 1:8 revealed to us that the mission of this book is witnessing about the Lord Jesus to the end of the world, and here in Rome Paul has finally arrived to fulfill both missions. I see four traits of God's mission in this world.

HOSPITALITY

Paul gets to exercise his gift of preaching and defending and explaining because others offer hospitality. In Puteoli, a location near modern Naples, the contingent ("We") "found some brothers and sisters who invited us to spend a week with them" (28:14). Before he even arrives in Rome more "brothers and sisters" come out on the Appian Way approximately 40 miles to meet him, and here the language, LOL, is not unlike what is used to welcome an imperial ruler (28:15). With Rome's permission, the prisoner "was allowed to live by himself, with a soldier to guard him" (28:16), which means Rome is all but showing hospitality too! And he remained in this "rented house" for "two whole years" and was able to show hospitality to all who came to him (28:30).

How many of us get to do what we are called to do because of the generosity of others? And, conversely, how many of us provide so others can exercise their gifts without having to be bi-vocational?

COURAGE

The NIV's "encouraged" in 28:15 could perhaps lead readers to think Paul was encouraged in the sense of being uplifted, but the Greek word *tharsos* floats in meaning from "courage" to outright "audacity." We might think then of the apostle meeting up with siblings in the Roman house churches stimulating his imagination, faith, and strong courage to stand before Nero and declare not only his innocence about the accusations but also preach the gospel to the emperor himself. "We can do this!" is the spirit Paul has as he enters the Eternal City itself (in more than one sense, of course).

CAPTIVE

Nothing has changed. He's been accosted, he's been on trial, he's gospeled about everyone in his path, he's survived storm and shipwreck and a snake bite, but he's still a prisoner of Rome sent to Rome to defend himself before the emperor. He's done enough to be set free but is still under guard. The wheels of justice for the marginalized move backwards as much as they grind slowly forward, and Paul knows that reality.

SPEAKING

Paul knows gospel. Wherever the man is planted gospel conversations grow. The focus for Luke is preaching the gospel in Rome. Like all the mission church plants, the audience and response are the same. "The local Jewish leaders," and Rome had a huge Jewish population at the time with at least a dozen or so synagogues, find an audience with Paul, and he describes the story we have read that started in Acts 21. Then he defends himself for having done nothing against the law (28:17–18). His zealous opponents would not relent, so Paul tells the locals that he had to appeal to Caesar as a citizen (28:19).

His last word to the local Jewish leaders is a subtle explanation of the gospel: "It is because of the hope of Israel," which means the resurrection launched on Easter, "that I am bound with this chain" (28:20). That group of leaders has not heard a word, which always relieves the ears of the one who suspects everyone's gossiping about him, but they'd like to hear more (28:21–22). Which is an open invitation for Paul to create more turbulence. So they come back "in even larger numbers" and he gospeled them up and down, talking God's empire (kingdom) and especially attempting to show them that Jesus of Nazareth, the crucified one, is Israel's Messiah (28:23). Same message, same response, all based on the same experience. Some were persuaded, others thought he was wrong. So, he quotes at length from scripture (Isaiah 6:9–10; cf. Luke 8:10), a text used by Jesus for those who heard him but were split into two groups, affirmers and deniers. Paul's response draws from another theme in Acts, namely, that their rejection leads him to preach to the gentiles.

Luke closes down his account with Paul preaching the gospel "with all boldness and without hindrance" in the heart of the empire (28:31). His message was God's empire and God's Messiah. It's the only thing he has known for some thirty years.

Mission accomplished!

But, please Luke, why not tell us what happened when Paul was put on trial! After all, you're the one who made a big deal of his appealing to Caesar.

QUESTIONS FOR REFLECTION AND APPLICATION

1. How does the entire book of Acts end up flowing from the verse Acts 1:8?

2. What role does hospitality play in Paul's ministry?

3. What is the content of the message Paul continues to preach, even in chains?

4. Why do you think Luke doesn't tell us what happened to Paul?

5. As you reach the end of this study, what has impacted you the most? What do you want to implement in your life, with the transforming help of the Spirit of Jesus?

The Blue Parakeet

Rethinking How You Read the Bible

Scot McKnight, author of
The Jesus Creed

Why Can't I Just Be a Christian?

Parakeets make delightful pets. We cage them or clip their wings to keep them where we want them. Scot McKnight contends that many, conservatives and liberals alike, attempt the same thing with the Bible. We all try to tame it.

McKnight's *The Blue Parakeet* has emerged at the perfect time to cool the flames of a world on fire with contention and controversy. It calls Christians to a way to read the Bible that leads beyond old debates and denominational battles. It calls Christians to stop taming the Bible and to let it speak anew for a new generation.

In his books *The Jesus Creed* and *Embracing Grace*, Scot McKnight established himself as one of America's finest Christian thinkers, an author to be reckoned with.

In *The Blue Parakeet*, McKnight again touches the hearts and minds of today's Christians, this time challenging them to rethink how to read the Bible, not just to puzzle it together into some systematic theology but to see it as a Story that we're summoned to enter and to carry forward in our day.

In his own inimitable style, McKnight sets traditional and liberal Christianity on its ear, leaving readers equipped, encouraged, and emboldened to be the people of faith they long to be.

Available in stores and online!

We hope you enjoyed this Bible study from Scot McKnight.
Here are some other Bible studies we think you'll like.

N.T. Wright and
Michael F. Bird

Sandra Richter

Derwin Gray

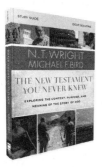

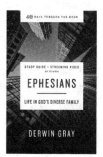

*The New Testament
You Never Knew*
Video Study

The Epic of Eden: Psalms
Video Study

*40 Days Through
the Book: Ephesians*
Video Study

ALSO AVAILABLE FROM SCOT MCKNIGHT

How to Know, Read, Live, and Show the Gospel

We want to follow King Jesus, but do we know how?

Author and professor Scot McKnight will help you discover what it means to follow King Jesus through 24 lessons based on four of his writings (The King Jesus Gospel, The Blue Parakeet – 2nd edition, One.Life, and A Fellowship of Differents). McKnight's unique framework for discipleship is designed to be used for personal study and within disciple-making groups of two or more. In this workbook, McKnight will help you:

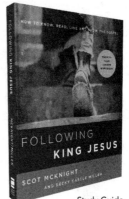

Study Guide
9780310105992

- Know the biblical meaning of the gospel
- Read the Bible and understand how to apply it today
- Live as disciples of Jesus in all areas of life
- Show the world God's character through life together in the church

Each lesson, created by Becky Castle Miller, has both Personal Study and Group Discussion sections. The Personal Study section contains a discipleship reading from Scot McKnight, an insightful Bible study, an insightful Bible study, and a time for individual prayer, action, and reflection. The Group Discussion section includes discussion questions and activities to do together with a discipleship group. You'll share insights from your personal study time with each other and explore different ways of living out what you're learning.

Whether you have been a Christian for many years or you are desiring a fresh look at what it means to be a disciple, this workbook is an in-depth guide to what it means to follow King Jesus and to discover how to put that kind of life into practice.

Harper*Christian*
Resources